TOP 10
ROME

REID BRAMBLETT &
JEFFREY KENNEDY

Left **Palatine Hill** Right **Piazza Navona**

LONDON, NEW YORK,
MELBOURNE, MUNICH AND DELHI
www.dk.com

Produced by Sargasso Media Ltd, London

Reproduced by Colourscan, Singapore
Printed and bound in China by Leo Paper
Products Ltd

First published in Great Britain in 2002 by
Dorling Kindersley Limited
80 Strand, London WC2R 0RL
A Penguin Company

**Copyright 2002, 2011 © Dorling Kindersley
Limited, London**

**Reprinted with revisions 2003, 2004, 2006,
2007, 2008, 2009, 2010, 2011 (001)**

A CIP catalogue record is available from the
British Library.

ISBN: 978-1-40535-875-0

Within each Top 10 list in this book, no hierarchy
of quality or popularity is implied. All 10 are, in
the editor's opinion, of roughly equal merit.

MIX
Paper from
responsible sources
FSC
www.fsc.org   FSC™ C018179

Contents

Rome's Top 10

The information in this DK Eyewitness Top 10 Travel Guide is checked regularly.
Every effort has been made to ensure that this book is as up-to-date as possible at the time of
going to press. Some details, however, such as telephone numbers, opening hours, prices,
gallery hanging arrangements and travel information are liable to change. The publishers cannot
accept responsibility for any consequences arising from the use of this book, nor for any
material on third party websites, and cannot guarantee that any website address in this book
will be a suitable source of travel information. We value the views and suggestions of our
readers very highly. Please write to: Publisher, DK Eyewitness Travel Guides,
Dorling Kindersley, 80 Strand, London, Great Britain WC2R 0RL, or email: travelguides@dk.com.

Cover: Front **DK Images** Mike Dunning clb; **Hemispheres Images** Pawel Wysocki main. Spine **DK Images** John
Heseltine b. Back **DK Images** cr; Mike Dunning c, cl.

Left **Rome rooftops** Right **Campidoglio at night**

Left **Interior, the Pantheon** Right **Trinità dei Monti church**

As a guide to abbreviations in visitor information blocks: Adm = admission charge; DA = disabled access; D = dinner; L = lunch

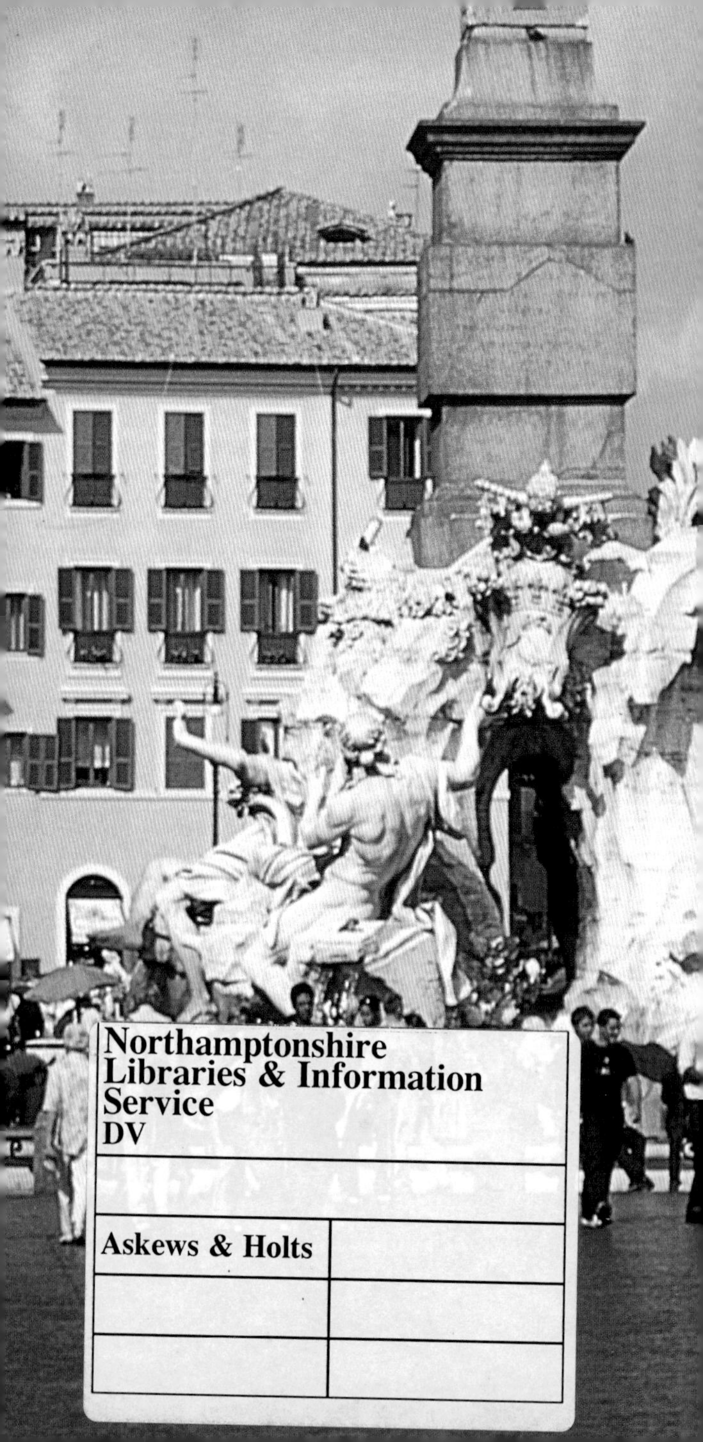

ROME'S
TOP 10

ROME'S TOP 10

🔟 Rome Highlights

Although functioning as a vibrant, modern capital akin to any in Europe, the unique appeal of Rome is that the entire city is a vast, 3,000-year-old, indoor-outdoor museum. In every quarter you'll find ancient monuments, art treasures and timeless architecture in churches, galleries and protected ruins. Home to the world's smallest country, the Vatican, Rome has religion at its heart and history in its soul – a city that dazzles and inspires visitors time and time again.

Vatican City [1]
This tiny city-state is home to the Pope, the world's greatest museum, largest church, and the most astounding work of art ever created – Michelangelo's Sistine Chapel ceiling *(see pp8–13)*.

The Pantheon [2]
The most perfectly preserved of all ancient temples, this marvel of architectural engineering has a giant oculus forever open to the sky *(see pp14–15)*.

Roman Forum [3]
At the once-bustling heart of ancient political, judicial and commercial power, there's now an evocative emptiness, punctuated by grandiose arches, solitary columns and carved rubble *(see pp16–19)*.

Prati

Città del Vaticano

Giardini Vaticani

VIA LEONE IV

VIA COLA DI RIENZO

VIA CRESCENZIO

PIAZZA S. PIETRO

VIA D. CONCILIAZIONE VATICANO LUNGOT. CASTELLO

Borgo

LUNGOT. TOR DI NONA

V. PORTA CAVALLEGGERI

GALLERIA PRINCIPE AMEDEO SAVOIA AOSTA

Ponte [7]

PIAZZA APOLLINA

PIAZZA NAVO

CORSO V.

VITTORIO EMANUEL

Parione

CAMPO DE' FIORI

Gianicolo

VIA G. CARIBALDI

Trastevere

LUNGOT. R. SAN

600 ⎯ yards ⌐ 0 ⌐ metres ⎯ 600

20km
[10]

Galleria Borghese [4]
A stunningly beautiful pleasure-palace, this was the vision of an immensely rich, hedonistic papal nephew, who filled it with Graeco-Roman, Renaissance and Baroque works by the greatest masters *(see pp20–21)*.

Museo Nazionale Romano

These collections, housed at two sites, feature some of the world's finest ancient art, including Classical sculpture and stunning mosaics *(see pp28–31)*.

Colosseum and Imperial Fora

Imperial Rome constructed many impressive monuments, including the spectacular amphitheatre *(see pp22–3)*.

Santa Maria del Popolo

Built over emperors' tombs, this church offers one of Rome's richest displays of Renaissance and Baroque art, including masterpieces by Pinturicchio, Raphael, Caravaggio and Bernini *(see pp32–3)*.

San Clemente

With its mysterious passages and legends, this fascinating church provides first-hand experience of the layers that comprise Rome; here you can descend to a depth of 18m (60 ft) and go back over 2,000 years *(see pp34–5)*.

Musei Capitolini

At the ancient centre of religious Rome are found some of the world's greatest masterpieces, from 4th-century BC Greek sculptures to Caravaggio's revolutionary – even scandalous – paintings *(see pp24–7)*.

Ostia Antica

Extending over several square kilometres, the remarkable ruins of ancient Rome's main port city hold many surprises and convey a powerful sense of everyday Imperial life *(see pp36–7)*.

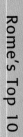

ᴛᴏᴘ10 Vatican City

The Vatican is the world's smallest nation, covering just 50 ha (120 acres), and is a theocracy of just over 550 citizens, headed by the Pope, but its sightseeing complex is beyond compare. Within its wall are the ornate St Peter's Basilica (see pp12–13), the astonishing Sistine Chapel (see pp10–11), lush gardens, apartments frescoed by Fra' Angelico, Raphael and Pinturicchio, and some 10 museums. The latter, detailed on these pages, include collections of Egyptian, Greek, Etruscan and Roman antiquities; Paleochristian, Renaissance and modern art; and a world-class ethnographic collection.

Vatican courtyard

🍴 There is a café inside the Vatican Museums although it is often crowded.

🕐 When in town, the Pope gives a mass audience on Wednesday mornings. Book the free tickets in advance through the Prefecture of the Papal Household (Fax 06 6988 5863).

• Map B2
• www.vatican.va
• Museums and Sistine Chapel: Viale Vaticano 100; 06 6988 4947; Open 8:30am–6pm (last admission 4pm) Mon–Sat and 8:30am–2:30pm last Sun of month. Closed 1 & 6 Jan, 11 Feb, Easter, 1 May, 29 Jun, 14–15 Aug, 1 Nov 8, 25, 26 Dec. Adm €15 (€8 ISIC students under 26); DA (partial). • St Peter's Basilica: Piazza S Pietro; 06 6988 3731 (information line); Open 7am–7pm daily; Free (basilica); Adm €6 (treasury), €5 (dome – steps), €7 (dome – lift).

Top 10 Features

1 Sistine Chapel
2 Raphael Rooms
3 Apollo Belvedere
4 Raphael's *Transfiguration*
5 Chapel of Nicholas V
6 Laocoön
7 Caravaggio's *Deposition*
8 Borgia Apartments
9 Belvedere Torso
10 Leonardo da Vinci's *St Jerome*

1 Sistine Chapel
Michelangelo's ceiling *(right)* is one of the most spectacular works of art in the world *(see pp10–11)*.

2 Raphael Rooms
Raphael decorated Julius II's apartments between 1508 and 1520. The Stanza della Segnatura features the School of Athens, a convention of ancient philosophers bearing portraits of Renaissance artists such as Leonardo da Vinci as bearded Plato in the centre.

3 Apollo Belvedere
This Roman copy of a 4th-century BC Greek statue *(left)* is considered a model of physical beauty. It inspired Bernini's *Apollo* in Galleria Borghese *(see pp20–21)*.

Raphael's Transfiguration
Raphael was labouring on this gargantuan masterpiece (1517–20) when he died at 37, leaving students to finish the base. It depicts Christ appearing to the Apostles in divine glory *(below)*.

Chapel of Nicholas V
The Vatican's hidden gem is this closet-sized chapel colourfully frescoed (1447–50) with early martyrs by Fra' Angelico.

Plan of Vatican City

Caravaggio's Deposition
Caravaggio's *chiaroscuro* technique accentuates a diagonal composition (1604) filled with peasant figures and grisly realism.

Belvedere Torso
The highly crafted, bulging muscles of this 1st-century BC torso of the god Hercules were regularly used as a prime sketching model for Michelangelo and many other Renaissance masters.

Borgia Apartments
Pope Alexander VI had these beautiful rooms frescoed by Pinturicchio (Raphael was once his junior collaborator) between 1492 and 1495. The walls are now hung with lesser pieces from the Modern Art collection.

Leonardo da Vinci's St Jerome
Sketchy and unfinished – Leonardo was often a distracted genius – this 1482 painting is nevertheless an anatomical masterpiece.

Museum Guide

The Vatican Museums (a 15-minute walk around the Vatican walls from St Peter's) are made up of 10 collections plus the Sistine Chapel and papal apartments. To see highlights only, first visit the Pinacoteca, to the right of the entrance turnstile. The Sistine and other collections are to the left.

Laocoön
One of antiquity's most famous sculptures *(right)* is this 1st-century AD Trojan prophet and his sons being strangled by serpents as they try to warn against the besieging Greeks' sneaky gift horse.

Left **Adam and Eve** Right **Ezekiel, Prophets**

Sistine Chapel Works

1 Adam and Eve
God imparts the spark of life to Adam in one of western art's most famous scenes, then pulls Eve from Adam's rib.

2 Creation
God separates darkness from light, water from land and creates the Sun and Moon. Michelangelo veers towards blasphemy by depicting God's dirty feet.

3 The Sacrifice, Flood, and Drunkenness of Noah
After disassembling his scaffolding and gazing from floor level, Michelangelo noticed that these three tumultuous scenes were too minutely drawn.

4 Last Judgment
This vast work identifies saints by their medieval icons: Catharine with her wheel, Bartholomew with the knife which flayed him.

5 Sibyls and Prophets
Hebrew prophets, including Jonah shying away from the whale, mingle with the Sibyls who foretold Christ's coming.

6 Old Testament Salvation Scenes and Ancestors of Christ
Portraits from Jesus's family tree are above the windows, and bloody Salvation scenes, including David and Goliath, are on corner spandrels.

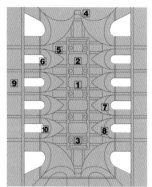

Plan of the Sistine Chapel

7 Life of Christ Scenes
The chapel's right wall stars Botticelli's *Cleansing of the Leper*, Ghirlandaio's *Calling of Peter and Andrew*, as well as Perugino's work below.

8 Giving the Keys to St Peter
Classical buildings form the backdrop to this pivotal scene of transferring power from Christ to the popes. Each scene is divided into three parts.

9 Life of Moses Scenes
Left wall highlights include Botticelli's *Burning Bush* and Signorelli and della Gatta's *Moses Giving his Rod to Joshua*.

10 Botticelli's Punishment of the Rebels
Schismatics question Aaron's priestly prerogative to burn incense. A vengeful Moses opens the earth to swallow them.

For more Roman masterpieces **See pp48–9**

Understanding the Sistine Chapel Art

The Sistine's frescoes are not merely decorations by some of the greatest Renaissance artists – the images tell a story and make a complex theological argument. Pope Sixtus IV commissioned wall frescoes for the Pope's Chapel in 1481–83. They were intended to underscore papal authority, in question at the time, by drawing a line of power from God to the pope. In the Life of Moses cycle, Moses' and Aaron's undisputed roles as God's chosen representatives are affirmed by the fate of those who oppose Aaron – significantly and anachronistically wearing a papal hat – in the Punishment of the Rebels. Directly across from this work, Perugino's Giving the Keys to St Peter bridges the Old Testament with the New as Christ hands control of the church to St Peter – and therefore to his successors, the popes (who are pictured between the Sistine windows). Michelangelo's ceiling (1508–12) later added Genesis, Redemption and Salvation to the story.

Original Sin
Part of Michelangelo's Genesis cycle shows Adam and Eve being expelled from Paradise for eating the forbidden fruit from the Tree of Knowledge.

The Life of Moses, Sandro Botticelli

Left **The Dome** Right **Baldacchino**

🔟 Features of St Peter's Basilica

Pietà
Michelangelo carved this masterpiece *(see p48)* in 1499 at the age of 25. It is at once graceful and mournful, stately and ethereal. It has been protected by glass since 1972, when a man screaming "I am Jesus Christ!" attacked it with a hammer, damaging the Virgin's nose and fingers.

The Dome
When Michelangelo designed a dome to span St Peter's massive transept, he made it 42 m (138 ft) in diameter, in deference to the Pantheon's 43.3-m (142-ft) dome. You can ride an elevator much of the way, but must still navigate the final 330 stairs between the dome's inner and outer shell to the 132-m-high (435-ft) lantern and sweeping vistas across the city.

Piazza San Pietro
Bernini's remarkable semi-elliptical colonnades transformed the basilica's approach into a pair of welcoming arms embracing the faithful *(see p46)*. Sadly, the full effect of entering the square from a warren of medieval streets was spoiled when Mussolini razed the neighbourhood to lay down pompous Via della Conciliazione. The obelisk came from Alexandria.

Baldacchino
Whether you view it as ostentatious or glorious, Bernini's huge altar canopy is at least impressive. Its spiralling bronze columns are claimed to have been made from the revetments (portico ceiling decorations) of the Pantheon *(see p14)*, taken by Pope Urban VIII. For his desecration of the ancient temple the Barberini pope and his family *(see p51)* were castigated with the waggish quip: "What even the barbarians wouldn't do, Barberini did."

Statue of St Peter
A holdover from the medieval St Peter's, this 13th-century bronze statue by the sculptor Arnolfo di Cambio has achieved holy status. The faithful can be seen lining up to rub (or kiss) Peter's well-worn foot for luck.

Michelangelo's Pietà

Treasury

Among the ecclesiastical treasures here is a 6th-century, jewel-encrusted bronze cross (the Crux Vaticana), various fragments of the medieval basilica including a ciborium by Donatello (1432), and Antonio Pollaiuolo's masterful bronze slab tomb (1493) for Sixtus IV, the pope's effigy surrounded by representations of theological virtues and liberal arts.

Alexander VII's Monument

Apse

Bernini's exuberantly Baroque stained-glass window (1666) centres on a dove representing the Holy Ghost, surrounded by rays of the sun and a riot of sculptural details. Beneath the window sits the Chair of St Peter (1665), another Bernini concoction; inside is a wood and ivory chair said to be the actual throne of St Peter. Bernini also crafted the multicoloured marble *Monument to Urban VIII* (1644) to the right, based on Michelangelo's Medici tombs in Florence. It is of far better artistic quality than Guglielmo della Porta's similar one for Pope Paul III (1549) to the left.

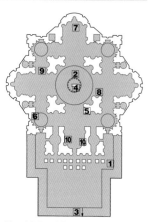

Plan of St Peter's Basilica

Crypt

Many of the medieval basilica's monuments are housed beneath the basilica's floor. During excavations in the 1940s workers discovered in the Necropolis the legendary Red Wall behind which St Peter was supposedly buried. The wall was covered with early medieval graffiti invoking the saint, and a box of bones was found behind it. The late Pope John Paul II is buried in the crypt.

Alexander VII's Monument

One of Bernini's last works (1678) shows figures of Justice, Truth, Chastity and Prudence gazing up at the pontiff seated in the deep shadows of the niche. A skeleton crawls from under the flowing marble drapery to hold aloft an hourglass as a reminder of mortality.

Central Piers

Until modern times, a church was judged by its relics. St Peter's Basilica houses the spear of St Longinius, which jabbed Jesus's side on the Cross, St Veronica's handkerchief bearing Christ's face, and a fragment of the True Cross.

⯅ 10 The Pantheon

When Emperor Phocas donated this pagan temple to Pope Boniface IV in 608, he unwittingly ensured that one of the marvels of ancient Rome would be preserved, virtually unaltered, in its new guise as the Christian church Santa Maria ad Martyres. Emperor Hadrian, an amateur architect, designed this lovely structure in AD 118–25. It has been lightly sacked over the ages – barbarians took portable pieces, Constans II stole its gilded roof tiles and, in 1625, Urban VIII melted down the portico's bronze ceiling panels to make cannon for Castel Sant' Angelo. Yet the airy interior and perfect proportions remain, a wonder of the world even in its own time.

Agrippa inscription, Pantheon façade

🅰 There's a good gelateria, Cremeria Monteforte, on the Pantheon's right flank, and an excellent coffee shop, La Tazza d'Oro, just off the square *(see p71).*

🅖 Rather than bemoan a rainy day in Rome, scurry to the Pantheon to watch the water fall gracefully though the oculus and spatter against the marble floor and down a drain. Snowfalls are even better.

• Piazza della Rotonda
• Map M3
• 06 6830 0230
• Open 8:30am–7:30pm Mon–Sat, 9am–6pm Sun (9am–1pm during hols); Mass: 10:30am Sun and 5pm Sat; closed 1 Jan, 1 May, 25 Dec • Free

Top 10 Features

1 Dome
2 Oculus
3 Portico
4 Doors
5 Walls
6 Royal Tombs
7 Raphael's Tomb
8 Fountain
9 Marble Decorations
10 Basilica of Neptune Remains

Dome
The widest masonry dome in Europe *(above)* is precisely as high as it is wide: 43.3 m (142 ft). Its airy, coffered space, cleverly shot through with a shaft of sunlight from the oculus, is what lends the Pantheon an ethereal air.

Oculus
The bold, 8.3 m-diameter (27-ft) hole at the dome's centre provides light and structural support: the tension around its ring helps hold the weight of the dome.

Portico
The triangular pediment *(below)* is supported by 16 pink and grey granite columns, all original save the three on the left (17th-century copies).

4 Doors
The massive bronze doors *(right)* are technically original, but were so extensively renovated under Pius IV (1653) they have been practically recast.

7 Raphael's Tomb
Raphael, darling of the Roman Renaissance art world but dead at 37, rests in a plain, ancient stone sarcophagus. Poet Bembo's Latin epitaph translates as: "Here lies Raphael, whom Nature feared would outdo her while alive, but now that he is gone fears she, too, will die." Other artists buried here include Baldassare Peruzzi.

8 Fountain
Giacomo della Porta designed this stoop *(below)* Leonardo Sormani carved it in 1575. The Egyptian obelisk of Rameses II was added in 1711.

9 Marble Decorations
Red porphyry, giallo antico, and other ancient marbles grace the interior. More than half the polychrome panels cladding the walls are original, the rest careful reproductions, as is the floor *(below)*.

10 Basilica of Neptune Remains
Of the Pantheon's old neighbour, all that remains are an elaborate cornice and fluted columns against the Pantheon's rear wall.

The First Pantheon
Emperor Augustus's son-in-law, Marcus Agrippa, built the first Pantheon in 27 BC, replaced in AD 118-125 by Hadrian's rotunda. The pediment's inscription "*M. Agrippa cos tertium fecit*" ("M. Agrippa made this") was Hadrian's modest way of honouring Agrippa. The pediment also provided the illusion of a smaller temple, making the massive space inside even more of a surprise (the Pantheon was originally raised and you couldn't see the dome behind). Bernini's "ass ears", tiny towers he added to the pediment, were removed in 1883.

5 Walls
The 6.2-m (20-ft) thick walls incorporate built-in brick arches to help distribute the weight downwards, relieving the stress of the heavy roof.

6 Royal Tombs
Two of Italy's kings are honoured by simple tombs. Vittorio Emanuele II (1861–78) unified Italy and became its first king. His son, Umberto I, was assassinated in 1900.

TOP 10 Roman Forum

Gazing on it today, a picturesque shambles of ruins and weeds, you would hardly guess that the Forum was the symbol of civic pride for 1,000 years. Its humble beginning, more than 3,000 years ago, was as a swampy cemetery for the original village on Palatine Hill. Gradually it rose, ever more glorified, as Rome's power grew. After the marsh was finally drained off in the 6th century BC, it took on its central role in the life of the Republic. The Forum showed its most elegant face starting with the reign of Augustus, the first Roman emperor, who is said to have turned the city from brick to marble.

The Curia

📍 The only option in the immediate area for drinks and snacks is one of the mobile refreshment vendors. For something more substantial, there are plenty of cafés and restaurants on Via Cavour.

🕐 In summer, it's best to visit the Forum either early or late in the day, to avoid the intense heat.

• Via dei Fori Imperiali • Map Q5 • 06 3996 7700 • Open 1 Nov–15 Feb: 8:30am–4:30pm daily; 16 Feb–15 Mar: 8:30am–5pm daily; 1 Apr–31 Aug: 8:30am–7:15pm; Sep: 8:30am–7pm daily; Oct: 8:30am–6:30pm daily. Closed 1 Jan, 25 Dec • Forum: Adm €12 (includes Palatine and Colosseum; valid for 48 hours). Free for EU citizens under 18 and over 65.

Top 10 Features

1. Arch of Septimius Severus
2. Temple of Vesta and House of the Vestal Virgins
3. Curia
4. Temple of Castor and Pollux
5. Arch of Titus
6. Basilica of Maxentius and Constantine
7. Temple of Vespasian
8. Via Sacra
9. Temple of Saturn
10. Temple of Antoninus and Faustina

Arch of Septimius Severus

This well-preserved triumphal arch *(below)* celebrates the emperor's Middle Eastern victories. It was erected in AD 203 by his sons, Geta and Caracalla, then co-emperors.

Temple of Vesta and House of the Vestal Virgins

A graceful round temple and its adjacent palace *(right)* were the centre for one of Rome's most revered cults. Noble priestesses tended the sacred flame and enjoyed the greatest privileges.

Curia

The 3rd-century-AD Senate retains its original polychrome inlaid floor, its risers, where the 300 senators sat in deliberation, and the speaker's platform. For 2nd-century views of the Forum, examine the large marble reliefs, showing Emperor Trajan's good works.

For more ancient sights in Rome See pp40–41

Temple of Castor and Pollux

Three Corinthian columns remain of this temple to the *Dioscuri* – twin brothers of Helen of Troy and sons of Jupiter and Leda. The shrine marked the spot where they miraculously appeared in 499 BC to announce a crucial Roman victory.

Basilica of Maxentius and Constantine

Three vast, coffered barrel vaults *(below)* proclaim the Forum's largest structure, built around AD 315 and used as the legal and financial centre of the Empire.

Original Plan of the Roman Forum

Temple of Saturn

Eight grey-and-red Ionic columns constitute what's left of this temple (also the state treasury) to the ruler of agriculture and of a mythic "Golden Age." Saturnalia, celebrated each December, was very similar to modern-day Christmas.

Temple of Antoninus and Faustina

Dedicated by Antoninus Pius in AD 41 to his deified wife Faustina, this is one of the best preserved temples *(centre)*. With its Baroque-style top-knot, it is also one of the oddest. Note the carvings of griffins along the side frieze.

Temple of Vespasian

Until 18th-century excavations were undertaken, these graceful corner columns (AD 79) of the temple to a former emperor stood mostly buried beneath centuries of detritus.

Arch of Titus

The oldest extant arch in Rome *(above)* was erected in AD 81 by Emperor Domitian to honour his brother, Titus, and his father, Vespasian, for putting down the Jewish Revolt. Reliefs show soldiers sacking Jerusalem's Holy of Holies and taking sacred objects, such as a golden menorah.

Via Sacra

Paved with broad, flat, black basalt stones, Rome's oldest road wound from the Arch of Titus through the Forum and up to the Capitoline. Republican heroes staged triumphal processions here, but it degenerated into a hangout for gossips, pickpockets and other idlers.

Forum Guide

You can access the Forum from Via Dei Fori Imperiali. However, for a great view of the whole site, enter from one of the high points at either end. From the northwest end, begin on the Capitoline (to the right and behind the huge, white Victor Emmanuel Monument) and take the stairs down from Largo Romolo e Remo. From the southeast end, start at the Colosseum *(see p22)* and climb the small hill just to the northwest. Enter by the Arch of Titus, which is also near the main entry gate to the Palatine.

Left **Farnese Gardens** Centre **Stucco relief, Cryptoporticus** Right **Domus Flavia**

Palatine Hill Features

1 Domus Flavia
Marked today mainly by the remains of two fountains, this imposing edifice was the official wing of a vast emperors' palace, built by Domitian in AD 81.

2 Livia's House
This 1st-century BC structure, now below ground level, formed part of the residence of Augustus and his second wife. Here you can examine a number of mosaic pavements and wall frescoes.

3 Palatine Museum and Antiquarium
This former convent houses a wealth of artifacts unearthed here, including pottery, statuary, ancient graffiti and very fine mosaics. You can also study a model of the Iron Age Palatine.

4 Romulus's Iron-Age Huts
Traces of the three 9th-century BC huts were uncovered in the 1940s. Legend says that this tiny village was founded by Romulus, who gave Rome its name *(see p38)*.

5 Stadium
Possibly a racetrack, or just a large garden, this sunken rectangle formed part of Domitian's palatial 1st-century abode.

6 Domus Augustana
All that remains of the private wing of Domitian's imperial extravaganza are the massive substructure vaults.

Plan of Palatine Hill

7 Temple of Cybele
The orgiastic Cult of the Great Mother was the first of the Oriental religions to come to Rome, in 191 BC. Still here is a decapitated statue of the goddess. Priests worshipping Cybele ritually castrated themselves.

8 Farnese Gardens
Plants and elegant pavilions grace part of what was once an extensive pleasure-garden, designed by Vignola and built in the 16th century over the ruins of Tiberius's palace.

9 Cryptoporticus
This series of underground corridors, their vaults decorated with delicate stucco reliefs, stretches 130 m (425 ft). It connected the Palatine to Nero's fabulous Golden House *(see p41)*.

10 Domus Septimius Severus
Huge arches and broken walls are all that remain of this emperor's 2nd-century AD extension to the Domus Augustana.

Top 10 Ancient Roman Belief Systems

1. State Religion of Graeco-Roman Gods (especially the Capitol Triad: Jupiter, Juno, Minerva)
2. Household Gods: Ancestors and Genii
3. Cult of Cybele, the Great Mother
4. Deification of Emperors, Empresses and Favourites
5. Orgiastic Fertility Cults
6. Mithraism
7. Cult of Attis
8. Cult of Isis
9. Cult of Serapis
10. Judeo-Christianity

Roman Bathhouses

As the centre of Roman social life, bathhouses were grandiose affairs, as seen in the remains *(below)* in the Baths of Caracalla *(see p119).*

A Day in the Life of a Roman Household

Most Romans lived in insulae, *apartment buildings of perhaps six floors, with the poorest residents occupying the cheaper upper floors. An average Roman male citizen arose before dawn, arranged his toga, and breakfasted on a glass of water. Then out into the alleys, reverberating with noise. First, a stop at a public latrine, where he chatted with neighbours. Next a visit to his honoured patron, who paid him his daily stipend. Lunch might be a piece of bread washed down with wine. Bathing waited until late afternoon, when he met his friends at a public bathhouse. There he lingered – conversing, exercising, reading, or admiring the artwork – until dinnertime. The main meal of the day was taken lying on couches, with his slaves in attendance. Then it was bedtime. Roman matrons, apart from their time at the baths, spent the entire day at home, running the household.*

Roman toga

🔟 Galleria Borghese

The Borghese Gallery is one of the world's greatest small museums. A half dozen of Bernini's best sculptures and Caravaggio paintings casually occupy the same rooms as Classical, Renaissance and Neo-Classical works. The setting is the beautiful frescoed 17th-century villa set in the greenery of Villa Borghese park, all of which once belonged to the great art-lover of the early Baroque, Cardinal Scipione Borghese. Scipione patronized the young Bernini and Caravaggio, in the process amassing one of Rome's richest private collections.

Bernini's David
Young Bernini's *David* (1623–4) *(above)* was the Baroque answer to Michelangelo's Renaissance version. The frowning face is a self-portrait.

Façade, Galleria Borghese

🍴 There's a decent café in the museum basement, although the Caffè delle Arti (06 3265 1236) at the nearby Galleria Nazionale d'Arte Moderna is better, with a park view.

🎫 Entrance to the gallery is strictly by reservation. Book well ahead of time – entries are timed and tickets often sell out days, even weeks, in advance, especially if an exhibition is on.

• Villa Borghese, off Via Pinciana • Map E1
• 06 32810 • www. galleriaborghese.it
• www.ticketeria.it (for reservations) • Open 9am–7pm Tue–Sun. Closed 1 Jan, 25 Dec.
• Adm €8.50; €5.25 EU citizens 18–25; €2 EU students, EU citizens under 18 and over 65 and journalists
• Max. viewing time 2 hours

Top 10 Exhibits

1. Bernini's *Apollo and Daphne*
2. Bernini's *Rape of Persephone*
3. Bernini's *David*
4. Caravaggio's *Madonna of the Serpent*
5. Canova's *Pauline Bonaparte*
6. Caravaggio's *Self-Portrait as a Sick Bacchus*
7. Raphael's *Deposition*
8. Bernini's *Aeneas and Anchises*
9. Titian's *Sacred and Profane Love*
10. Correggio's *Danae*

Bernini's Apollo and Daphne
A climactic moment frozen in marble (1622–5). As Apollo is inches from grabbing Daphne, the pitying gods transform her into a laurel *(right)*.

Bernini's Rape of Persephone
Bernini carved this masterpiece at age 23 (1621–2). Muscular Hades throws his head back with laughter, his strong fingers pressing into the maiden's soft flesh as she struggles to break free of his grasp.

Caravaggio's Madonna of the Serpent
Baroque tastes disliked this altarpiece's lack of ornamentation (1605). It spent only weeks on St Peter's altar before being moved to a lesser church then sold to Borghese.

For more masterpieces in Rome **See pp48–9**

5 Canova's Pauline Bonaparte

Napoleon's sister caused a scandal with this half-naked portrait (1805–8), lounging like a Classical goddess on a carved marble cushion.

6 Caravaggio's Self-Portrait as a Sick Bacchus

This early self-portrait (1593) as the wine god was painted with painstaking detail, supposedly when the artist was ill. It shows finer brushwork than later works.

7 Raphael's Deposition

The Borghese's most famous painting (1507), although neither the gallery's nor Raphael's best *(right).* The Perugian matriarch Atalanta Baglioni commissioned the work to honour her assassinated son (perhaps the red-shirted pall-bearer).

8 Bernini's Aeneas and Anchises

Pietro Bernini was still guiding his 15-year-old son in this 1613 work. The carving is more timid and static than in later works, but the genius is already evident.

10 Correggio's Danae

A sensual masterpiece (1531) based on Ovid's *Metamorphoses.* Cupid pulls back the sheets as Jupiter, the golden shower above her head, rains his love over Danae *(below).*

Key

First floor

Ground floor

9 Titian's Sacred and Profane Love

Titian's allegorical scene (1514), painted for a wedding, exhorts the young bride that worldly love is part of the divine, and that sex is an extension of holy matrimony *(below).*

The Borghese Collectors

Scipione used this 17th-century villa as a showplace for a stupendous antiquities collection given to him by his uncle, Pope Paul V, to which he added sculptures by the young Bernini. When Camillo Borghese married Pauline Bonaparte, he donated the bulk of the Classical sculpture collection to his brother-in-law Napoleon in 1809. They now form the core of the Louvre's antiquities wing in Paris.

🔟 The Colosseum and Imperial Fora

This rich archaeological zone, rudely intruded upon by Mussolini's Via dei Fori Imperiali, contains some of the most grandiose and noteworthy of Rome's ancient remains. Dominating the area is the mighty shell of the Colosseum, constructed in AD 72–80 under the Flavian emperors and originally known as the Flavian Amphitheatre. The quarter also holds other imperial wonders, such as the Arch of Constantine, the gigantic fora of various emperors, most notably Trajan's, and the 1st century AD folly of Nero's Golden House, now a subterranean revelation of Roman interior design. Plans are under way to turn the area into one great archaeological park, and the broad thoroughfare crossing the zone is more and more frequently closed to traffic, as those aims are gradually realized.

Loggia, House of the Knights of Rhodes

🔵 One of the friendliest places for a light meal is Caffè Valorani, at Largo Corrado Ricci 30.

🔶 At the Colosseum, use one of the student guides – they work for tips and really bring the place to life.

• 06 3996 7700 (reservations for all archaeological sites)
• Colosseum: Piazza del Colosseo, Map R6, Open 8:30am–1 hr before sunset daily. Closed 1 Jan and 25 Dec. Adm €12 (includes the Palatine and Roman forum).
• Trajan's Markets: Via IV Novembre, Map P4, 06 6978 0532, Open 9am–7pm Tue–Sun, Adm €6.50 (€3.20 for EU students. Free for EU citizens under 18 and over 65.)

Top 10 Sights

1. Colosseum
2. Trajan's Markets
3. Nero's Golden House
4. Trajan's Forum and Column
5. Arch of Constantine
6. Mamertine Prison
7. House of the Knights of Rhodes
8. Forum of Nerva
9. Forum of Julius Caesar
10. Forum of Augustus

Colosseum

Here the imperial passion for bloody spectacle reached its peak of excess. When Emperor Titus inaugurated the amphitheatre *(right)* in AD 80, he declared 100 days of celebratory games, some involving the massacre of 5,000 wild beasts. All such slaughter-as-sport was legal until AD 523 *(see p40)*.

Trajan's Markets

The emperor and his visionary architect, Apollodorus of Damascus, built this attractive, very modern looking shopping and office mall *(left)* in the early 2nd century AD. There were 150 spaces in all, the top floor utilized by welfare offices, the lower levels by shops of all kinds.

 For more sights in Ancient Rome See pp118–21

3 Nero's Golden House (Domus Aurea)

This mad emperor's self-indulgence resulted in the largest, most sumptuous palace Rome ever saw, yet it was for amusement only. It covered several acres and had every luxury, including its own forest. Currently closed for restoration. *(See p41).*

Original Plan of the Imperial Fora

4 Trajan's Forum and Column

Trajan's Forum was so splendid that it left all who beheld it awed by its nobility. Now cut off by modern streets, all that stands out is the magnificent column *(right)*, commemorating in fine graphic detail the emperor's victories in what is now Romania. Access to part of it is through Trajan's Market.

6 Mamertine Prison

Legend holds that St Peter was imprisoned here. Prisoners were dropped down through a hole in the floor and the only exit was death. Currently closed to the public.

8 Forum of Nerva

If Pope Paul V hadn't stripped it to build the Acqua Paola fountain in the 17th century, the main attraction here would have been the Temple of Minerva. Two Corinthian columns remain, and a frieze above, depicting the myth of Arachne.

9 Forum of Julius Caesar

The first of Rome's Imperial Forums. Caesar's line, the Julians, traced their ancestry back to Venus herself, so he erected the Temple of Venus Genetrix (46 BC) and placed there statues of himself and Cleopatra, his great love.

10 Forum of Augustus

Julius Caesar's successor *(see p38)* made the focus of his forum the Temple of Mars the Avenger, identified by the broad staircase and four Corinthian columns.

5 Arch of Constantine

This arch *(right)* marks the victory of the first Christian emperor over his rival emperor Maxentius *(see p38)*. Yet it is mostly a pastiche of pagan elements taken from several earlier monuments – the beautiful hunt-scene roundels come from a temple dedicated to Emperor Hadrian's male lover, Antinous.

7 House of the Knights of Rhodes

This 12th-century priory was owned by the crusading order of the Knights of Rhodes. Inside are the original portico, three shops and the Chapel of St John.

Area Guide

Expect to take three hours to see everything. There are likely to be queues for the Colosseum and for Nero's Golden House, which is currently closed to the public. Use the Via IV Novembre entrance to Trajan's Markets. The fora of Augustus and Nerva can be viewed from Via dei Fori Imperiali.

▒10 Musei Capitolini

Capitoline Hill was ancient Rome's religious heart, and is now home to a magnificent museum. A gently stepped grade, the Cordonata leads you up the hill and provides an unforgettably theatrical experience, just as Michelangelo planned it in the 16th century. At the top you notice the outstretched hand of Emperor Marcus Aurelius, as he dispenses peace from astride his horse. The sides of the star-shaped piazza are graced by twin palaces that contain some of Rome's greatest treasures. The collections in the Palazzo Nuovo, detailed below, and in the Palazzo dei Conservatori (see pp26–7) were inaugurated in 1471 with a donation of bronzes by Pope Sixtus IV, and have been judiciously added to ever since.

Façade, Palazzo dei Conservatori

🍴 The café behind the Palazzo dei Conservatori (Caffè Capitolino) has a terrace with a spectacular panorama of the city.

🔁 Part of the underground passage between the museums is the Tabularium, ancient Rome's Hall of Records, from which you can get unusual views of the Forum.

• Piazza del Campidoglio
• Map N5
• 06 0608
• Open 9am–8pm Tue–Sun. Closed 1 Jan, 1 May, 25 Dec.
• Adm €6.50 (Free for EU citizens under 18 and over 65).
• The Capitolini Card costs €8.50 and is valid for 7 days. The card also gives admission to the Montemartini Art Centre (see p152)

Top 10 Features

1. Hall of the Emperors
2. Dying Gaul
3. Capitoline Venus
4. Mosaic of the Doves
5. Marforio
6. Resting Satyr
7. Hall of the Philosophers
8. Cupid and Psyche
9. Mosaic of the Masks
10. Drunken Old Woman

Key

▨ First floor

▨ Ground floor

1 Hall of the Emperors

The hall contains several portraits of the emperors and empresses of the Imperial Age. Among them is a bust of the brutal ruler Caracalla *(right)* from the 3rd-century AD.

2 Dying Gaul

The collection's most renowned piece *(below)* conveys great pathos. It is probably a 1st-century AD Roman copy of a Hellenistic bronze from the 3rd century BC.

3 Capitoline Venus

The shimmering goddess of love gets a room of her own. This fine 1st-century BC copy of a Praxiteles' Aphrodite from the 4th century BC shows her risen voluptuously from her bath, attempting to cover herself, as if reacting to someone's arrival.

4 Mosaic of the Doves

Originally the centre-piece of a floor decoration in Hadrian's Villa *(see p154)*, this jewel-like composition *(right)* uses tiny marble and glass chips *(tesserae)* to achieve a sense of texture and volume.

5 Marforio

This hirsute reclining giant *(below right)* was originally a river god, and is believed to come from the Forum of Augustus *(see p23)*. A Renaissance sculptor added the attributes of the god Ocean and placed him here, as overseer of this courtyard fountain.

8 Cupid and Psyche

The god of love embracing the personification of the soul, the two lovers are eternally united. This Roman copy of a Hellenistic original has inspired many sentimental variations.

9 Mosaic of the Masks

This floor decoration of two Greek theatre masks is probably from the 2nd-century AD. The use of perspective, light and shadow is highly skilled, employing small squares of coloured marble to create dramatic effects.

6 Resting Satyr

Used to adorn an ancient grove or fountain, this young mythological creature is a copy of a 4th-century BC original by Praxiteles. His pointed ears, panther-skin cape and flute are attributes of the nature-god Pan. The statue inspired Nathaniel Hawthorne's novel *The Marble Faun (see p56)*.

10 Drunken Old Woman

This copy of a Hellenistic original from the 3rd-century BC is from a series of sculptures depicting the wages of vice.

Museum Guide

The Palazzo Nuovo, on the left as you enter the piazza, contains mostly restored ancient sculpture. The finest pieces are on the upper floor. Then take the stairs down to the underpass that leads to the Palazzo dei Conservatori *(see pp26–7)*. The courtyard displays ancient marble fragments. The next floor up has 16th- and 17th-century decorations and Classical statuary. On the top floor are Renaissance and Baroque paintings.

7 Hall of the Philosophers

Roman copies of idealized Greek portrait busts of the greatest Hellenic poets and thinkers fill this room, including the blind epic poet Homer *(right)*.

Left **Lo Spinario** Right **Bronze she-wolf**

Palazzo dei Conservatori Exhibits

1 Colossal Statue of Constantine Fragments

Found in the ruins of the Basilica of Maxentius and Constantine, these surreal outsized body parts (c.AD 313–24) formed the unclothed segments of an overwhelming seated effigy of the first Christian emperor, recognizable by his protuberant eyes. The rest of the sculpture was made of carved wood dressed in sheets of bronze.

2 Lo Spinario

One of the precious bronzes that comprised Sixtus IV's donation to the people of Rome, this charming sculpture dates from the 1st century BC. Hellenistic in its everyday subject matter, the head recalls more archaic models. The boy's unusual and graceful pose inspired many works during the Renaissance.

3 Caravaggio's St John the Baptist

Shocking in its sensuality, the boy's erotic pose, his arm around the ram, created an iconographic revolution when it was unveiled around 1600. Masterful *chiaroscuro* brought the holy image even more down to earth.

4 Bronze she-wolf

The most ancient symbol of Rome, from the 5th century BC, of Etruscan or Greek workmanship. The she-wolf stands guard, at once a protectress and a nurturer, as the twins Romulus

Key to Palazzo dei Conservatori

▣	Second floor
▣	First floor
▣	Ground floor

and Remus *(see p38)* feed on her milk. This was also part of the 1471 donation of Pope Sixtus IV.

5 Guercino's Burial of St Petronilla

The influence of Caravaggio is clearly evident in this huge altarpiece, executed for St Peter's Basilica between 1621 and 1623. Powerful effects of light and dark combined with pronounced musculature and individuality of the figures bring the work directly into the viewer's physical world.

6 Caravaggio's Gypsy Fortune-Teller

An earlier work by Caravaggio, but just as revolutionary as his St John the Baptist. This subject is taken from everyday street life in

Caravaggio's Gypsy Fortune-Teller

late 16th-century Rome, which the painter knew intimately. Notice that the gypsy is slyly slipping the ring from the unsuspecting young dandy's finger.

7 Bust of L. Junius Brutus

Dating from between the 4th and 3rd centuries BC, this bronze bust is possibly the rarest object in the museum. Its identification as the first Roman consul is uncertain, because it also resembles Greek models of poets and philosophers. Its intense, inlaid glass eyes make it one of the most gripping portraits.

8 Pietro da Cortona's Rape of the Sabines

Baroque painting is said to have begun with this work (c.1630), where symmetry is abandoned and all is twisting, dynamic movement. It depicts an early episode in Roman history:

the new city had been founded but the population lacked women, so they stole those of the neighbouring Sabine tribe (see p38).

9 Bust of Commodus as Hercules

The 2nd-century emperor, who loved to fight wild animals in the Colosseum, had himself represented as the demigod Hercules, to promote his own divinity. The club in his right hand, the lion's mantle and the apples of the Hesperides in his left hand are all symbols of Hercules' labours.

10 Equestrian Statue of Marcus Aurelius

A copy of this 2nd-century AD bronze masterpiece *(left)* stands in the centre of the Capitoline star; the original is displayed on the first floor of the Palazzo dei Conservatori.

Marcus Aurelius on horseback

TOP 10 Museo Nazionale Romano

The National Museum of Rome, with its excellent Classical art collection, grew too vast for its home in the Baths of Diocletian, which closed in 1981. In 1998 the collection was split between various sites, becoming a truly modern, 21st-century museum. The Ludovisi, Mattei and Altemps collections of sculpture moved into the gorgeous 16th-century Palazzo Altemps near Piazza Navona (see pp30–31). The 19th-century Palazzo Massimo alle Terme, a former Jesuit College near Termini, received some of the best individual sculptures, as well as ancient mosaics and fantastic frescoes, some never previously displayed, as detailed below. The ancient Aula Ottagona inherited the oversized bathhouse sculptures; the Baths of Diocletian re-opened in 2000 with an important epigraphic collection and exhibition space (see p133).

Façade, Palazzo Massimo alle Terme

From Palazzo Altemps, pop into Piazza Navona for refreshments at Tre Scalini *(see p88).*

Call ahead for Palazzo Massimo tickets, as the frescoes and mosaics on the top floor are timed entry-only.

• Palazzo Massimo alle Terme: Largo di Villa Peretti 1, Map F3, 06 3996 7700, Open 9am–7:45pm Tue–Sun
• Palazzo Altemps: Piazza Sant'Apollinare 44, Map L2, 06 3996 7700, Open 9am–7:45pm Tue–Sun
• Closed 1 Jan and 25 Dec • A €7 ticket (valid for 7 days) gives admission to all Museo Nazionale Romano sites, the 7-day Archeo Pass costs €23 and gives entry to all of the above plus many other archaeological sites. Free for EU citizens under 18 and over 65

Top 10 Exhibits

1. Statue of Augustus
2. Triclinium Frescoes
3. Four Charioteers Mosaic
4. Wounded Niobid
5. Leucotea Nursing Dionysus
6. Bronze Dionysus
7. Discus Thrower
8. Ostia Altar
9. Scenes from the Basilica of Giunio Basso
10. Numismatic Collection

1 Statue of Augustus

This statue of Rome's first emperor *(below right)* once stood on Via Labicana. It shows Augustus wearing his toga draped over his head – a sign that, in AD 12, he added the title *Pontifex Maximus* (high priest) to the list of honours he assigned himself.

2 Triclinium Frescoes

These frescoes (20–10 BC) depicting a lush garden came from the villa of Augustus's wife, Livia. They were in the *triclinium*, a dining pavilion half-buried to keep it cool in summer.

3 Four Charioteers Mosaic

The imperial Severi family must have been passionate about sports to have decorated a bedroom of their 3rd-century AD villa with these charioteers *(above)*. They are dressed in the traditional colours of the Roman circus's four factions.

For more museums in Rome See pp42–3

4 Wounded Niobid

This hauntingly beautiful figure of Niobid (daughter of Queen Niobe), reaching for the fatal arrow that killed her siblings *(right)*, was sculpted around 440 BC for a Greek temple, and was later acquired by Julius Caesar.

6 Bronze Dionysus

Few large Classical bronzes survive today, making this 2nd-century AD statue special beyond its obvious grace, skill and preserved decoration. You can still see the yellow eyes, red lips and a comb band in the grape-festooned hair.

7 Discus Thrower

This 2nd-century AD marble copy *(below)* of the famous 450 BC Greek original by Myron is faithful to the point of imitating the original bronze's imperfect dimensions.

5 Leucotea Nursing Dionysus

A luxuriously frescoed villa, discovered in 1879, included this bedroom scene of the nymph nursing the wine god *(below)* with additional scenes in the niches.

8 Ostia Altar

This Trajan-era altar connects the foundation of Rome to the divine consorts Mars and Venus. Mars is shown as father to Rome's legendary founder Romulus (see p38); Venus bears the hero Aeneas, who fled Troy for Rome and consequently founded the Iulia dynasty (Julius Caesar's own, invented family tree).

9 Scenes from the Basilica of Giunio Basso

Colourful marble inlays represent paganism's dying grasp among prominent Roman families *(below)*. The empire had converted to Christianity by AD 331 when consul Giunio Basso (pictured as a charioteer in one panel) commissioned the scenes for his meeting hall.

10 Numismatic Collection

Italian coinage and currency is on display here, from the Roman Republic and Empire coins through to the medieval and Renaissance principalities, to the lira and the euro.

Gallery Guide

The Palazzo Massimo exhibits all its statuary relating to Republican and Early Imperial Rome (up to Emperor Augustus) on the ground floor, along with a few precious earlier, Greek pieces. The first floor exhibits detail art in the political, cultural and economic spheres of Imperial Rome up to the 4th century. The second floor, which must be visited on a timed-entry ticket, preserves ancient mosaics and frescoes. The numismatic collection is in the basement, alongside some gold jewellery and a mummified eight-year-old girl.

Left **Grande Ludovisi sarcophagus** Right **Relief, Ludovisi throne**

Palazzo Altemps Collection

Garden of Delights Loggia
The loggia frescoes (c.1595) are a catalogue of the exotic fruits, plants and animals then being imported from the New World.

Athena Parthenos
The 1st-century BC Greek sculptor Antioco carved this statue to match the most famed sculpture in antiquity, the long-lost Athena in Athens' Parthenon.

"Grande Ludovisi" Sarcophagus
This mid-3rd century AD sarcophagus, deeply carved and remarkably well-preserved, shows the Romans victorious over the barbarian Ostrogoth hordes.

Orestes and Electra
This 1st-century AD statue was carved by Menelaus, an imitator of the great Greek artist Praxiteles. The scraps of 15th-century fresco nearby depict some wedding gifts from the marriage of Girolamo Riario and Caterina Sforza.

Ludovisi Throne
This set of 5th-century BC reliefs depicting the birth of Aphrodite came to Rome from a Calabrian Greek colony and were discovered in the 19th century.

Dionysus with Satyr
Imperial Rome was in love with Greek sculpture, producing copies such as this grouping of Dionysus, a satyr and a panther.

Apollo Playing the Lute
There are two 1st-century AD Apollos in the museum, both restored in the 17th century.

Suicidal Gaul
This suicidal figure supporting his dead wife's arm was part of a trio, including the Capitoline's Dying Gaul (see p24) commissioned by Julius Caesar to celebrate a Gaulish victory.

Egyptian Statuary
The Egyptian collections are divided into three sections related to that culture's influence on Rome: political theological, popular worship and places of worship. The showpiece is the impressive granite *Bull Api*, or *Brancaccio Bull* (2nd century BC).

Colossal Head of Ludovisi Hera

Colossal Head of Ludovisi Hera

Colossal Head of Ludovisi Hera
German writer Goethe called this his "first love in Rome". It is believed to be a portrait of Claudius's mother, Antonia.

Ancient Roman Art

Ancient Rome's art was as conservative as its culture. Sculpture, the most durable art form, was also the least original. From the middle Republican period through to the Imperial age, Romans shunned original pieces for copies of famous Greek works. The Caesars imported shiploads of Golden Age statuary from Greece and its old colonies in southern Italy; Roman workshops churned out headless, toga-wearing figures in a variety of stock poses to which any bust could be affixed. It was at bust portraiture that Romans truly excelled, especially up to the early Imperial age when naturalism was still in vogue. Roman painting is divided into styles based on Pompeii examples. The First Style imitated marble panels; the Second Style imitated architecture, often set within the small painted scenes that became a hallmark of the Third Style. The Fourth Style was trompe-l'oeil decoration. Mosaic, initially developed as a floor-strengthening technique, could be simple black-on-white or intricate wall-mounted scenes using tiny marble chips to create shading and contour. Opus sectile (inlaid marble) was a style that was imported from the East.

Roman Goddess

Marble carving, such as this sitting figure of a goddess, was one of the most popular and enduring of Roman art forms. The fluidity of the woman's robes is particularly impressive.

Mosaic of Virgil and the Muses

🔟 Santa Maria del Popolo

Few churches are such perfect primers on Roman art and architecture. Masters from the Early Renaissance (Pinturicchio, Bramante), High Renaissance (Raphael) and Baroque (Caravaggio, Bernini) exercised their genius in all disciplines here: painting, sculpture, architecture and decoration. It's also one of the few churches with major chapels still intact, preserving the artworks that together tell a complete story (most Italian chapels have been dismantled, their paintings now in museums). In the Cerasi Chapel, Caravaggio and Carracci collaborated with a frescoist to create a depiction of Peter, Paul and Mary and, on the vault, their connections to Heaven. Bernini altered Raphael's Chigi Chapel to help clarify the interplay of its art across the small space.

Façade, Santa Maria del Popolo

🍽 Canova and Rosati cafés *(see p116)* are both on Piazza del Popolo.

✪ Some of the church's treasures are behind the High Altar in the choir and apse. When mass is not in session, you are allowed to go behind the curtain to the left of the altar and switch on the lights in the fuse box to see them.

- Piazza del Popolo 12
- Map D2
- Open 8am–noon, 4–7pm daily
- Free

Top 10 Features
1. Crucifixion of St Peter
2. Conversion of St Paul
3. Raphael's Chigi Chapel
4. Bernini's Chigi Chapel
5. Pinturicchio's *Adoration*
6. Sansovino Tombs
7. Marcillat's Stained-Glass Window
8. Bramante's Apse
9. Cybo Chapel
10. Sebastiano del Piombo's *Nativity of the Virgin*

Crucifixion of St Peter
Caravaggio has avoided the melodrama and goriness of his earlier works and packed drama into this *chiaroscuro* work (1601). The naturalistic figures quietly go about their business, the tired workers hauling the cross into place, Peter looking sad and contemplative *(below)*.

Conversion of St Paul
Again, Caravaggio leaves all drama to the effects of light, depicting an awe-struck Paul transfixed by blinding light (1601).

Raphael's Chigi Chapel
Raphael designed this exquisite chapel for papal banker Agostini Chigi, including the frescoes and niche statues (1519–23).

For more Roman churches See pp44–5

Bernini's Chigi Chapel

Cardinal Fabio Chigi hired Bernini to finish the job begun by Raphael 130 years earlier. The artist only deviated from the original plan in two Biblical niche statues *(above)*.

Pinturicchio's Adoration

Raphael's elder contemporary retained more of their teacher Perugino's limpid Umbrian style in this 1490 work in the della Rovere chapel. Also in the chapel is Cardinal Cristoforo's tomb sculpted by Francesco da Sangallo (1478), while Domenico's tomb (1477) features a *Madonna with Child* by Mino da Fiesole.

Sansovino Tombs

Under triumphal arch tombs, Tuscan Andrea Sansovino gave a Renaissance/Etruscan twist to the traditional lying-in-state look (1505–07). These effigies of Cardinal Girolamo Basso della Rovere and Cardinal Asciano Sforza recline on cushions as if merely asleep *(below)*.

Marcillat's Stained-Glass Window

The only Roman work by Guillaume de Marcillat (1509), the undisputed French master of stained glass, depicts the Infancy of Christ and Life of the Virgin *(below)*.

Bramante's Apse

The Renaissance architect's first work in Rome, commissioned by Julius II around 1500, was this beautiful light-filled choir and scallop shell-shaped apse.

Plan of Santa Maria del Popolo

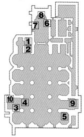

Cybo Chapel

Carlo Fontana managed to make this Baroque confection of multicoloured marbles and a Carlo Maratta *Immaculate Conception* altarpiece blend together in his 1682–7 design.

Sebastiano del Piombo's Nativity of the Virgin

This altarpiece in the Chigi Chapel (1530–34) is in contrast to the dome's Neo-pagan themes, the Eternal Father blessing Chigi's horoscope of planets symbolized by pagan gods.

The People's Church

The ghost of Nero, buried in the Domitia family crypt on the Pincio *(see p62)*, terrorized this neighbourhood in the form of demon crows that lived in a cursed tree. Pope Paschal II reassured the locals in 1099 by replacing the tree with a chapel paid for by the people *(il popolo)*. It was enlarged in 1227 and rebuilt in Lombard style in 1472–7. Andrea Bregno may have added the Renaissance façade, and Bernini a Baroque touch to the interior.

San Clemente

Nowhere else in Rome can give such a clear idea of the city's layering and millennia of cultural riches than this wonderful church. The very lowest level remains largely unexplored, dating back to Republican Rome, probably the 2nd century BC. At the deepest excavated level there are 1st-century AD buildings, including an early house of Christian worship and a temple dedicated to the Persian god, Mithras. Above that is a partially intact 4th-century AD basilica. When that edifice was burned in the Norman sacking of 1084, the space was filled in and a new church was built, using some of the original architectural elements. In 1857, the Irish Dominican prior, Father Mullooly, accidentally discovered the lower church and began the long process of emptying out the rubble.

Façade, San Clemente

○ Cafés and restaurants abound in the area. Try Cannavota *(see p131)* for a traditional Roman meal.

○ Bring a small torch, so that you can make out the ancient decorations in the shadowy Mithraeum. But no photos or videos are allowed, and they mean it!

• Via di S Giovanni in Laterano 108
• Map F4
• 06 774 0021
• Open 9am–12:30pm, 3–6pm daily (from 10am Sun)
• Adm €5 to lower levels

Top 10 Features

1 Apse Mosaic
2 Legend of Sisinius Frescoes
3 Mithraeum
4 St Catherine's Chapel
5 Miracle of San Clemente Frescoes
6 Schola Cantorum
7 1st-century BC Domus
8 Cosmatesque Pavement
9 Paschal Candlestick
10 Courtyard and Façade

Apse Mosaic
Few images are more joyous than this 12th-century variation on the tree-of-life, in the Upper Church *(below)*. Plump cupids, winsome animals and lush foliage evoke a new-found Paradise. The stone and glass squares were taken from a similar work in the destroyed 4th-century church below it.

Legend of Sisinius Frescoes
These frescoes in the Lower Church relate how a wealthy pagan, Sisinius, was struck deaf and blind for suspecting his Christian wife of infidelity. St Clement cures him but incurs his wrath and Sisinius's furious commands are the first known inscriptions in Italian.

Mithraeum
The triclinium, with its platforms along both sides, was used for ritual banqueting, where the male-only congregation imitated the gods' last meal before they re-ascended to heaven. The altar painting shows Mithras slaying the Cosmic Bull to bring about Creation.

St Catherine's Chapel
The restored frescoes *(above)* in the Upper Church by the 15th-century Florentine artist Masolino show vibrant scenes from the life of St Catherine of Alexandria. These provide one of the few opportunities in Rome to appreciate the painting of the early Florentine Renaissance.

Miracle of San Clemente Frescoes
These frescoes in the Lower Church show how St Clement saved a boy from drowning.

Schola Cantorum
The enclosure for the choir in the Upper Church *(above right)*, a gift from Pope John II (AD 535–55), was retained when a new choir was built. It is walled with panels of white marble inlaid with colourful mosaics and carved with early Christian symbols.

1st-century BC Domus
This mansion belonged to a man named Clemens, perhaps a relative of an early Christian martyr and of St Clement, or perhaps a freed man of Jewish birth. The 4th-century church was built precisely over the 1st-century site.

Cosmatesque Pavement
This technique *(below)*, developed by the Cosmati family in the 12th century, involved using fragments of stone from Roman ruins, to create intricate, geometric patterns.

Paschal Candlestick
This 12th-century spiralling motif *(left)*, striped with glittering mosaics of ancient glass, is another magnificent example of work by Cosmati artisans in the Upper Church.

Courtyard and Façade
The original entrance was through the *quadroporticus*, the medieval colonnaded square forecourt. The fountain and the scrolled façade were added in the early 18th century.

Church Guide
You can usually enter both through the balconied front gate or by a side door, off the small piazza on Via di San Giovanni in Laterano. The entrance to the Lower Church and archaeological areas is through the sacristy vestibule, where you'll also find books, slides and attractive postcards of the two churches and the Mithraic temple's works of art. The 1st-century alleyways beneath are no place for claustrophobics, but the refreshing sound of the underground spring down below may provide some relief.

📖 Ostia Antica

Some 2,000 years ago, ancient Rome's lively international port city was right on the beach and at the mouth of the Tiber (ostium means "river mouth"). In the ensuing millennia the sea has retreated several kilometres and the river has changed course dramatically. Ostia was founded in the 4th century BC, first as a simple fort, but as Rome grew, the town became ever more important as the distribution point for imports from around the Mediterranean. Grain was the most vital commodity, to feed Rome's one million inhabitants, and so huge storage bins (horrea) were built here. Goods were sent up to Rome on river barges. Ostia's heyday ended in the 4th century AD, and it died completely as an inhabited area about 1,000 years ago.

Forum

🍴 There's a snack bar behind the museum, which is a great place to refuel and refresh on a hot day.

🔊 The ruined walls can look confusingly similar, so rent one of the audioguides where you buy your entrance ticket.

- Viale dei Romagnoli 717
- Metro B, trams 3 and 30, or buses 23, 75, 95, 280 to Piramide, then local train from Porta San Paolo Station to Ostia Antica
- 06 5635 8003
- Open Nov–Feb: 8:30am–5pm daily; Mar: 8:30am–6pm daily; Apr–Oct: 8:30am–7:30pm daily, closed 1 Jan, 1 May, 25 Dec
- Adm €6.50 (reduced €3.25)
- The port area (Trajan's Port) can be visited on request, 06 6501 0089

Top 10 Features

1. Decumanus Maximus
2. Theatre
3. Casa di Diana and Thermopolium
4. Museum
5. Forum
6. Capitolium
7. Terme dei Sette Sapienti
8. House of Cupid and Psyche
9. Terme di Nettuno
10. Mithraeum of the Serpents

1 Decumanus Maximus

You enter the park by way of the ancient Via Ostiensis. The white marble goddess on the left marks the beginning of city's main street, the Decumanus Maximus *(above)*.

2 Theatre

The original theatre was twice as tall as it now stands *(centre)*. Behind the stage was a temple, of either Ceres (goddess of grain) or Dionysus (god of theatre). Around the square, mosaics *(right)* advertise various import businesses: grain, wild animals, ivory and shipping.

3 Casa di Diana and Thermopolium

You can climb up to the top of this *insula* (apartment block) for a great view. Across the street is the Thermopolium, a tavern with a wall-painting of menu items.

For more ancient sights in Rome See pp40–41

Museum
Beautifully organized, the displays include precious sculptures, sarcophagi and mosaics found among the ruins. One of the highlights is a marble statue of the god Mithras about to sacrifice the Cosmic Bull.

Forum
The rectangular heart of officialdom was originally surrounded by columns. In the centre was a shrine to the Imperial Lares (household gods).

Ostia Antica

Terme di Nettuno
Built in the 2nd century, this bath complex *(left)* was enhanced with fine mosaics of sea-gods and sea-monsters, which you can view from a small terrace. You can also go down along to the left to study close-up the baths' ingenious heating system.

Mithraeum of the Serpents
This was one of 18 Ostian temples to Mithras. The cult was very popular with Roman soldiers, and flourished especially well in port towns. The frescoes of snakes invoked the earth's fertility, while the platforms were for lying on during mystic banquets.

Park Guide
Arrival by local train is very easy, and takes about 20 minutes from Porta San Paolo station, next to the Piramide underground stop. The cost of the trip is one regular bus ticket. From the Ostia Antica train station, walk straight out to the footbridge that goes over the highway. Continue straight on past the restaurant until you get to the ticket booth. The park is very extensive and a decent visit will take at least three hours. Wear sturdy shoes, and bring sunscreen and a bottle of water on hot days.

Terme dei Sette Sapienti
This elaborate bath complex contains a painting of Venus, floor mosaics of hunters and animals and nude athletes and marine scenes.

Capitolium
Dominating the city was the monumental temple to the Capitoline Triad – Jupiter, Juno and Minerva. Climb the staircase *(above)* to examine the threshold stone of rare Lucullan marble.

House of Cupid and Psyche
The wealthy had villas like this refined example of a 3rd-century AD *domus*. You can still admire the Doric columns, the fountain *(nymphaeum)* and the inlaid marble decorations.

Left **Rome burns** Right **Mussolini and Fascists march on Rome, 1922**

10 Moments in History

1 Romulus and Remus

The foundation of Rome is said to have occurred in 753 BC. Twins Romulus and Remus, sons of Mars and a Vestal Virgin, were set adrift by their evil uncle and suckled by a she-wolf. They then founded rival Bronze Age villages on the Palatine, but Romulus killed Remus during an argument, and his "Rome" went on to greatness.

2 Rape of the Sabine Women

To boost the female population in the 750s BC Romulus's men kidnapped women from the neighbouring Sabine kingdom. As Rome began to expand, however, the kingdoms were united. Rome was later conquered by the Etruscan Tarquin dynasty. In 510 BC, a patrician-ruled Republic was formed that lasted more than 450 years.

3 Assassination of Caesar

A series of military victories, adding Gaul (France) to Rome, increased General Julius Caesar's popularity. He marched his army to Rome and declared himself Dictator for Life, but on 15 March 44 BC he was assassinated. Caesar's adopted son Octavian changed his name to Augustus and declared himself emperor in 27 BC.

Bust, Julius Caesar

4 Rome Burns

In AD 64 fire destroyed much of Rome. Emperor Nero rebuilt many public works, but also appropriated vast tracts of land to build his Golden House. Hounded from office, he committed suicide in AD 68 *(see p41)*.

5 Battle at Milvian Bridge

In 312 Emperor Constantine, whose mother was a Christian, had a vision of victory under the sign of the Cross and defeated co-emperor Maxentius at Milvian Bridge. He declared Christianity the state religion.

6 Fall of the Empire

By the late 4th century Rome was in decline, as Barbarians from across the Rhine and Danube conquered outlying provinces. In 476, the last emperor was deposed and the Empire fell.

7 Papacy moves to Avignon

Following the departure of the papacy to France in 1309, the city became a backwater ruled by petty princes who built palaces out of marble from the great temples. In 1377 the papacy returned to Rome, and the city was reborn.

Papal Palace, Avignon

Sack of Rome

8 Rome was conquered for the first time in more than a millennium in 1527. Emperor Charles V's Germanic troops held the city for seven months until Pope Clement VII surrendered and promised to address concerns of the new Protestant movement.

Unification of Italy

9 Piemontese King Vittorio Emanuele II and his general, Garibaldi, spent years conquering the peninsula's kingdoms and principalities to create a new country called Italy. In 1870, Garibaldi breached the Aurelian walls and took the ancient capital, completing Italian Unification.

Mussolini Takes Power

10 Benito "Il Duce" Mussolini, leader of the nationalistic Fascist Party, marched on Rome in 1922 and was declared prime minister. Delusions of imperial grandeur led him to excavate many of the ruins we see today. He allied Italy with Hitler, but when the tides turned, Mussolini was deposed and Italy joined Allied troops. The current Republic was set up in 1946.

Top 10 Influential Popes

1 St Peter
The Apostle (AD 42–67) tapped by Jesus to lead the church. After his martyrdom in Rome the city became the epicentre of Christianity.

2 St Leo the Great
Rome's bishop (440–61) made himself *pontifex maximus* of the Christian church.

3 St Gregory the Great
Affirmed the papacy as the western secular leader and converted England to Christianity (590–604).

4 Innocent III
This medieval pope (1198–1216) hand-picked emperors and approved monkish orders.

5 Boniface VIII
Imperious, pragmatic and power-hungry, Boniface (1294–1303) instituted the first Jubilee to make money.

6 Alexander VI
Ruthless Borgia pope (1492–1503) used the pontificate to destroy rival families.

7 Julius II
Warrior pope and patron of the arts (1513–21), he hired Michelangelo for the Sistine Chapel and Raphael to decorate his apartment (see p8).

8 Paul III
Scholarly and secular, but fighting Protestant reforms, Paul III (1534–49) founded the Jesuits and the Inquisition.

9 Sixtus V
Cleansed Papal States of corruption (1585–90) and masterminded a Baroque overhaul of Rome.

10 John Paul II
The first non-Italian Pope for over 400 years, John Paul II (1920-2005), was famed for his extensive travelling.

Left **Roman Forum and Colosseum** Centre **Palatine fresco** Right **Domus Augustana, Palatine Hill**

Ancient Sights

Roman Forum

In the centre of the Forum stands a humble ruined structure where fresh flowers are placed year-round. This is the foundation of the Temple to Julius Caesar, built by Augustus in the 1st century BC. The flowers indicate the exact spot of Caesar's cremation *(see pp16–17)*.

Pantheon

Originally worshippers approached this temple to all the gods by a steep staircase, but the street level has risen since the 2nd century. The present temple was built by Hadrian, after the 1st-century BC temple burned down *(see pp14–15)*.

Imperial Fora

The largest temple and one of the most commanding of this imposing zone was the 2nd-century AD Temple of Venus and Rome, its columns standing high on the hill between the Forum and the Colosseum. Its back-to-back design was Hadrian's, and when the great architect Apollodorus criticized it, Hadrian had him put to death *(see pp22–3)*.

Colosseum

Colosseum

The backbreaking labour to build the greatest of amphi-theatres was carried out by a horde of Jewish slaves, brought here following the suppression of their revolt in Judaea. The structure has been the archetype for the world's sports stadiums ever since *(see p22)*.

Palatine Hill

Most European languages derive their word for palace from the name of this hill. All-important in the history of early Rome, first as its birthplace, then as the home of its leaders' opulent homes, it now serves as a bucolic setting for a romantic stroll *(see pp18–19)*.

Baths of Diocletian

A large section of this huge 3rd-century AD complex now houses an excellent archaeo-logical museum, including a marble sculpture of Mithras that still retains its gold leaf and paint. A vast Michelangelo cloister is decorated with ancient statuary *(see p133)*.

Column of Marcus Aurelius

A 2nd-century AD commemoration of conquests along the Danube, this colossus stands 30 m (100 ft) high and is composed of 28 marble drums. The 20 spiral reliefs realistically chronicle scenes from two wars. A statue of the emperor and his

For more on Ancient Rome **See pp118–21**

wife once stood on top of the column, but it was replaced by one of St Paul in 1589 (see p92).

Baths of Caracalla

The most popular spa of ancient Rome, the Baths of Caracalla included exercise areas, hot and cold pools, social lounges, art centres, brothels and libraries. Incredibly, access to the *terme* was free. Today, the archaeological complex hosts Rome's most important opera festival (see p19).

Largo di Torre Argentina

Discovered in the 1920s, four Republican temples stand out distinctly, with the columns of a portico at the north end. The drainage gutters of an Imperial public latrine are behind one temple, and behind others stands the tufa-block platform of the Curia of the Theatre of Pompey. Caesar was killed here on 15 March 44 BC (see p99).

Largo di Torre Argentina

Theatre of Marcellus

The theatre was inaugurated by Augustus in 23 BC and dedicated to his nephew and son-in-law Marcellus, who had just died, aged 19. Not much remains of the once huge structure, which held up to 20,000 people. In later ages, what was left of it was used as support for medieval and Renaissance fortresses and palaces (see p101).

Top 10 Roman Emperors

1 Augustus
The first and most brilliant emperor (31 BC–AD 14) brought a reign of peace after 17 years of civil war.

2 Nero
The most notorious for his excesses, Nero (54–68) fancied himself a great singer and showman. He eventually committed suicide.

3 Vespasian
This emperor (69–79) ended civil war and the Jewish revolt, and started construction of the Colosseum.

4 Trajan
One of the most just rulers and successful generals, Trajan (98–117) pushed the Empire to its furthest reaches.

5 Hadrian
A great builder and traveller, Hadrian (117–38) revived Greek ideals, including the fashion of growing a beard.

6 Marcus Aurelius
The closest Rome came to having a philosopher-king of the Platonic ideal (161–80).

7 Septimius Severus
Brought order after civil war, promoted cultural life and left an important architectural legacy (193–211).

8 Diocletian
Diocletian (284–305) set up a governing system of multiple emperors. A virulent persecutor of the Christians.

9 Constantine
Constantine (306–37) established Christianity as the state religion and moved the capital to Constantinople.

10 Romulus Augustulus
The last of the emperors (475–6), deposed by the German warrior Odoacer.

Left **Sala dei Misteri, Vatican Museums** Right **Palazzo dei Conservatori, Musei Capitolini**

Museums and Galleries

1 Vatican Museums

Occupying papal palaces dating from the 13th century onwards, these galleries include the Graeco-Roman antiquities, the Etruscan Museum, four Raphael Rooms, the Collection of Modern Religious Art, the Sistine Chapel and the Picture Gallery (see pp8–11).

2 Museo Nazionale Romano

Founded in 1889, this museum's holdings include archaeological finds and antiquities unearthed since 1870, plus pre-existing collections. The works are spread around five separate locations: the Baths of Diocletian, the Aula Ottagona – a part of the baths, nearby Palazzo Massimo, Palazzo Altemps, and the Crypta Balbi (see pp28–31).

3 Galleria Borghese

A tribute to the unbridled power of favoured papal nephews in the 1600s, this pleasure-palace, its priceless collections of art and its restored gardens comprise one of the most gorgeous sights in Rome (see pp20–21).

4 Musei Capitolini

The glorious square, designed by no less than Michelangelo, is home to smaller papal art collections than the Vatican's, but equally invaluable (see pp24–7).

Hellenistic faun, Galleria Borghese

5 Galleria Nazionale d'Arte Antica

This state art collection is divided between two noble family residences: Palazzo Barberini (see p133) and Palazzo Corsini (see p142). The first boasts the Gran Salone, with its dazzling illusionistic ceiling by Pietro da Cortona, along with works by Filippo Lippi, El Greco, Holbein and Caravaggio. The second houses a Fra Angelico triptych, and paintings by Rubens, Van Dyck and Caravaggio.

6 Villa Giulia

The building itself is a 16th-century country retreat designed for Pope Julius III by Vignola. Since 1889, it has housed the state collection of pre-Roman art, including Etruscan artifacts and relics of the Latins and other tribes. The prize Etruscan work is the 6th-century BC Husband and Wife Sarcophagus, a large terracotta showing a serenely smiling couple on a couch (see p112).

7 Galleria Doria Pamphilj

This aristocratic family's palace is filled with master-pieces by such painters as Raphael, Titian and Velázquez, whose portrait of the Pamphilj pope is famous for its psychological depth. This exhibit is fortunate to have a superb audio-guide, narrated by the present-day Prince Jonathan Doria Pamphilj (in English) that gives rare insight into the history of the collection *(see p91)*.

Palazzo and Galleria Spada

This superb 16th-century palace contains a specially built 17th-century gallery to hold the cardinals' collection of Renaissance, Baroque and later works, including paintings by Rubens and Jan Brueghel the Elder. One of the high points is Borromini's whimsical *trompe-l'oeil* gallery, a clever study in illusory perspective that appears to be four times longer that it really is *(see p104)*.

Villa Giulia

Galleria Nazionale d'Arte Moderna

The *belle époque* home to this collection offers sculptures by Canova and an exhaustive view of 19th-century Italian and European painting. There is also an eclectic selection of modern works, including pieces by artists such as Rodin, Cézanne, Modigliani, Van Gogh, Monet, Klimt and Jackson Pollock *(see p112)*.

Palazzo delle Esposizioni

This garishly triumphant palazzo was designed by architect Pio Piacentini and opened in 1883 as part of a project to revamp the city to Capital status. Today it houses a gallery and expo centre that hosts various exhibits, from contemporary art collections to retrospectives of renowned film directors. Via Nazionale 194 • Map E3 • 06 3996 7500 • 9:30am–8pm Tue–Thu, 9:30am–10:30pm Fri & Sat, 10am–8pm Sun • Adm

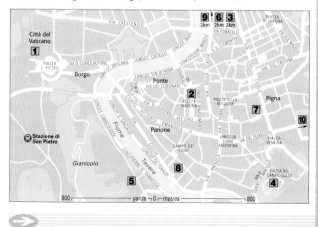

Left **Sarcophagus, San Clemente** Centre **Santa Maria Maggiore** Right **Santa Maria sopra Minerva**

🔟 Churches

1 St Peter's Basilica
Should the opportunity arise, don't miss seeing the basilica's cavernous interior when all the lights are on – only then can you fully appreciate this giant jewel-box of colour *(see pp12–13).*

2 Santa Maria del Popolo
Legend recounts that on this spot, where a magnificent oak grew, Nero died and was buried. The site was thought cursed, but in 1099, in a vision, the Virgin told Pope Paschal II to fell the oak, dig up the evil emperor's bones and build a chapel *(see pp32–3).*

3 San Clemente
This modest yet compelling church provides a concise Roman history lesson in one concentrated location *(see pp34–5).*

4 Santa Maria Maggiore
One of Rome's greatest basilicas, this richly decorated church dates from the 5th century, as do its earliest mosaics, full of Byzantine splendour. The 16th-century Cappella Sistina's rare marbles were "quarried", in typical papal fashion, by destroying an ancient wonder – the Palatine's Septizonium, a tower erected by Septimius Severus in AD 203 *(see p127).*

5 Santa Maria sopra Minerva
Raised over an ancient temple of wisdom, this is Rome's only Florentine Gothic church, built around 1280. In the 16th century it was the stronghold of the Inquisition in Rome. Among its great art is Michelangelo's *Risen Christ*, created nude but now sporting a skewed, gilt-bronze loincloth. The body of St Catherine of Siena, who convinced the papacy to return from France in 1377, reclines under the altar *(see p91).*

6 San Giovanni in Laterano
The "Mother of All Churches", the cathedral of Rome's bishopric was founded by Constantine in the 4th century. It was the chief papal residence until 1309, and popes were crowned here up until the 19th century. Its most recent renovation was ordered in 1650, explaining its present-day heavy Baroque grandeur, containing mammoth depictions of saints. The remarkable cloisters are 13th-century Cosmatesque *(see p127).*

San Giovanni in Laterano

7 Santa Maria in Trastevere

This is probably Rome's oldest church and certainly one of the most intimate and charming. Dating from the time of Pope Calixtus I (AD 217–222), it was an early centre of Marian devotion and is Rome's only medieval church that has not been transmogrified by either decay or enthusiastic Baroque renovators. Legend claims it was founded on a spot where olive oil miraculously sprang forth on the day of Christ's birth *(see p139)*.

San Luigi dei Francesi statue

8 San Luigi dei Francesi

The priceless attraction in the national church of France in Italy is Caravaggio's famous trio of enormous paintings in the Chapel of St Matthew *(see p49)*. These were his first great religious works. The central oil on canvas, *St Matthew and the Angel*, is the second version. The first was rejected by the church because the saint was shown with dirty feet – and, some say, because his relationship with the young angel seemed inappropriately intimate *(see p83)*.

9 San Paolo fuori le Mura

Despite its rather soulless 19th-century reconstruction following a fire, the grandeur of this 4th-century basilica can still impress. Some restored 5th-, 12th- and 13th-century mosaics survive, along with the original 11th-century bronze door and a grand Paschal candlestick. Fortunately, the cloisters of inlaid double columns (1214), considered the most beautiful in Rome, escaped the flames *(see p151)*.

10 Sant'Andrea della Valle

Most visitors seek out this church as the setting of the first act of Puccini's opera *Tosca*, but the Counter-Reformation giant is also important in its own right. It has

Sant'Andrea della Valle

the city's second-largest dome, a flamboyant Baroque façade and some wonderful frescoes by Domenichino inside *(see p99)*.

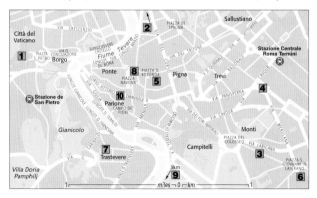

Left **Fontana delle Tartarughe** Right **Piazza San Pietro**

🔟 Squares and Fountains

Piazza Navona
The elongated oval of Rome's loveliest square hints that it is built atop Domitian's ancient stadium *(see p86)*. This pedestrian paradise is filled with cafés, street performers and artists, milling tourists, kids playing football, and splashing fountains. Bernini designed the central Fountain of Four Rivers, and added the Moor figure to the most southerly of the piazza's other two fountains, constantly altered from the 16th to 19th centuries *(see p83)*.

Trevi Fountain

Trevi Fountain
Tradition holds that if you throw coins into this 1732 Nicola Salvi fountain, you ensure a return to Rome. Ingeniously grafted on to the back of a palazzo (even the windowsills mutate into rough rocks), the Trevi marks the end of the Acqua Vergine aqueduct, built by Agrippa in 19 BC from a spring miraculously discovered by a virgin *(see p109)*.

Campo de' Fiori
This "field of flowers" bursts with colour during the morning market, and again after dark when its pubs and bars make it a centre of Roman nightlife. The dour hooded statue overlooking all is in honour of Giordano Bruno, a theologian who was burned at the stake here for his progressive heresies in 1600 during the Counter-Reformation *(see p99)*.

Piazza del Popolo
Architect Giuseppe Valadier expanded this site of festivals and public executions into an elegant piazza in 1811–23, adding four Egyptian-style lion fountains to the base of one of Rome's oldest obelisks. The 1200 BC Ramases II monolith was moved to the Circus Maximus by Augustus then placed here by Pope Sixtus V *(see p110)*.

Piazza San Pietro
Bernini's gargantuan colonnade, 196 m (640 ft) across, embraces the hordes of worshippers and tourists arriving at St Peter's. Its perfect ellipse is confirmed by the optical illusion of disappearing columns afforded by standing at one of the focus points – marble discs set between the central 1st-century BC obelisk, carved in Egypt for a Roman Prefect, and either fountain: Bernini's on the left, Domenico Fontana's on the right *(see p12)*. ◈ Map B3

6 Fontana delle Tartarughe
Giacomo della Porta designed this delightful fountain between 1581 and 1584. The turtles *(tartarughe)* struggling up over the lip, however, were added in 1658, perhaps by Bernini *(see p101)*.

7 Piazza Barberini
This busy piazza is centred on Bernini's Triton Fountain (1642–3), the merman spouting water from a conch shell. It was commissioned by Pope Urban VIII and features his family symbol (bees) on its base *(see p133)*.

8 Piazza Venezia
The de facto centre of Rome and convergence of traffic patterns, during evening rush hour conducted with balletic brio by a white-gloved policeman. The piazza is flanked by the Palazzo Venezia, from whose balcony Mussolini once exhorted hordes to the joys of Fascism *(see p104)*.

Piazza del Popolo

9 Fountain of the Naiads
The water spouting from Bernini's Triton is puny compared to the gushes rising from Glaucus in this huge fountain and traffic circle. The fountain is surrounded by naiads and horses in this 1888 confection by Mario Rutelli (grandfather of Francesco, the city's mayor from 1993 to 2001). ◉ *Piazza della Repubblica • Map C3*

10 Piazza Santa Maria in Trastevere
A perfect neighbourhood square: cafés, shops, a fine restaurant and a 17th-century palazzo abutting a medieval church, its mosaics romantically floodlit at night. A fountain fitted with shells by Carlo Fontana (1682) atop a pedestal of stairs serves as benches for backpackers to strum guitars and tourists to eat ice cream *(see p139)*.

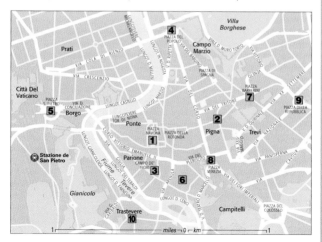

Left **Ceiling, Sistine Chapel** Right **Michelangelo's Pietà**

🔟 Artistic Masterpieces

1 Caravaggio's Deposition

Caravaggio strove to outdo Michelangelo's *Pietà* by making his Mary old and tired. Rather than a slender slip of a Christ, Caravaggio's muscular Jesus is so heavy (emphasized by a diagonal composition) that Nicodemus struggles with his legs and John's grasp opens Christ's wound *(see p9)*.

2 Raphael's Transfiguration

Raphael's towering masterpiece and his final work was found, almost finished, in his studio when he died. It is the pinnacle of his talent as a synthesist, mixing Perugino's clarity, Michelangelo's colour palette and twisting figures, and Leonardo's composition *(see p8)*.

3 Michelangelo's Pietà

The Renaissance is known for naturalism, but Michelangelo warped this for artistic effect. Here, Mary is too young, her dead son, achingly thin and small, laid across her voluminous lap. Hearing the work being attributed to better known sculptors, the artist crept into the chapel of St Peter's one night and carved his name in the band across the Virgin's chest *(see p12)*.

4 Raphael's School of Athens

When Raphael first cast his contemporary artists as Classical thinkers in this imaginary setting, one was missing. After he saw the Sistine ceiling Michelangelo was painting down the hall, Raphael added the troubled genius, sulking on the steps, as Heraclitus *(see p8)*.

5 Michelangelo's Sistine Chapel

Although he considered himself a sculptor first, Michelangelo managed to turn this almost flat ceiling into a soaring vault peopled with Old Testament prophets and *ignudi* (nude men). He did it virtually alone, firing all of his assistants save one to help him grind pigments *(see pp10–11)*.

Raphael's School of Athens

6 Bernini's Apollo and Daphne

Rarely has marble captured flowing, almost liquid movement so gracefully. Bernini freezes time, wind-blown hair and cloak, in the instant the fleeing nymph is wrapped in bark and leaves, transformed into a laurel by her sympathetic river god father *(see p20)*.

Caravaggio's Calling of St Matthew

7 Caravaggio's Calling of St Matthew

Caravaggio uses strong *chiaroscuro* techniques here. As a naturalistic shaft of light spills from Christ to his chosen chronicler, St Matthew, Caravaggio captures the precise moment of Matthew's conversion from tax collector to Evangelist *(see p83)*.

8 Leonardo da Vinci's St Jerome

Barely sketched out, yet compelling for its anatomical precision and compositional experimentation. Jerome forms a spiral that starts in the mountains, runs across the cave entrance and lion's curve, up the saint's outstretched right arm, then wraps along his left arm and hand into the centre *(see p9)*.

9 Michelangelo's Moses

This wall monument is a pale shadow of the elaborate tomb for Julius II that Michelangelo first envisaged and for which he carved this figure. Some claim there is a self-portrait in the beard and what are commonly thought to be horns may have been an attempt to create a radiating light effect *(see p127)*.

10 Bernini's Ecstasy of St Teresa

The saint here is being pierced by a smirking angel's lance, and is Bernini at his theatrical best. He sets this religious ecstasy on a stage flanked by opera boxes from which members of the commissioning Cornaro family look on *(see p133)*.

Left **Palazzo Venezia** Right **Fresco, Villa Farnesina**

10 Villas and Palaces

1 Villa Farnesina
A little gem of gracious living, decorated by some of the greatest artists of the Renaissance, including Raphael. The loggias are now glassed in to protect the precious frescoes, but they were originally open, embodying the ideal of blending indoor and outdoor spaces – a concept borrowed from ancient Roman villa designers *(see p139)*.

2 Palazzo del Campidoglio
When Emperor Charles V visited Rome in 1536, Pope Paul III was so embarrassed at the Capitol's state that he enlisted Michelangelo's help. Work started 10 years later, but Michelangelo died long before its completion. True to his design, however, are the double flight of steps for the Palazzo Senatorio, the addition of Palazzo Nuovo, the fine façades and placement of ancient sculptures *(see p99)*.

3 Palazzo Borghese
Called "the harpsichord" because of its unusual shape, this 17th-century palace was once the centre of fashionable entertainments for Rome's papal high society. Its Mannerist courtyard, in particular, was the stage for lavish affairs. You can peek in to see the oversize statuary, columns supporting the double loggias, and the "Bath of Venus" fountain *(see p94)*.

4 Palazzo Massimo alle Colonne
Architect Peruzzi overcame a number of technical problems to build this 16th-century masterpiece. Primarily, he had to follow the curve of the foundations of the ancient Theatre of Domitian. His colonnaded portico is an elegant solution along the street side; the other façade is decorated with monochrome frescoes, known as *grisaille (see p85)*.

5 Palazzo Farnese
Considered the Renaissance palace *par excellence*, reflecting the genius of both Antonio da Sangallo the Younger and Michelangelo. Home to one of Rome's most unscrupulous families, it was commissioned in 1517 by Alessandro Farnese, later Pope Paul III *(see p104)*.

Villa Farnesina courtyard

Villa Giulia

Intended for hedonistic pleasure, this was a perfect papal retreat where Pope Julius III could indulge his tastes for young boys and Classical statuary. Designed by Vignola, Ammannati and Vasari, this 16th-century marvel is all loggias, fountains and gardens (see p112).

Palazzo Farnese

Palazzo Barberini

When Maffeo Barberini became Pope Urban VIII in 1623, he decided to build a family palace on the (then) edge of town. Architect Carlo Maderno designed it as an outsize country villa with three floors of arcades. Bernini added the square staircase on the left; Borromini the spiral staircase on the right (see p133).

Palazzo della Cancelleria

One of the loveliest palaces from the Early Renaissance (late 1400s) – the purity of its façade and courtyard is unparalleled. Several ancient monuments were pillaged to provide the marble and the 44 portico columns inside (see p104).

Palazzo Spada

Built around 1550 for a wealthy cardinal, the architect unknown, this palace has one of the most ornate Renaissance façades in Rome, featuring reliefs evoking the city's glorious past. However, the inner courtyard is the masterpiece, decorated with stucco figures of the 12 Olympian gods and goddesses (see p104).

Palazzo Venezia

Rome's first great Renaissance palace (1455–64) was built for the Venetian cardinal Pietro Barbo. It is attributed to one of two Florentine architects, Alberti or Maiano. You can admire the beautiful palm court with an 18th-century fountain from the museum café (see p104).

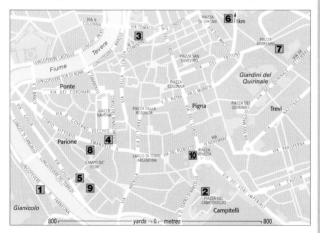

Left **Catacombs of San Sebastiano** Centre **Ceiling, San Clemente** Right **Crypta Balbi**

Top 10 Underground Sights

San Clemente
The many layers of this fascinating church reveal the changing ideals of Rome in various eras *(see pp34–5)*.

Catacombs of Domitilla
This is the largest catacomb network in Rome. Many of the chambers from the 1st and 2nd centuries have no Christian connection; burial of this sort was practised by several religions. The chambers have frescoes of both Classical and Christian scenes, including one of the earliest images of Christ as the Good Shepherd *(see p65)*. Ⓢ *Via delle Sette Chiese 282* • *Buses 118, 218, 660, 760* • *Open Feb–Dec: 9am–noon, 2–5pm Wed–Mon (to 5:30pm in summer)* • *Adm*

Vatican Grottoes
The famous Red Wall behind which Peter was supposedly buried was discovered under the Vatican in the 1940s *(see p13)*.

Catacombs of San Sebastiano
Underground cemeteries outside the city walls were created in accordance with laws at the time, not as a response to suppression (it was thought that the ghosts of the dead could interfere with the living). However, the remains of saints Peter and Paul may have been moved here, away from the centre, during one of the city's periods of persecution. There are also several 4th-century mausoleums. Ⓢ *Via Appia Antica 136* • *Buses 118, 218* • *Open mid-Dec–mid-Nov: 9am–noon, 2–5pm Mon–Sat (to 5:30pm in summer)* • *Adm*

Catacombs of San Callisto
Rome's first official Christian cemetery features some rooms decorated with stucco and frescoes, and special crypts for early popes and saints. Built over four levels, the rooms and passageways were hewn out of relatively soft volcanic tufa. The niches, called *loculi*, were designed to hold two or three bodies. Ⓢ *Via Appia Antica 110* • *Buses 118, 218* • *Open Mar–28 Jan: 9am–noon, 2–5pm Thu–Tue (to 5:30pm in summer)* • *Adm*

Crypta Balbi
A jumble of excavations from several eras, including a piece of 13 BC *crypta* (porticoed courtyard)

Underground font, San Clemente

attached to a destroyed theatre. The museum's didactic panels, which are an excellent introduction to Rome's layer effect, and the medieval frescoes are more interesting than the excavations. ◈ *Via delle Botteghe Oscure 31* • *Map M4* • *Open 9am–7:45pm Tue–Sun* • *Adm*

Casa di SS Giovanni e Paolo (Celian)

The house under this church belonged to two Constantinian officials, martyred in AD 362. There is a series of buildings, including a frescoed nymphaeum dating from the 1st to 4th centuries. ◈ *Clivio di Scauro/Piazza SS Giovanni e Paolo* • *Map E5* • *06 7045 4544* • *Open 10am–1pm, 3–6pm Thu–Mon* • *Adm* • *DA*

Museo Barracco

The museum's basement dates from the 4th century AD: walls, flooring, column stumps, a bit of cornice and sculpted relief, a marble basin and a large double pestle for hand-grinding grains can be seen *(see p55)*.

Pompey's Theatre

Pompey's 61–55 BC theatre is still evident in the curve of medieval buildings on Largo del Pollaro. Its fabric is visible only in the basements, including the downstairs rooms of the da Pancrazio restaurant in the ancient travertine corridors. ◈ *Piazza del Biscione 92* • *Map L4* • *Open 12:30–2:30pm, 7:30–11pm Thu–Tue* • *Free*

Mithraeum under Santa Prisca

This 3rd-century AD shrine to Mithraism was popular among soldiers and the lower classes while Christianity was gaining status with the patricians *(see p128)*. ◈ *Via di Santa Prisca 13* • *Map D5* • *06 3996 7700* • *Open 2nd and 4th Sun of the month, 4pm. By reservation only* • *Adm*

Top 10 Vistas

1 Roman Forum from Campidoglio

Walk around the right side of Palazzo Senatorio for a postcard panorama – floodlit at night. ◈ *Map P5*

2 Il Vittoriano

Climb the "Wedding Cake" (or take the lift) for vistas over the Imperial Fora *(see p104)*.

3 Gianicolo

The Eternal City is laid out at your feet from a lover's lane perch across the Tiber *(see p141)*.

4 The Spanish Steps

Views spill down the steps to the tourist-filled piazza *(see p109)*.

5 Musei Capitolini Café

A bird's-eye sweep over the archaeological park at Rome's heart can be seen from here *(see p24)*.

6 St Peter's Dome

St Peter's colonnade and Castel Sant'Angelo can be seen from Michelangelo's dome *(see p12)*.

7 Knights of Malta Keyhole

St Peter's Dome is perfectly framed through a gate keyhole in this garden *(see p120)*.

8 Castel Sant'Angelo Ramparts

Lazy Tiber River vistas with the Ponte Sant'Angelo directly underneath *(see p140)*.

9 Pincio

Valadier carefully designed this view from his gardens, across Piazza del Popolo to St Peter's *(see p111)*.

10 Villa Mellini

A different panorama, near Rome's observatory above Piazzale Clodio, taking in the city and hills beyond from the northwest. ◈ *Map B1*

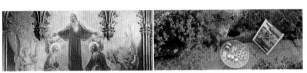

Left **Museo delle Anime del Purgatorio** Right **Cat Sanctuary at Largo Argentina**

Hidden Rome

Capuchin Crypt

If you like a good haunted house, this is your first stop. The bones of thousands of deceased monks have been used to decorate every conceivable surface in the most ghoulish designs. Those corpses that weren't taken to bits have been hung on walls, decked out in cowled robes *(see p134)*.

Museo della Casina delle Civette

One of the restored buildings in Villa Torlonia, Mussolini's abode as prime minister, this Art Nouveau cottage displays ceramic and stained-glass decorations, including owl motifs, which gives it its name, "The Little House of the Owls." The setting is now a public park. ◈ *Via Nomentana 70 • Map G1 • Open Apr–Sep: 9am–7pm; Mar & Oct: 9am–5:30pm; Nov–Feb: 9am–4:30pm (museum). Closed Mon • 060608 • Adm*

Façade, Museo della Casina delle Civette

Criminology Museum

Torture instruments, letters from jail and weapons used by the Mafia are among the items on display in this museum recounting the history of Italian crime. The different sections cover the themes of capital punishment, criminal anthropology and psychology, and the modern prison system. ◈ *Via del Gonfalone 29 • Map J3 • Open 9am–1pm Tue–Sat; 2:30–6:30pm Tue & Thu • Adm • www. museucriminologco.it*

Museo delle Anime del Purgatorio

The Gothic Sacro Cuore del Suffragio church is host to a truly spooky display. A glass case preserves various types of physical "evidence" (mostly handprints burned on to surfaces) of visitations from dead souls, waiting in Purgatory to move up into Heaven. ◈ *Lungotevere Prati 12 • Map L1 • Open 7–11am, 4:30–7pm daily • Free*

Pyramid of Caius Cestius

Following the Egyptian fashion, many ancient Romans used to build their tombs as pyramids, but this is the only survivor. It was made to form part of the defensive wall around the city *(see p121)*.

Cat Sanctuary at Largo Argentina

Dr Silvia Viviani is the guiding genius of this loving undertaking, but what makes it work is the

volunteers' enthusiasm. Tourists are welcome to visit the veterinary clinic, and are also encouraged to adopt one of the cats. The sanctuary has a "no-kill" policy.
⚇ Largo di Torre Argentina (southwest corner of square) • Map M4 • Open noon–6pm daily • Donation

Doorway, Palazzo Zuccari

Palazzo Zuccari

Noted for its door and window frames shaped into screaming mouths of grotesque ogres, this bit of 16th-century Mannerist fantasia was the atelier of the painters Taddeo and Federico Zuccari. ⚇ Via Gregoriana 28 • Map D2 • Closed to public

Museo Barracco

This select collection traces the development of sculptural art in the ancient world. Assyrian and Egyptian works are highlighted, along with Etruscan, Roman and paleo-Christian art. Its original

Greek sculpture is second only to the Vatican's (see p104).

Museo della Civiltà Romana

A Fascist Art Deco Temple of Karnak is home to this fascinating museum. The most striking exhibit is a 1:250 scale model of what Rome looked like in the 4th century. Other items include models of ancient furniture and musical instruments. ⚇ Piazza Giovanni Agnelli 10 • Metro EUR Fermi • Open 9am–2pm Tue–Sat, 9am–1:30pm Sun • Adm • DA

Museo delle Mura

Porta San Sebastiano is the most impressive gate surviving in the Aurelian Wall (see p152). It now houses a museum containing prints and models illustrating the wall's history.
⚇ Via di Porta San Sebastiano 18 • Bus 118, 218 • Open 9am–2pm Tue–Sun. By reservation only (06 0608). • Adm

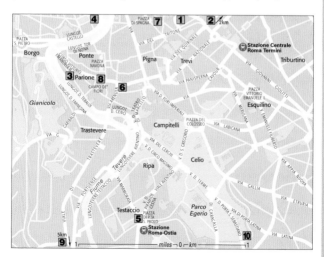

Left **Lord Byron** Right **Mark Twain**

🔟 Writers in Rome

1 Wolfgang Goethe
The first Grand Tourist, German author Goethe (1749–1832) rented rooms on the Corso, now a museum, between 1786 and 1788 *(see p112)*. His book *Italian Journey* laid the blueprint for later tourists who came to Italy to learn from its history and to complete their education.

Wolfgang Goethe

2 John Keats
The English Romantic poet (1795–1821) came to Rome in 1820 for the antiquities and Italian lifestyle – and to bolster his ailing health, which nevertheless failed. Keats died at age 25 of tuberculosis in an apartment by the Spanish Steps *(see p109)*.

3 Henry James
The New York author (1843–1916) spent half his life in Europe. Rome features in *Daisy Miller, A Roman Holiday, Portrait of a Lady* and his travelogue *Italian Hours*. In an 1869 letter he

proclaimed "At last – for the first time – I live! It beats everything: it leaves the Rome of your fancy – your education – nowhere."

4 Nathaniel Hawthorne
During his Italian sojourn from 1857 to 1859, the American man of letters (1804–64) was so moved by an ancient sculpture in the Capitoline museums he crafted his final novel *The Marble Faun* around it.

5 Alberto Moravia
One of Italy's top modern authors (1907–90) wrote about Rome in *Racconti Romani, La Romana, La Ciociara, Gli Indifferenti* and *La Noia*, most of which have been translated.

6 Lord Byron
The ultimate Romantic poet (1788–1824) who lived, to varying degrees, the cavalier life so beloved by his genre. He spent years in Italy in the company of the Shelleys and other friends, and based a large part of *Childe Harold's Pilgrimage* and *Don Juan* on his experiences here.

7 Edward Gibbon
When English parliamentarian Gibbon (1737–94) stood in the Forum for the first time in 1764, he was struck by how "...each memorable spot where

Romulus stood, or Tully spoke, or Caesar fell, was at once present to my eye." He resolved to write the history of Rome, and by 1788 had finished his seminal work, *The Decline and Fall of the Roman Empire*.

Gore Vidal
The prolific American writer (b.1925) has been a resident of Rome and Ravello, south of Naples, for decades. His Roman experiences have informed such books as *The Judgment of Paris*, *Julian* and his memoir *Palimpsest*.

Mark Twain
The American writer (1835–1910) spent little time in the Eternal City during his Grand Tour, but his satirical impressions in *The Innocents Abroad* have become among the most quoted and memorable of any visitor.

Percy Bysshe Shelley
The English poet (1792–1822) lived in Italy with his wife Mary from 1818 until he drowned near Pisa. He visited Rome often, and penned the masterpiece *The Cenci* about the scandal of Roman patrician Beatrice Cenci.

Percy Bysshe Shelley

Top 10 Classical Writers in Rome

1 Plautus
Formulaic comedies of errors by Plautus (250–184 BC) influenced Shakespeare.

2 Caesar
General, dictator and writer (100–44 BC). *De Bello Gallico* describes his campaigns in Gaul (France), *The Civil War* his fight against Pompey.

3 Cicero
Great orator and staunch republican (106–43 BC). His speeches grant insight into Roman political life.

4 Virgil
Poet and propagandist (70–19 BC). His epic *The Aeneid* tied Rome's foundation to the Trojan War.

5 Ovid
Greatest Roman Classical poet (43 BC–AD 17). His *Metamorphoses* codified many Roman myths, but *Ars Amatoria* detailed how to entice women and got him exiled.

6 Tacitus
Tacitus (55–117) wrote *Annals and Histories* covering Rome's early Imperial history; *Life of Agricola* his father-in-law's governorship of Britain.

7 Juvenal
Romans invented satire; Juvenal (60–130) perfected the form in his poems.

8 Pliny the Younger
The letters *(Epistulae)* of Pliny (61–113) to prominent figures give us a glimpse of imperial society.

9 Suetonius
Historian (70–125) who wrote the lives of the Caesars.

10 Petronius
Petronius (70–130) parodied Roman life in *Satiricon*.

Left **Ben Hur** Right **La Dolce Vita**

Cinecittà Studio Films

1 La Dolce Vita
Fellini's 1960 classic on "the sweet life" of 1950s Rome, when the Eternal City was a hot-spot for international glitterati. Marcello Mastroianni plays a reporter sucked into this deca-dent lifestyle, while a character named Paparazzo, snapping stars at Via Veneto cafés, gave a name to his occupation.

2 Fellini's Roma
Fellini's 1972 tribute to his adopted home town. Rome's heritage gets in the way of modernization, and the absurdity of the Vatican is shown in a frighteningly funny papal fashion show. Fellini built a highway at the Cinecittà studios so he could film rush hour without the bother of real traffic.

3 Ben Hur
The original big budget ($50 million) gladiator epic from 1959. William Wyler directed Charlton Heston as a Jewish prince betrayed into slavery. He bares his chest, wins his freedom and engages in a chariot race that has influenced every cinematic race since. The film won 11 Academy Awards.

4 The Bicycle Thieves
The ultimate neo-realist film, Vittorio de Sica's 1948 work is a recreated documentary of late 1940s Rome. An honest family man struggling to make ends meet in postwar Rome watches everything fall apart when his precious bicycle, so necessary for his livelihood, is stolen and he tries to track it down.

Roman Holiday

Cleopatra
5 Despite the lavish sets and costumes, a cast of thousands and Elizabeth Taylor and Richard Burton steaming up the place, Joseph Mankiewicz's 1963 epic was one of Hollywood's first spectacular box office flops.

Rome, Open City
6 Powerful 1946 drama about the Roman Resistance during World War II. Roberto Rossellini tried to create a documentary feel, filming in the streets mere months after the war ended, using real soldiers and recreating actual events. A young Fellini helped write the script.

Roman Holiday
7 Romantic comedy which made a star of newcomer Audrey Hepburn in 1953, when she won the Academy Award as a rebellious princess who runs around the city with Gregory Peck, a penniless writer.

Caro Diario
8 This most personal of films (1994) opens with the director, Nanni Moretti, riding his scooter around suburban Rome.

Life is Beautiful
9 Surprisingly successful 1998 mix of comedy and fable set against Nazi-occupied Italy. Writer/director Roberto Begnini's Jewish bookseller uses comedy to shield his son from the horror of their Nazi concentration camp by pretending it's all a big game. It won three Academy Awards.

Gangs of New York
10 Hollywood director Martin Scorsese spent $100 million to recreate 1840s New York and an ocean liner at the Cinecittà studios for his 2002 film.

Top 10 Italian Film Directors

1 **Federico Fellini**
The five-time Academy Award-winner (1920–1993) embodied styles from neo-realism to magico-realism.

2 **Roberto Rossellini**
Neo-realist master director (1906–77) of *Rome, Open City* and *Paisà*.

3 **Vittorio De Sica**
De Sica (1901–74) was the founder of neo-realism, with films such as *Shoeshine* and *Yesterday, Today and Tomorrow*.

4 **Luchino Visconti**
Visconti (1906–1976) is most famous for filming *The Leopard* and *Death in Venice*.

5 **Pier Paolo Pasolini**
Poet, Communist and film-maker (1922–75). Filmed notorious versions of *Oedipus Rex* and *The Decameron*.

6 **Sergio Leone**
Leone (1929–89) turned Italy into America's Wild West and Clint Eastwood into a star with "spaghetti westerns" such as *A Fistful of Dollars*.

7 **Michelangelo Antonioni**
Antonioni (b.1912) helped create the Italian New Wave (*Red Desert*) and has enjoyed Hollywood success (*Blow Up*).

8 **Nanni Moretti**
Often autobiographical writer/director (b.1953), likened to Woody Allen.

9 **Bernardo Bertolucci**
Poet and film-maker (b.1941). After great success outside Italy he returned home for *Stealing Beauty*.

10 **Roberto Benigni**
Writer-director-actor (b.1952), often using slapstick, achieved worldwide fame with *Life is Beautiful*.

Left **Villa Borghese** Centre **Casina Valadier, Pincio** Right **Church, Via Appia Antica**

🔟 Romantic Spots

1 Gianicolo
Saunter around arm-in-arm in this elegant park and take in a traditional puppet show, perhaps buy a puppet or two and check out the carousel. But most of all, enjoy the views, considered by many to be the best in the city. If you happen to be here at noon, get ready for a shock when the cannon booms – a daily routine *(see p141)*.

2 Pincio
These gardens are the other most famous view of Rome, much cherished by Romantic writers since the early 19th century, when the gardens were designed by Giuseppe Valadier. If the exclusive Casina Valadier café/restaurant should be open for business, no place is more romantic for a drink or a meal *(see p111)*.

3 Rose and Orange Gardens, Parco Savello
The public Rose Gardens are a gracious, fragrant place to stroll in season, and then make your way on up the hill to the Orange Garden, where you can relax under umbrella pines and orange trees, and enjoy the view of the river, Trastevere and St Peter's. Take the ancient Clivo di Rocca Savella back down the hill.
◈ *Map A3*

4 Villa Borghese
A huge park with innumerable fountains, benches, shady lanes, niches and glades. But by far the most appealing activity is taking a rowboat out on the lake, around the island with its Classical temple *(see p111)*.

5 Antico Arco
This historic restaurant perched on the Gianicolo Hill is set in a homely villa and serves inventive dishes based on traditional recipes. There are sommeliers on hand to help choose the perfect accompanying wine. The stone and brick walls add to the atmosphere, and seating upstairs is particularly cosy. End the evening with their famed chocolate soufflé with a molten centre *(see p149)*.

Campidoglio at night

For a guide to restaurant price ranges **See p89**

Arco Degli Acetari
A walk through the tangled cobblestone alleys around Campo de'Fiori would not be complete without a visit to the Arco Degli Acetari. Time seems to have stood still in this hidden medieval courtyard, accessible through a small, shabby archway on Via del Pellegrino. ◈ *Via del Pelegrino • Map K4*

Campidoglio by Night
With the subtle yet dramatic lighting, the three palaces on this hill take on an almost magical beauty at night *(see pp24–7)*. Make your way up the gentle incline, circumambulate the piazza once or twice, then head across and down to imbibe the vision of the Roman Forum and Colosseum, which are also evocatively floodlit.

Trevi Fountain
Too often thronged with tourists, yet the sheer beauty and power of this creation are nevertheless overwhelming, day or night. It's also a perfect opportunity to make any wishes you may have in mind, the more romantic the better. Have some coins ready for tossing in – backwards, of course – to ensure your return to Rome *(see p109)*.

Appian Way on a Sunday
One day a week, part of the old Via Appia Antica is closed to all traffic except tour buses, making it perfect for a bucolic bike ride, or a very long walk if you want to cover it all. Lined

Trevi Fountain

with pines and cypresses, this is where the ancient Romans came to bury their dead, and many tombs still remain along the roadside *(see p151)*.

Gelato at Tre Scalini
A triple-chocolate bomb with a cherry in the middle and topped with whipped cream is the famous *tartufo* produced by this café. If you get it "to go", it's a bargain, but it's probably more romantic to sit inside and share one – as long as you don't fight over the cherry *(see p88)*.

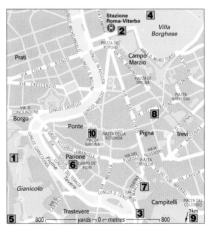

Left **Villa Doria Pamphilj** Right **Orto Botanico**

🔟 Green Spaces

1 Villa Borghese

Extensive, elegant and full of shady glades and beautiful fountains, this is a great park for a stroll, a picnic or a jog. You can also go boating on the artificial lake, rent a bicycle or in-line skates *(see p111)*.

2 Pincio

The traditional time to enjoy the most famous panorama of Rome is at sunset. Other charms here include the water clock, the busts of various notables and an Egyptian-style obelisk Emperor Hadrian erected on the tomb of his beloved Antinous *(see p111)*.

3 Villa Celimontana

Picnics have been a tradition here since 1552, when San Filippo Neri instituted the Visit of the Seven Churches and the Mattei family offered pilgrims a simple repast. In summer it's the venue for wonderful dinner-concerts. ◈ *Piazza della Navicella 12* • *Map E5* • *Open dawn–dusk* • *DA*

4 Villa Doria Pamphilj

Rome's largest green area, extending from the Gianicolo along the ancient Via Aurelia. It's a terrific place for a run and offers a course of exercise posts. Its hills are adorned with villas, fountains, lakes and orangeries and are perfect for strolls; enjoy a picnic under the umbrella pines *(see p142)*.

5 Orto Botanico

The graceful botanical gardens and grounds of Palazzo Corsini now provide one of the most enjoyable places to while away an hour or two and breathe in air richly perfumed by more than 7,000 plant species that thrive here. The gardens, which now belong to the University of Rome, include indigenous and exotic varieties, grouped according to ecosystems *(see p142)*.

6 Villa Sciarra

This small park is replete with fountains, gazebos, ponds, loggias and statuary. There are leafy lanes for walking and lawns

Villa Borghese

For squares and fountains in Rome **See pp46–7**

for relaxing. It's a good place for children, too *(see p64).* ◈ *Via Calandrelli • Map C5 • Open dawn–dusk • Villa Sciarra is temporarily closed to the public • DA*

Villa Ada
This huge public park, originally the hunting reserve of King Vittorio Emanuele III, has rolling lawns, serene waters and copses. It's worth the trip out if you need an antidote to the fumes and noise of the city. On summer nights the lake at the far end hosts food stalls and concerts. ◈ *Via Salaria 265 • Map E1 • Open dawn–dusk • DA*

Water clock, Pincio

Parco Della Caffarella
Combining farmland and wilderness with abundant wildlife, the meadows and fields of Parco Della Caffarella are dotted with the remains of Roman temples. There is also a large playground. ◈ *Via della Caffarella • www.caffarella.it*

Colle Oppio
After hours of walking around the Forum and the Colosseum in the high summer heat, these green slopes can be a welcome sight. Most of the Colle Oppio park is actually the roof of Nero's Golden House *(see p41)*, and you can see skylight structures for its rooms. If you haven't had enough of sightseeing, you can also examine the massive remains of the Baths of Trajan scattered about the area. ◈ *Via Labicana, Parco Oppio • Map E4 • DA*

Parco della Resistenza dell'8 Settembre
This former dustbowl has now been turned into a pleasant slice of greenery, where local people picnic and children play. Since it's one of the few parks in the city without walls or gates, it's perfect for enjoying a moonlight stroll here after dinner. ◈ *Viale della Piramide Cestia, Viale M Gelsomini • Map D5 • DA*

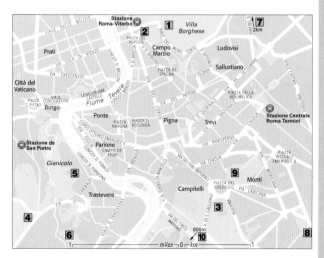

Left **Villa Borghese park** Right **Villa Borghese funfair**

🔟 Rome for Children

1 Villa Borghese

Scipione Borghese's private Renaissance park and the adjacent 19th-century Pincio gardens, with statues and fountains, are a joy to explore, especially on two wheels. There are bike rental stands scattered throughout the park. You can also rent paddle boats for the little lake or take the kids to the park's small funfair *(see p111)*.

2 Explora

This museum offers a child's eye view of the way the world works. Children can interact with life-size dioramas and models. There is a popular create-your-own TV show. ◉ *Via Flaminia 82 • Map C1 • Children admitted with adults only • Hour-long visits 10am, noon, 3pm, 5pm Tue–Sun • Booking recommended • Adm*

3 Capuchin Crypt

Fantastically creepy chapels festively decorated with mosaics made from the bones of dead monks, a few of whose skeletons remain propped up in bone-built niches. It rarely fails to impress, and for adolescents and adults can be a highlight of the trip, although it may be a bit too much for the very young or overly squeamish *(see p134)*.

4 Bioparco (Zoo)

Rome's zoo, once a depressing conglomeration of badly kept cement cubicles, has been overhauled to become a pretty "biological garden" set into a corner of Villa Borghese park. ◉ *Piazzale del Giardino Zoologico 1 • Map E1 • Open 9:30am–6pm Mon–Fri, 9:30am–7pm Sat & Sun (to 5pm Nov–Mar) • Adm*

5 Technotown

Occupying a 20th-century house on the grounds of lush Villa Torlonia gardens, Technotown is a multimedia playhouse for kids, with fun and educational interactive exhibits including robotics and 3D photography.

◉ *Via Lazzaro Spallanzani 1 • Map F2 • 06 4288 8888 • Open 9am–7pm Tue–Sun; Jul & Aug: 10am–11pm Tue–Sun • www.technotown.it*

6 Puppet Shows on the Gianicolo

You don't need to understand Italian to appreciate a Punch and Judy show (the pugilistic characters are native to Italy). This is the last of the old puppet kiosks that

Roman puppets

For information about Bateaux Rome river cruises visit www.battellidiroma.it; 06 9774 5498

once peppered Rome's public parks, offering a dying art form for free. ⊛ *Teatro di Pulcinella, Gianicolo • Map B4 • Show times variable, Tue–Sun • Free • DA*

7 Casina Di Raffaello

This city-run playhouse for kids aged 3–10 offers educational toys and games, a library and a mini-theatre. There are weekly events and workshops. Entrance to the park is free. ⊛ *Via della Casina di Raffaello (Villa Borghese) • Map D2 • 06 4288 8888 • www.casinadiraffaello.it • Adm*

Roman children

8 Exploring the Catacombs

There is nothing more spooky in Rome than wandering these mazes of tight, dimly lit corridors, roughly carved in the tufa and lined with tomb niches. At the San Domitilla complex, some guides let you touch a few

of the bones. At most others, all human remains have been removed to ossuaries on lower levels *(see p151)*.

9 Piscina delle Rose

When traipsing around ruins has sapped your energy, spend some time cooling down with the locals. This open-air swimming pool in EUR is Rome's largest and most pleasant, with a special area for kids. ⊛ *Viale America 20 • Metro EUR Palasport • Open Jun–mid-Sep 9am–7pm daily • Adm*

10 Time Elevator

Kids of all ages will enjoy the panoramic movies shown at Time Elevator, complete with surround-sound, flight simulator and 5D technology. Not advisable for those suffering from motion sickness. ⊛ *Via dei Santi Apostoli 20 • Map D3–4 • 06 9774 6243 • Open 10:30am–8:15pm (last show 7:30pm) daily • www.timeelevator.it • Adm • DA*

Left **Piano recital, RomaEuropa Festival** Right **Easter, St Peter's Square**

🔟 Cultural Festivals

1 RomaEuropa Festival
A fast-growing performing arts festival with a pronounced emphasis on the provocative, held every autumn in various superlative venues, including the French Academy, Palazzo Farnese and the Spanish Academy. All kinds of music, dance and theatre, including several international artists. ✎ *end Sep–early Dec*

2 Testaccio Village
This well-run multi-event happens all summer long in a purpose-built area near an old slaughterhouse. Every evening there's live music until midnight, followed by several discos, each featuring a different type of music, and lots of food choices. There's a new decor theme every year, often quite elaborate.
✎ *Via Monte Testaccio 16 • Map D6 • Jun–Sep: 8:30pm–3am nightly*

¡Fiesta!

3 Festa dell'Unità
Put on by the PD, the former Communist Party, this is a lively evening event, featuring music, films, dancing, games and more. The venue changes every year, as do the dates, but it's usually held in a central park, sometime around July, for about a month.

4 Rome's Birthday
Every 21 April there's a gala civic observance in the Piazza del Campidoglio, celebrating Rome's traditional founding in 753 BC *(see p38)*. Music, fireworks and a speech by the mayor mark the event, but the best news is that the Musei Capitolini *(see pp24–7)* are free of charge and open until 10pm.

5 Summer Opera Festivals
Not only does the Rome Opera Company offer its usual summer programme in the Baths of Caracalla *(see p119)*, but there are also a number of other opera programmes all over the city, with singers from around the globe.

6 ¡Fiesta!
Celebrating all forms of Latin music, this festival takes place every night throughout the summer. In recent years, world, jazz, rock and pop music have been added to the schedule. The event is held in the vast grounds of a converted racetrack.
✎ *Ippodromo delle Capannelle, Via Appia Nuova 1245 • Metro Colli Albani then bus • www.fiesta.it • mid-Jun–mid-Aug*

7 Luglio Suona Bene
This "July Sounds Good" concert brings pop, jazz and folk music artists to Auditorium Parco della Musica's outdoor arena. ◈ *Viale Pietro de Coubertin 30* • *06 802 41281* • *www.auditorium.com*

8 International Horse Show
Villa Borghese's annual splash-out for the equestrian classes. International show-jumping in a garden setting. Much of the park is closed off for the event and parties. ◈ *Piazza di Siena, Villa Borghese* • *Map E1* • *last week May*

International Horse Show

9 Villa Celimontana Jazz
A magnificent setting among dramatically lit umbrella pines, where you can enjoy gourmet cuisine and jazz every night all summer long. ◈ *Piazza della Navicella* • *Map E5* • *06 589 7807* • *Jun–Sep* • *www.villacelimontanajazz.com*

10 May Day Concert
Held in front of the Basilica of San Giovanni in Laterano (*see p127*), this is a vast, free event, boasting a line-up of top Italian popstars and the occasional international luminary. It's in celebration of socialist Italy's "Day of the Worker", when just about everything shuts down. ◈ *Piazza S Giovanni* • *Map F5* • *1 May*

Top 10 Religious Festivals

1 Pentecost
Rose petals shower down through the Pantheon's oculus (*see p14*), followed by pageantry. ◈ *Map M3* • *Whitsunday*

2 Christmas Market
Sugar candy, nativity figurines and all the Christmas trimmings. ◈ *Piazza Navona* • *Map L3* • *1 Dec–6 Jan*

3 Epiphany
Friendly witches land in Piazza Navona to give free candy to well-behaved children. ◈ *6 Jan*

4 Easter Week
Events include the Good Friday Procession of the Cross at the Colosseum and the Easter Sunday blessing from the balcony of St Peter's.

5 Madonna della Neve
Commemorating a papal vision of an August snowfall in the 4th century, white petals float down from the ceiling of S Maria Maggiore. ◈ *5 Aug*

6 Christmas Eve Midnight Mass
Most churches celebrate the Saviour's birth, but tickets are required for St Peter's.

7 "Urbi et Orbi"
The noontime Christmas Day blessing by the pope from St Peter's balcony.

8 Carnival
Dressing up, parties and pranks. ◈ *Late Jan–Feb*

9 All Saints' Day
Romans visit the graves of loved ones. ◈ *1 Nov*

10 Feast of Sts Peter and Paul
Fireworks and partying to celebrate the founders of the Catholic Church. ◈ *Piazza S Paolo and Via Ostiense* • *Map D6* • *28–29 Jun*

Left **Dolce e Gabbana** Right **Via dei Condotti**

Top 10 Shopping Streets

Via dei Condotti
The chicest shops are here, where all the biggest names in *haute couture* have staked out their turf: Gucci, Bulgari, Prada, Hermès, Ferragamo, Armani, Trussardi, Valentino and more. It's a foregone conclusion that this street offers no bargains, but the staff will make you feel like visiting royalty *(see p111)*.

Via del Corso
Up and down Rome's central axis street, more commonly known as the Corso, you'll find the entire range of shopping options. Music stores and trendy young styles predominate. There are also good shoe shops.
Map N1–3

Via Cola di Rienzo
This is Rome's best street for middle-range clothing. There are also a few shoe shops and a department store. For hard-to-find international and traditional food items, Castroni is the city's best shop, while nearby Franchi is famous for its cheese selection *(see p143)*.

Via Borgognona
The other major street for top-name fashion, second only and parallel to Via dei Condotti. Here's where Dolce e Gabbana, Fendi, Ferrè, Givenchy and Versace have all set up shop. Don't omit nearby Piazza di Spagna, which is home to Fendi, Missoni and Krizia *(see p114)*.

Via dei Coronari
Named for the rosary makers and sellers that used to line the way when it was on the main pilgrimage route to St Peter's, this street now has a reputation for antiques. Only partly deserved, however, since prices are generally exaggerated and most pieces are imported *(see pp86–7)*.

Via del Babuino
An imposing blend of high fashion (Armani, Chanel, Tiffany & Co.) and antiques make this street one of Rome's most elegant. Worth a stroll just to peek into some of the finer antiques shops – they're full of Baroque furniture, paintings and antiquities *(see p113)*.

Via Margutta
A wonderful range of art, antiques and antiquities shops has made this little street famous. Nos. 45 and 86 often have stunning

Glassware, Via del Babuino

 For shopping tips See p164

Antiques shop, Via Margutta

merchandise for sale, whereas No. 109 specializes in more affordable copies of antiquities (see p113).

Via Bocca di Leone
One of the side streets that joins Via dei Condotti and Via Borgognona, in the heart of Rome's *haute couture* shopping area, has several high-style boutiques including Valentino and Gianni Versace (see p114).

Via Nazionale
A solidly mid-range shopping experience, lined with shoe and clothing boutiques, Oriental rug stores, an international bookshop and a reliable bag and luggage emporium. Frette, with its elegant range of bed linen, also has an outlet here. ⊗ Map R2

Via dei Giubbonari
Named for the traditional *giubbotti* (jackets) whose makers and sellers used to populate this street, Via dei Giubbonari is still noted for its stylish clothing and down-to-earth prices. Sportswear, shoes, trendy styles and classics for men and women are all available here (see p105).

Top 10 Markets

1 Porta Portese
Rome's mammoth flea market, for genuine and fake antiques, memorabilia, art, clothing, plants and more. Sunday morning. ⊗ Via Ippolito Nievo • Map C5

2 Campo de' Fiori
Rome's famous outdoor fruit, vegetable and fish market in one of the most authentic medieval squares. ⊗ Map L4

3 Via Mamiani
Rome's largest market for the freshest meat and fish, as well as clothing and housewares. Monday to Saturday mornings (see p130).

4 Via Sannio
Vintage clothing and designer fakes. Weekday mornings and Saturday (see p130).

5 Antique Print Market
Antique and reproduction prints. Monday to Saturday mornings. ⊗ Largo della Fontanella di Borghese • Map M1

6 Piazza Testaccio
A covered market with lavish displays of nature's bounty. Monday to Saturday mornings. ⊗ Map D6

7 Via Trionfale Flower Market
Fresh cut flowers and all sorts of plants at bargain prices. Tuesday morning. ⊗ Map B2

8 Borghetto Flaminio
A flea market in a former bus depot. Every Sunday, Sep–Jul. ⊗ Piazza della Marina 32 • Map D1 • Adm

9 Piazza San Cosimato
Trastevere's lively fruit and vegetable market. Monday to Saturday mornings. ⊗ Map C5

10 Quattro Coronati
Quaint produce market. Monday to Saturday mornings. ⊗ Map E4

Left and centre **Antico Caffè Greco** Right **Giolitti**

🔟 Cafés and Gelaterie

Antico Caffè Greco
Rome's 1760 answer to all the famed literary cafés of Paris. Just off the Spanish Steps on the busiest shopping street in town, it is an elegant holdover from yesteryear, its tiny tables tucked into a series of genteel, cosy rooms plastered with photos, prints and other memorabilia from the 19th-century Grand Tour era. The A-list of past customers runs from Goethe to Byron, Casanova to Wagner *(see p116)*.

Caffè Sant'Eustachio
Rome's most coveted *cappuccini* come from behind a chrome-plated shield that hides the coffee machine from view so no one can discover the skilled owner's secret formula. All that is known is that the water comes from an ancient aqueduct and the brew is pre-sweetened. Always crowded *(see p96)*.

San Crispino
Navigate the glut of inferior ice cream parlours infesting the Trevi neighbourhood to reach this elegantly simple little *gelateria*. The signature ice cream contains honey but there are other velvety varieties made with fresh fruit or nuts and sinful delights laced with liqueurs. ✪ *Via della Panetteria 42 • Map P2*

Tre Scalini
This café's claim to fame is Rome's most decadent *tartufo* (truffle) ice cream ball, which is almost always packaged in other outlets. Dark chocolate shavings cover the outer layer of chocolate ice cream, with a heart of fudge and cherries *(see p88)*.

Giolitti
This 19th-century café is the best known of Rome's *gelaterie*. Touristy but excellent *(see p96)*.

Gran Caffè Doney
Still the top café on the famous Via Veneto, but long past its prime as the heartbeat of Rome's 1950s heyday (along with rival Café de Paris across the road) – when celebrities in sunglasses hobnobbed with starlets draped over the outdoor tables. The lifestyle was documented in

Giolitti

(and in part created by) Fellini's seminal film *La Dolce Vita (see p58)*, whose shutterbug character Paparazzo lent a name to his profession of bloodhound photographers *(see p136)*.

Caffè Rosati
The older, more left-wing of Piazza del Popolo's rival cafés (the other is Caffè Canova) was founded by two of the Rosati brothers (a third continued to manage the family's original Via Veneto café). It sports a 1922 Art Nouveau decor and its patrons park their newest Ferrari or Lotus convertibles out front *(see p116)*.

Caffè Novecento
Exuding a cosy, 19th-century teahouse charm, this café contains a series of parlour-like nooks accessorized with antique furniture and serves delicate sweets or light salads, tarts and quiche. ◎ *Via del Governo Vecchio 12 • Map K3 • 06 686 5242 • DA • €*

Gelateria della Palma
Modern ice cream parlour with more than 100 flavours of *gelato* plus *semifreddi* (half-

La Tazza d'Oro

frozen mousse) and frozen yoghurt. It's open late and constantly thronged with Rome's young and beautiful. Mere steps from the Pantheon *(see p96)*.

La Tazza d'Oro
Strictly the highest quality Brazilian beans go into the coffee here. There's nothing fancy in this unassuming place and no touristy gimmicks (despite being just off the Pantheon's piazza). Just a long, undulating bar counter where regulars enjoy a heavenly *espresso* that, amazingly, manages to be both among the best and the cheapest in Rome *(see p96)*.

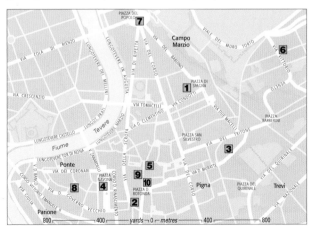

Left **Pizzeria da Ricci** Right **Pizzeria da Baffetto**

Pizzerias

Pizzeria da Baffetto
The pizza here is the best in Rome, but they are open only for dinner and, beyond pizza, only serve *bruschetta* and other simple appetizers *(see p162)*. The thin-crust, wood-oven pizzas come *piccola* (small) or *grande* (large). Service is not always good. ⬡ *Via del Governo Vecchio 114 • Map K3 • 06 686 1617*

Pizzeria da Ivo
The most famous pizzeria in Trastevere, definitely discovered by the tourist crowds, but local fans never let them take it over completely. The pizza is great, but skip the other second-rate main meals *(see p148)*.

Pizzeria da Ricci
This Liberty-style pizzeria, in the Ricci family since 1905, is hidden away on a quiet dead-end street off Via Nazionale. The pizzas are tiny (many people order two) but excellent; complement them with the sweet northern Lazio white wine Est! Est! Est!, after which the place is nicknamed *(see p77)*. ⬡ *Via Genova 32 • Map R2 • 06 488 1107 • Closed Mon • €*

Pizzeria dar Poeta
There's a merry war between ultra thin-crust Roman pizza and thicker, chewier Neapolitan pizza. Dar Poeta goes its own road, letting the dough rise a full day (rather than the usual hour), resulting in a thin yet light and airy pie loaded down with the freshest of toppings. Tucked into a quiet Trastevere side street, with tables out front and an air-conditioned brick-walled dining room *(see p148)*.

Pizzeria da Ivo

For a guide to restaurant prices **See p89**

Pizzeria dar Poeta

Pizzeria da Vittorio

Vittorio Martini's unassuming little place with its wood beams and a few tables on the cobblestones out front serves fantastic Neapolitan-style pizza, courtesy of award-winning *pizzaiolo* Angelo Jezzi. The mixed *antipasti* plate is generous and a great bargain (see p148).

Achiappafantasmi

The award-winning pizza is shaped vaguely like a ghost with olives for eyes at this restaurant (the pizzeria's name means "ghostbusters"). A half-dozen Calabrese snacks are also available. The service can be slow. ❧ *Via dei Cappellari 66 • Map K4 • 06 687 3462 • Closed Mon, Tue–Fri L • €*

PizzaRé

Roman mini-chain serving thicker, Neapolitan-style wood oven pies. Cheap lunch menus include cover charge, drink, and a pizza, a pasta, or a roast meat dish. ❧ *Via di Ripetta 14 • Map D2 • 06 321 1468 • €*

Gaudì

Thick Neapolitan-style pizza in a modern room or on the roof terrace, with red lamps to click on for rapid service. Lots of pastas and desserts as well. No bookings and long queues, so arrive early. ❧ *Via R Giovannelli 8–12 • Map F1 • 06 884 5451 • Closed Sat & Sun L • €*

Panattoni "L'Obitorio"

This Trastevere institution's nickname ("the morgue") refers to the chilly effect of the marble that sheathes the walls and acts as tabletops. The reception is as warm as the decor is cold, however, and the Roman pizza as excellent as the *supplì al telefono* (fried rice balls with a melted mozzarella heart that makes a long "telephone" cord when you pull them apart). Open late. ❧ *Viale Trastevere 53 • Map C5 • 06 580 0919 • Closed Wed, L • No credit cards • €*

Pizzeria La Montecarlo

Late opening hours have kept this simple Roman-style pizzeria packed with locals and students for years (see p89).

Left **Checchino dal 1887** Right **'Gusto**

Top 10 **Restaurants**

1 Checchino dal 1887
The premier restaurant of Testaccio since 1887 boasts Rome's largest wine cellar. Working-class dishes – this is the place that invented *coda alla vaccinara (see p77)* – and more elegant fare are prepared divinely, with the best selection of Italian and French cheeses in town *(see p125)*.

2 Agata e Romeo
Romeo Caraccio runs the dining room in this Liberty-style temple to creative Roman cuisine near Santa Maria Maggiore. His wife Agata Parisella reigns in the kitchen, preparing rich and highly original concoctions of meat, fish and fresh vegetables.

Logo, Agata e Romeo

Don't miss her heavenly desserts, including the *millefoglie* – puff pastry filled with cream *(see p131)*.

3 La Gensola
This small, intimate trattoria was formerly a meeting place for painters in the 1800s. Today, La Gensola is a stronghold for Sicilian cuisine in Rome, with menus based on the freshest fish and Mediterranean flavours. Ask for a table in the front dining room *(see p149)*.

4 Sabatini
One of Rome's most famed restaurants, favoured by the likes of Fellini in the days before it became too hyped for its own good. Killer location on the piazza, but terribly steep prices. The cuisine is refined Roman and seafood *(see p149)*.

5 Sapori del Lord Byron
The location, inside one of Rome's most exclusive small hotels, and the chef's renowned ability to turn both Italian classics and inventive new dishes into works of art, keeps this elegant restaurant on the A-list – and makes it a great place for celebrity-spotting. ◈ *Via G. de Notaris 5, Hotel Lord Byron • Map E1 • 06 322 0404 • Closed Sun • €€€€€*

Terrace, Checchino dal 1887

Da Cesaretto

Also known as Fiaschetteria Beltramme, little has changed since this *osteria* opened in 1886. Prices are relatively low and dishes are solid Roman specialities *(see pp76–7)*. There is no phone and no reservations so come early. The tables are shared. ◎ *Via della Croce 39 • Map D2 • Closed Sun • No credit cards • €€*

Piperno

Very good Roman Jewish cooking in the Ghetto since 1856 (although also very pricey). Hosts of TV shows have been seen sneaking in to try and unlock the chef's secrets. Service can be slightly off-hand, but the artichokes can't be beat *(see p107)*.

Da Augusto

Archetypal Trastevere *trattoria*. Block-style wooden tables and butchers' paper mats form the decor; the menu is recited by the busily indifferent waiters rather than printed. Good table wine and the food comprises excellent, simple traditional dishes. In fine weather there is seating on the tiny piazza-cum-car park out front *(see p148)*.

'Gusto

The see-and-be-seen restaurant, kitschily installed in one of Mussolini's pompous travertine buildings lining the piazza. Glass walls and outdoor tables overlook Augustus's Mausoleum *(see p92)*. Several dining choices, each excellent: *cucina creativa* is served in

Piperno

the restaurant proper, and there's a pizzeria (open until 1am), and a wine bar (open 11am to 2am) serving Thai cuisine. Booking is recommended *(see p117)*.

Antica Birreria Peroni

Local businessmen regularly take their lunchtime discussions to this 1906 beer hall sponsored by Italy's biggest brewery. The buffet snacks and scrumptious main dishes cross Roman and Germanic influences, and the Art Deco murals feature cherubs playing sports and promising "He who drinks beer lives to 100" *(see p117)*.

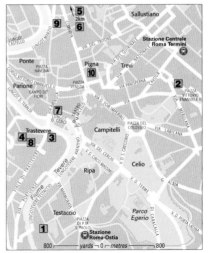

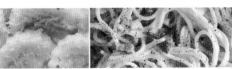

Left **Gnocchi** Right **Spaghetti alla carbonara**

🔟 Roman Dishes

1 Saltimbocca
This savoury veal dish is so good they call it "jumps-in-the-mouth". A veal escalope is layered with sage leaves and prosciutto then sautéed in white wine.

Bucatini all'amatriciana

2 Bucatini all'amatriciana
Named after Amatrice, the northern Lazio town high in the Abruzzi mountains where it originated. The sauce consists of tomatoes mixed with Italian bacon – *guanciale* (pork cheek) or *pancetta* (pork belly) – laced with chilli pepper and liberally dusted with grated Pecorino romano cheese. The classic pasta accompaniment are *bucatini* (thick, hollow spaghetti). The original *amatriciana bianca* version (before tomatoes, a New World food, entered Italian cuisine) adds parsley and butter.

3 Carciofi alla romana
Tender Italian artichokes, often laced with garlic and mint, are braised in a mixture of olive oil and water.

4 Abbacchio scottadito
Roasted Roman spring lamb, so succulent the name claims you'll "burn your fingers" in your haste to eat it. When *abbacchio* (lamb) is unavailable, once the spring slaughter is over, they switch to less tender *agnello* (young mutton).

5 Spaghetti alla carbonara
The piping hot pasta is immediately mixed with a raw egg, grated Parmesan and black pepper so that the eggy mixture cooks on to the strands of spaghetti themselves. It is then tossed with pieces of *pancetta* (bacon). There's a local legend that the recipe was born out of US army rations after World War II (powdered bacon and eggs mix), but no one seems to have proven or discarded the theory.

Carciofi alla giudia

6 Carciofi alla giudia
Artichokes, first flattened then fried. This typical Roman Jewish dish is often accompanied by fried courgette (zucchini) flowers stuffed with mozzarella cheese and anchovies.

For traditional Roman restaurants **See p125**

Pajata

It may sound revolting but it's actually delicious: suckling calf intestines boiled with its mother's milk still clotted inside. Usually the intestines are chopped, coated with a tomato sauce and served over pasta.

Coda alla vaccinara

Oxtail braised in celery and tomato broth. Like *pajata*, this is a product of trying to make something out of the *quinto quarto* (the unusable "fifth fourth" of the day's butchering), which was part of the take-home pay of 19th-century slaughterhouse workers.

Coda alla vaccinara

Checchino dal 1887, the restaurant that came up with this delicacy, is one of Rome's finest *(see p125)*.

Gnocchi

Dense and bite-sized potato and flour dumplings, gnocchi originated in Northern Italy but have infiltrated nearly every regional cuisine. Rome's version of the dish is made with semolina and/or corn flour, doused in butter and parmesan and oven-baked. The original gnocchi are served much more frequently, however. Try them with tomato sauce, gorgonzola cheese or simply "burro e salvia" with butter and sage.

Cacio e Pepe

Sometimes the simplest dishes are among the best. Perfectly *al dente* ("with a bite") spaghetti is tossed hot with cracked black pepper and grated Pecorino romano (a local sharp, aged sheep's milk cheese rather similar to Parmesan).

Top 10 Wines and Liqueurs

1 Frascati

Lazio's only high profile wine, a dry, fruity, not always perfect white from the hills south of Rome.

2 Castelli Romani

Cousin to Frascati, from neighbouring hilltowns, also made with Trebbiano grapes.

3 Colli Albani

Another Trebbiano-based white from the slopes of Lazio's dormant volcano.

4 Orvieto Classico

Dry white from southern Umbria – so good that the Renaissance artist Signorelli once accepted it as payment.

5 Est! Est! Est!

A bishop's taste-tester, sampling this sweet white in a northern Lazio lakeside village, excitedly ran to the door and scribbled "*Est! Est! Est!*" (Latin for "This is it!").

6 Torre Ercolana

One of Lazio's unsung reds, made from Cabernet and Cesanese grapes.

7 Chianti

This old favourite from over the border in Tuscany is one of the most common reds you'll find in Rome's bars and restaurants.

8 Lacrima Christi

"Tears of Christ", a white wine from the slopes of the infamous Mount Vesuvius near Pompeii *(see p154)*.

9 Campari

A bitter red apéritif, best diluted in soda water, or lemonade for a sweet drink.

10 Grappa

The most powerful of Italy's *digestivi* (drunk after a meal), this is quite a harsh-tasting liqueur.

For eating and drinking tips See p162

Left **Big Mama** Centre **Alexanderplatz** Right **Roman carousers**

Top 10 Pubs, Bars and Music Clubs

1 Alexanderplatz

This is definitely Rome's premier jazz venue. The management regularly books first-rate international talent as well as local musicians, and it serves excellent food, too. Advance reservations are highly recommended (see p147).

Alexanderplatz

2 Le Coppelle

A long-standing hub of flashy dressers and socialites, there's also a comfortable come-as-you-are feeling at this buzzing cocktail bar with a sophisticated wine list and expert mixology. Low tables spill out onto the piazza. Ⓢ Piazza delle Coppelle 52 • Map M2

3 Jonathan's Angels

A must-see for its outlandish decor, which was the brainchild of the proprietor Jonathan, a former circus performer and also the artist. Taking a cue from his Baroque forbears, he's covered practically every square inch of the place with squirming colour. There's a piano bar and floor shows (see p88).

4 Big Mama

Trastevere's historic jazz, blues, rhythm and blues and world music standby, with different acts performing every

night. Membership is by the month or year, but unfortunately Friday and Saturday night concerts are open only to those with annual memberships (see p147).

5 Fiddler's Elbow

One of the oldest Irish pubs in Rome and still going strong, frequented by both locals and out-of-towners. Italians seem to love everything Irish and the place really reels when some impromptu fiddlers get going. Ⓢ Via dell'Olmata 43 • Map F4

Est'd dal 1976

IRISH PUB
THE FIDDLER'S ELBOW
ROME
Via dell'Olmata, n° 43 (S. Maria Maggiore)
tel. 06.4872110 fax 06.48916763

Fiddler's Elbow

6 Trinity College

Rather like entering a time-warp that lands you up in Ireland. A warm, inviting two-floor place that can get very noisy and packed, but always stays cheerful. A very eclectic menu of simple, tempting fare available until 1am, and brunch on Sunday (see p96).

La Vineria

This historic wine bar is an established favourite with the locals. Smoky and definitely cosy during the winter, but spilling out onto the Campo de' Fiori in the summer. Prices for wine and beer are low, especially if you stand at the bar, and there are a few well-chosen snacks *(see p106).*

Bar della Pace

Bar della Pace

For those who crave to see and be seen, this is the place to drape your designer-clad self, especially on warm summer evenings when you can pose at an outdoor table. In the winter, it's a cosier, less self-conscious local favourite, although it's always pretty pricey, as are most places in the Piazza Navona area. ◈ *Via della Pace 5 • Map L3*

Micca Club

The DJ spins music from the 1950s to the 1970s at this atmospheric establishment housed in a former oil cellar. There are weekly burlesque shows, a vintage flea market on Sunday afternoons and special events attracting a colourful crowd. Get there early as the line outside is long. ◈ *Via Piero Micca 7A • Map G4 • www.miccaclub.com*

Les Affiches

This beloved Trastevere jazz joint moved across the bridge and got a makeover. The club hosts contemporary art exhibitions and live music in a modern, airy setting. There's always something unexpected happening, including live jam sessions. It is open until dawn and serves an excellent brunch at weekends. ◈ *Via di Santa Maria dell' Anima 52 • Map C3 • 06 686 8986*

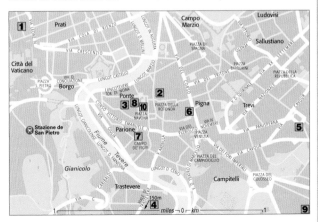

Recommend your favourite bar on traveldk.com

AROUND TOWN

ROME'S TOP 10

Left **Piazza Navona** Right **Cornice, Palazzo Madama**

Around Piazza Navona

THIS IS BAROQUE ROME IN ALL ITS THEATRICAL GLORY, *a collection of curvaceous architecture and elaborate fountains by the era's two greatest architects, Bernini and Borromini, and churches filled with paintings by the likes of Caravaggio and Rubens. The street plan was largely overhauled by 16th- to 18th-century popes attempting to improve the traffic flow from St Peter's – in fact, a 19th-century plan to turn Piazza Navona into a boulevard from Prati across Ponte Umberto I was only killed when wiser heads widened*

Corso del Rinascimento instead. However, ancient Rome does peek through in the shape of Piazza Navona and the curve of Palazzo Massimo alle Colonne. This is also a neighbourhood of craftsmen, shopkeepers and antiques restorers and dealers who line Via dei Coronari (see p87). More recently the narrow alleys around Via della Pace have become a centre of Roman nightlife, with tiny pubs, trendy cafés and nightspots where the clientele spills out into the streets in summer (see p88).

The Ganges, Four Rivers Fountain

🔟 Sights

1. Piazza Navona
2. Four Rivers Fountain
3. San Luigi dei Francesi
4. Sant'Ivo
5. Sant'Agostino
6. Santa Maria della Pace
7. Palazzo Altemps
8. Pasquino
9. Palazzo Massimo alle Colonne
10. Palazzo Madama

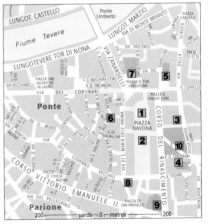

1 Piazza Navona

One of Rome's loveliest pedestrian squares *(see p46)* is studded with fountains and lined with palaces, such as the Pamphilj, the church of Sant'Agnese, and classy cafés such as Tre Scalini *(see p88)*. ✆ Map L3

2 Four Rivers Fountain

The statues ringing Bernini's theatrical 1651 centrepiece symbolize four rivers representing the continents: the Ganges (Asia, relaxing), Danube (Europe, turning to steady the obelisk), Rio de la Plata (the Americas, bald and reeling), and the Nile (Africa, whose head is hidden since the river's source was then unknown). The obelisk, balancing over a sculptural void, is a Roman-era fake, its Egyptian granite carved with the hieroglyphic names of Vespasian, Titus and Domitian. ✆ Piazza Navona • Map L3

3 San Luigi dei Francesi

France's national church in Rome has some damaged Domenichino frescoes (1616–17) in the second chapel on the right, but everyone bee-lines for the last chapel on the left, housing three large Caravaggio works. His plebeian, naturalistic approach often ran foul of Counter-Reformation tastes. In a "first draft" version of the *Angel and St Matthew*, the angel guided the hand of a rough labourer-type saint; the commissioners made the artist replace it with this more courtly one *(see p45)*. Underlying sketches in

Piazza Navona

Martyrdom of St Matthew and *Calling of St Matthew (see p47)* show how Caravaggio was moving away from symbolic compositions in favour of more realistic scenes. ✆ *Piazza S Luigi dei Francesi 5 • Map L2 • Open 10am–12:30pm, 4–7pm (closed Thu eve) • Free*

4 Sant'Ivo

Giacomo della Porta's Renaissance façade for the 1303 Palazzo della Sapienza, the original seat of Rome's university, hides the city's most gorgeous courtyard. The double arcade is closed at the far end by Sant'Ivo's façade, an intricate Borromini interplay of concave and convex curves. The crowning glory is the spiralling ellipse of the dome. The interior disappoints despite its Pietro da Cortona altarpiece. When the courtyard is closed, you can see the dome from Piazza Sant'Eustachio. ✆ *Corso Rinascimento 40 • Map L3 • Church and courtyard: 9am–noon Sun • Free*

Spire and lantern, Sant'Ivo

The Talking Statues

During the Renaissance, the most strident voices against political scandal and papal excess came from statues. Rome's *statue parlanti* "spoke" through plaques around their necks by anonymous wags (although Pasquino was a known local barber). Pasquino's colleagues included Marforio *(see p24)*, Babuino on Via del Babuino and "Madama Lucrezia" on Piazza San Marco. All four have been restored.

Stone relief, Palazzo Madama

5 Sant'Agostino

Raphael frescoed the prophet Isaiah (1512) on the third pillar on the right, and Jacopo Sansovino provided the pregnant and venerated *Madonna del Parto*; but Sant'Agostino's pride and joy is Caravaggio's *Madonna del Loreto* (1603–6). The master's strict realism balked at the tradition of depicting Mary riding atop her miraculous flying house (which landed in Loreto). The house is merely suggested by a travertine doorway and flaking stucco wall where Mary, supporting her overly large Christ child, is venerated by a pair of scandalously scruffy pilgrims. § *Piazza di Sant'Agostino 80 • Map L2 • Open 7:30am–12:30pm, 4–6:30pm daily • Free*

6 Santa Maria della Pace

Baccio Pontelli rebuilt this church for Pope Sixtus IV in 1480–84, but the lovely and surprising façade (1656–7), its curved portico squeezed into a tiny piazza, is a Baroque master-piece by Pietro da Cortona. Raphael's first chapel on the right is frescoed with *Sibyls* (1514) influenced by the then recently unveiled Sistine ceiling *(see pp10–11)*. Peruzzi decorated the chapel across the aisle and Bramante's first job in Rome was designing a cloister based on ancient examples. It now hosts frequent concerts. § *Via della Pace • Map L2 • Open 9am–noon Mon, Wed, Fri • Free*

7 Palazzo Altemps

This 15th-century palace was overhauled in 1585 by Martino Longhi, who is probably also responsible for the stucco and travertine courtyard (previously attributed to Antonio da Sangallo the Younger or Peruzzi). It now makes an excellent home to one wing of the Museo Nazionale Romano, its frescoed rooms filled with ancient sculptures *(see pp28–31)*.

8 Pasquino

That this faceless, armless statue was part of "Menelaus with the body of Patroclus" (a Roman copy of a Helle-nistic group) is almost irrelevant. Since this worn fragment took up its post here in 1501, it has been Rome's most vocal "Talking Statue" *(see box)*. § *Piazza Pasquino • Map L3*

Pasquino, Piazza Pasquino

Rear view, Palazzo Massimo alle Colonne

9 Palazzo Massimo alle Colonne

This masterpiece of Baldassare Peruzzi marks the transition of Roman architecture from the High Renaissance of Bramante and Sangallo into the theatrical experiments of Mannerism that would lead up to the Baroque. The façade is curved for a reason; Peruzzi honoured Neo-Classical precepts so much he wanted to preserve the arc of the Odeon of Domitian, a small theatre incorporated into the south end of the emperor's stadium *(see p50)*. ◉ *Corso Vittorio Emanuele II 141 • Map L3 • Open 7am–1pm 16 Mar only • Free*

10 Palazzo Madama

Based around the 16th-century Medici Pope Leo X's Renaissance palace, the Baroque façade of unpointed brick and bold marble window frames was added in the 17th century. Since 1870 it's been the seat of Italy's Senate, so public admission is obviously limited.

◉ *Piazza Madama 11 • Map L3 • Open for guided tours 10am–6pm 1st Sat of month • Free*

A Morning around Piazza Navona

🕐 Start in the courtyard of the Sapienza, marvelling at the remarkable façade of **Sant'Ivo** *(see p83)*. Head around the church's right side and out the back exit on to Via della Dogana Vecchia. If you need a morning pick-me-up, turn left and then right into Piazza Sant'Eustachio (if the namesake church is open, pop in for an early 18th-century interior). In the elongated piazza to the left are fine views of Sant'Ivo's dome and two great cafés to choose from, Camillo and Sant' Eustachio.

Return to Via della Dogana Vecchia and turn right to visit the Caravaggio works inside **San Luigi dei Francesi** *(see p83)*. Continue up the street to Via delle Coppelle and turn left for more Caravaggio at **Sant'Agostino**. Continue into Piazza delle Cinque Lune and walk a few yards to the left down Corso del Rinascimento *(see p83)* to **Ai Monasteri** *(see p87)* and browse the quality liqueurs and old-fashioned beauty products, all made by monks.

Around the corner is **Palazzo Altemps**, now full of Classical statuary. Spend a good hour inside. Then relax from the morning's sightseeing with a stroll amid the street performers and splashing fountains of **Piazza Navona** *(see p83)*. Enjoy a *tartufo* ice cream or a full lunch at the wonderful **Tre Scalini** *(see p88)*, before ending the morning window-shopping along the antiques of **Via dei Coronari** *(see pp86–7)*.

Left **Palazzo Pamphilj** Right **St Agnes statue, Sant'Agnese in Agone**

Best of the Rest

Sant'Agnese in Agone
This church was built in honour of a 13-year-old girl who was stripped in a brothel but whose hair miraculously grew to cover her nakedness. Borromini's façade is a wonderful play of concave and convex shapes. ✆ *Piazza Navona • Map L3 • Open 9:30am–12:30pm, 3:30–7pm Tue–Sat, 10am–1pm, 4–7pm Sun & hols • Free*

Domitian's Stadium
The outline of this AD 86 stadium is echoed in Piazza Navona, built on top of its remains. ✆ *Piazza di Tor Sanguigna 13 • Map L3 • 06 0608 • Open special occasions and by request • Adm*

Via dei Coronari
Lined with antiques shops, this street is at its torch-flickering best during the May and October antiques fairs *(see p68)*. ✆ *Map K2*

Palazzo Pamphilj
This 17th-century palace has a wonderful Pietro da Cortona fresco upstairs. ✆ *Piazza Navona 14 • Map L3 • Open by appointment only • Free*

Chiesa Nuova
Pietro da Cortona painted the dome and apse and Rubens three sanctuary canvases for this 1575 church. ✆ *Piazza della Chiesa Nuova/ Corso Vittorio Emanuele II • Map K3 • Open 7:30am– noon, 4:30–7:30pm daily • Free*

Palazzo Braschi
The last papal family palace, built 1791–1811. Cosimo Morelli used a Renaissance design to match the piazza. Inside is a small museum dedicated to Roman history. ✆ *Via San Pantaleo 10 • Map L3 • Open 9am–7pm Tue–Sun • Adm*

Sant'Antonio dei Portoghesi
A Baroque gem of a church. Out front is the Torre della Scimmia, a rare remnant of medieval Rome. ✆ *Via dei Portoghesi 2 • Map L2 • 8:30am–1pm, 3–6pm Mon–Fri, 8:30am– noon Sat, 9am–noon Sun • Free*

Santa Maria dell'Anima
Highlights in this gilded church are a Giulio Romano altarpiece and Peruzzi's Hadrian VI tomb (1523). ✆ *Vicolo della Pace 20 • Map L2 • Open 9am–12:45pm, 3–7pm daily • Free*

Museo Napoleonico
A collection of paintings, furnishings and *objets d'art* that once belonged to the Bonaparte clan. ✆ *Piazza di Ponte Umberto I • Map L2 • Open 9am–7pm Tue–Sun • Adm*

San Salvatore in Lauro
A chapel in this church houses da Cortona's *Adoration of the Shepherds* (1630). ✆ *Piazza S Salvatore in Lauro 15 • Map K2 • Open 4:30–7pm Mon–Sat, 8am– 1pm, 4:30–7pm Sun • Free*

Left **Antiques shop, Via dei Coronari** Right **Ai Monasteri**

⅒ Shops

1 Antica Cappelleria Troncarelli

Don't be fooled by the tiny size of this shop – it is still one of the best haberdashers in Rome, established in 1857. ◊ *Via della Cuccagna 15 • Map L2*

2 Ai Monasteri

Monasteries from all across Italy supply their home-made honey, liqueurs, beauty products, elixirs and other products to this shop. ◊ *Corso Rinascimento 72 • Map L2*

3 Antiqua Domus

Bring some of Rome's elegance into your own home. This sizeable showroom has mostly 18th- and 19th-century furnishings on sale; some nice Empire pieces are particularly worth a look. ◊ *Via dei Coronari 39 • Map K2*

4 Gea Arte Antica

Own your own piece of ancient Rome. Choose from a range of objects, from simple oil lamps to exquisite painted vases. ◊ *Via dei Coronari 233A • Map K2*

5 Massimo Maria Melis

This unique jewellery studio wraps 21-carat gold around coins, glass and stones preserved from the Etruscan, Roman and medieval eras. ◊ *Via dell'Orso 57 • Map L2*

6 D Cube

This tiny shop stocks cool and quirky design objects for the home and the garden, as well as what they call "gifts for people who already have everything". ◊ *Via della Pace 38 • Map K3*

7 Dott. Sergio de Sanctis

Exclusively Italian antiques, mostly elegant 18th- to early 20th-century furnishings and gilt-framed mirrors. ◊ *Via dei Coronari 218–19 • Map K2*

8 L'Art Nouveau

Antiques shop devoted to Art Nouveau and Liberty style furnishings, lamps, *objets d'art* and *chinoiserie* silk tapestries and gowns. ◊ *Via dei Coronari 221 • Map K2*

9 Calzoleria Petrocchi

Bruno Ridolfi keeps alive the high fashion, excellent quality, made-to-measure cobbler traditions of his uncle Tito Petrocchi, who regularly shod glamorous stars of stage and screen in the "*dolce vita*" heyday of the 1950s and 1960s. ◊ *Via dell'Orso 25 • Map L2*

10 Nardecchia

Prints, old photographs and watercolours are on sale here, from Piranesi originals to 20th-century works. ◊ *Piazza Navona 25 • Map L3*

Left **Tre Scalini** Right **Abbey Theatre Irish Pub**

Chic Cafés and Bars

Tre Scalini
This historic café, right on Piazza Navona, is renowned for its delectable chocolate home-made *tartufo* ice cream ball *(see p70)*. ⊗ *Piazza Navona 28 • Map L3*

Jonathan's Angels
Perhaps Rome's most unusual nightspot, which should be seen to be believed. Run by a former circus acrobat, it is eccentrically decorated, with a piano bar, tables out on the narrow alley strung with fairy lights, and the occasional impromptu floor show. ⊗ *Via della Fossa 16 • Map K3*

Abbey Theatre Irish Pub
Comfortable, cosy Guinness pub, pleasantly removed from the hubbub of the nightlife core that has sprouted down the road. Basic snacks are also served and there's an Internet terminal. ⊗ *Via del Governo Vecchio 51–53 • Map K3*

Cul de Sac
One of Rome's oldest wine bars, with lots of labels on offer. A bit of a squeeze inside and out, but a better option than the nearby bars of the Piazza Navona. ⊗ *Piazza Paquino 73 • Map L3*

Bull Dog Pub
American style bar positively hopping nightly with plenty of lively young students both foreign and Italian. ⊗ *Corso Vittorio Emanuele II 107 • Map L4*

Bloom
The former Clochard nightclub was reborn in 2001 as a jazzy modern bar. Known for its celebrity and football-player filled evenings. ⊗ *Via del Teatro Pace 30 • Map L3*

Bramante
Café/bar with a quirky elegance amid a sea of pubs. Light dishes are served to a chic young crowd. ⊗ *Via della Pace 25 • Map K3*

Societé Lutèce
The Romans love this small aperitivo bar, where beer and wine are accompanied by a buffet of couscous, salads, pastas and vegetables that costs no more than €5. ⊗ *Piazza Montevecchio 17 • Map K3*

La Botticella
Small, always crowded *birreria* (beerhouse) with some tables outside, in the heart of the area's nightlife action. Devil's Kiss and Castlemaine XXXX beer are on tap. ⊗ *Via di Tor Millina 32 • Map L2*

Old Bear
The eclectic but good food served at this establishment is accompanied by a wide range of beers. Live music is played in the basement. ⊗ *Via dei Gigli d'Oro 3 • Map L2*

Price Categories

For a three-course	€ under €30
meal for one with half	€€ €30–40
a bottle of wine (or	€€€ €40–50
equivalent meal), taxes	€€€€ €50–60
and extra charges.	€€€€€ over €60

Above **Il Convivio**

Places to Eat

1 Da Francesco

An abundant appetiser buffet offering hand-cut prosciutto, fresh seafood salads and many vegetarian options. ✎ *Piazza del Fico 29 • Map K2–3 • 06 686 4009 • Closed Tue, Aug: Mon, Tue & L • DA • €*

2 Terra di Siena

One of the best Tuscan restaurants in Rome. The family imports ingredients and classic seasonal recipes from the farmers around their hometown near Siena. ✎ *Piazza Pasquino 77–8 • Map L3 • 06 6830 7704 • Closed Sun • €€*

3 Lilli

An ex-footballer runs this ultra-traditional restaurant hidden away in a cul-de-sac next to the riverside boulevard. If you are looking for a true taste of Rome's cuisine, the recipes don't get more Roman than this. ✎ *Via Tor di Nona 23 • Map L2 • 06 686 1916 • Closed Mon, Sun D• €*

4 Il Convivio Troiani

For a special night out. One of the historic centre's best restaurants, with strictly seasonal cuisine based on Italian traditions and an excellent wine list.
✎ *Vicolo dei Soldati 28 • Map L2 • 06 686 9432 • Closed Sun • €€€€€*

5 Etabli

An informal eatery furnished in Provençal style. There is also a lounge area for pre-

and post-dinner drinks. The menu is Mediterranean with a creative touch. ✎ *Via delle Vacche 9 • Map K2 • 06 976 16694 • Open daily • DA • €€*

6 Pizzeria La Montecarlo

The offspring of Baffetto's owners run this joint. Has less ambience than its famous parent, but benefits from shorter queues (see p73). ✎ *Vicolo Savelli 12 • Map K3 • 06 686 1877 • Closed Mon • €*

7 Tre Archi

A local trattoria with two small rooms and a famed Roman set menu. ✎ *Via dei Coronari 233 • Map K2 • 06 686 5890 • Closed Sun • €*

8 Fraterna Domus

Communal dining in a hospice run by nuns. The set menu offers soup or pasta, a meat course and salad and fruit for dessert. ✎ *Via di Monte Brianzo 62 • Map L1 • 06 6880 5475 • Closed Thu • €*

9 Zio Ciro

This pizzeria is popular for its al fresco dining and the chance to order large pizzas with two or three different toppings. ✎ *Via della Pace 1 • Map K3 • 06 686 4802 • €*

10 Antica Taverna

The owners of this taverna get the goat's milk, ricotta and rabbit from their hometown in the Sabine Hills. ✎ *Via Monte Giordano 12 • Map K3 • 06 6880 1053 • €*

Recommend your favourite restaurant on traveldk.com

Left **Piazza Sant'Ignazio** Right **Frieze, Ara Pacis**

Around the Pantheon

DURING THE ROMAN EMPIRE the Tiber Bend area was a public training ground for soldiers called the Campo Marzio. With Rome's fall, the city turned its back on this riverside neighbourhood and, aside from a few foreign settlements, it wasn't until the 15th century that anything other than a few churches was built here. The Baroque boom gave the area's palaces their distinctive look. Mussolini cleaned up the neighbourhood in the 1920s and 1930s to bring out its ancient character. He cleared away the debris surrounding Augustus's Mausoleum, reassembled the Ara Pacis and surrounded the lot with reviled Fascist buildings, complete with self-aggrandizing bas-reliefs.

Marcus Agrippa, Ara Pacis

🔟 Sights

1. The Pantheon
2. Santa Maria sopra Minerva
3. Galleria Doria Pamphilj
4. Ara Pacis
5. Sant'Ignazio di Loyola
6. Column of Marcus Aurelius
7. Augustus's Mausoleum
8. Piazza di Sant'Ignazio
9. Bernini's Elephant Obelisk
10. Piazza della Rotonda

The Pantheon

"Simple, erect, severe, austere, sublime" – even Lord Byron struggled to find words to express this marvel of ancient Roman architecture, the only ancient Roman temple to survive the millennia virtually intact *(see pp14–15)*.

Relieving arches, Pantheon

Santa Maria sopra Minerva

The only truly Gothic church in Rome, possibly built, as the name suggests, atop a temple to Minerva. Michelangelo's *Risen Christ* (1514–21) is a muscular rendition of the Saviour so shockingly nude that church officials added the bronze wisp of drapery. Filippino Lippi frescoed the last chapel on the right; the lower scene on the right wall includes portraits of young Giovanni and Giulio de' Medici (known as Popes Leo X and Clement VII), who are buried in tombs by Antonio Sangallo the Younger, in the apse, with Fra' Angelico and (most of) St Catherine of Siena *(see p44)*. ✆ *Piazza della Minerva 42 • Map M3 • Open 7:10am–7pm Mon–Sat, 8am–noon, 2–7pm Sun • Free • DA*

Galleria Doria Pamphilj

The best of the private collection galleries in Rome. In addition to paintings by Rubens, Correggio, Tintoretto, Carracci and Brueghel, star works include Caravaggio's *Mary Magdalene*, *Rest on the Flight into Egypt*, and *Young St John the Baptist* (a copy he made of his Capitoline version); Titian's *Salome with the Head of John the Baptist*; and Bernini's bust of Pope Innocent X *(see p43)*. ✆ *Via del Corso 305 • Map N3 • Open 10am–5pm daily • Adm €9.50 • DA • www.doriapamphilj.it*

Ara Pacis Museum

Augustus Caesar built this "Altar of Peace" between 13 BC and 9 BC to celebrate the famed *pax romana* (Roman peace) he instituted – largely by subjugating most of Western Europe, the Levant and North Africa. Fragments of the altar were excavated over several centuries, and in the 1920s Mussolini placed the reconstituted Ara Pacis by Augustus's Mausoleum. The altar is now housed in a Richard Meier-designed museum, the first modern structure to rise in the centre of Rome in 70 years. ✆ *Lungotevere in Augusta • Map D2 • 060608 • Open 9am–7pm Tue–Sun • Adm • www.arapacis.it*

Nave, Santa Maria sopra Minerva

Relief, Column of Marcus Aurelius

career of Marcus Aurelius. The spiral of reliefs celebrates his campaigns against the Germans (169–73) on the bottom and the Sarmatians (174–6) on the top. In 1588, Pope Sixtus V replaced the statues of the emperor and his wife with that of St Paul.
🅢 *Piazza Colonna • Map N2*

Sant'Ignazio di Loyola
When the Jesuits' new Baroque church was finished in 1685, it still lacked a dome. Master of *trompe-l'oeil* Andrea Pozzo used his flawless technique to create the illusion of an airy dome on the flat circle of ceiling over the church's crossing; stand on the yellow marble disc for the full effect, then walk directly under the "dome" to see how skewed the painting actually is. Pozzo also painted the nave vault with the lovely *Glory of Sant'Ignazio*. 🅢 *Piazza di S Ignazio • Map N3 • Open 7:30am–12:20pm, 3–7:20pm daily • Free*

Column of Marcus Aurelius
Trajan's Column was such a success *(see p22)* that this 29.5-m (97-ft) one was erected in AD 180–93 to honour the military

Augustus's Mausoleum
Augustus built this grand imperial tomb in 27 BC, his ashes later joined by those of emperors Tiberius and Nerva, and worthies such as Agrippa and Marcellus. Barbarian invaders later made off with the urns and locals mined its travertine facing for their palaces. The ancient rotunda has served time as a hanging garden, fortress, circus for bear-baiting and concert hall. In the 1920s its crown was restored to the ancient style, covered with grass and cypress, and Mussolini laid out the Fascist piazza around it. Major architectural work is planned for this area.
🅢 *Piazza Augusto Imperatore • Map D2 • Closed for restoration • Adm*

Piazza di Sant'Ignazio
Francesco Raguzzini laid out this masterpiece of Baroque urban design for the Jesuits in

Recycled Temples
Romans are ingenious recyclers. The Pantheon became a church, Hadrian's Temple a stock exchange; San Clemente was built atop a temple to Mithras, Santa Maria sopra Minerva one to Minerva. In the 11th century, the walls of San Lorenzo in Miranda in the Forum and San Nicola in Carcere on Via Teatro di Marcello were both grafted onto temple columns.

Augustus's Mausoleum

Piazza della Rotonda

1727–8, creating a piazza carefully planned right down to the ornate iron balconies and matching dusty pink plaster walls. 🜂 *Map M2*

Bernini's Elephant Obelisk

An example of Bernini's fun-loving side. This baby elephant, carved to the master's designs by Ercole Ferrata in 1667, carries a miniature 6th-century BC Egyptian obelisk on its back. It is a tongue-in-cheek reference to Carthaginian leader Hannibal's war elephants, which carried tall siege towers across the Alps to attack the Roman Empire in 218 BC. 🜂 *Piazza della Minerva • Map M3*

Piazza della Rotonda

The square in front of the Pantheon was filled with a boisterous daily market until 1847; some of the Pantheon's portico columns still bear square holes from the stall posts once set into them. The square is now filled with tourists, outdoor tables of cafés, and horse-drawn carriages, all ranged around Giacomo della Porta's 1575 fountain, which supports a tiny Egyptian obelisk dedicated to Rameses II. 🜂 *Map M3*

A Morning Stroll around the Pantheon

🕙 Start with a *cappuccino* at **Caffè Sant'Eustachio** *(see p96)*. Follow Salita de' Crescenzi into **Piazza della Rotonda** and the stunning beauty of the **Pantheon** *(see pp14–15)*. Head down to Piazza di Minerva, with **Bernini's Elephant Obelisk** and the façade of **Santa Maria sopra Minerva** *(see p91)*, hiding masterpieces by Filippino Lippi and Michelangelo inside.

Via S Caterina da Siena becomes Via Pie' di Marmo (look right to see the famous ancient marble foot). The street spills into the long piazza in front of **Galleria Doria Pamphilj** *(see p91)*. After paying homage to works by Caravaggio, Tintoretto and Bernini continue out the east end of the piazza on Via Lata, then on to the Corso to **Santa Maria in Via Lata** *(see p94)*. Turn left up the Corso to the Baroque **Piazza Sant' Ignazio**, backed by Rome's best *trompe-l'oeil* frescoes in **Sant'Ignazio di Loyola**. Work your way behind the square's mini palaces onto Piazza di Pietra. A narrow alley leads to the **Column of Marcus Aurelius**. Head to **Giolitti** for a delicious ice cream *(see p96)*.

Walk west on Via del Leone into Piazza Borghese, home to an antiques print market and the **Palazzo Borghese** *(see p94)*. Two blocks north it opens out on to Piazza Augusto Imperatore, home to many churches, **Augustus's Mausoleum** and the **Ara Pacis** *(see p91)*. End your morning with lunch at trendy **'Gusto** *(see p117)*.

Left **Fontanella del Facchino** Right **Hadrian's Temple**

Best of the Rest

1 Hadrian's Temple
Eleven huge, worn columns still stand from a Temple to Hadrian built in AD 145 by his son. ◈ *Piazza di Pietra 9A • Map M2 • Access to the outside only*

2 Santa Maria Maddalena
The church is an elliptical Baroque gem. The 1735 façade by Giuseppe Sardi is Rome's best Rococo monument. ◈ *Piazza della Maddalena 53 • Map M2 • Open 7am–noon, 5–8pm Mon–Fri, 9:30am–noon, 5–8pm Sat, 9am–12:30pm, 5–8pm Sun • Free*

3 Pie' di Marmo
This large sandalled marble foot belonged to an unidentified ancient statue. ◈ *Via S Stefano del Cacco, Via Pie di Marmo • Map N3*

4 San Lorenzo in Lucina
Founded in the 5th century, and overhauled in 1090–1118. Guido Reni did the Crucifixion altarpiece, Bernini the second chapel on the right. ◈ *Piazza S Lorenzo in Lucina 16 • Map M2 • Open 8am–8pm daily • Free*

5 Palazzo di Montecitorio
Bernini's palace has housed Parliament's Chamber of Deputies since 1871. The south façade is original; the north is Art Nouveau. ◈ *Piazza di Montecitorio 33 • Map M1 • 06 676 01 • Open 10am–5:30pm 1st Sun of month • Free*

6 Piazza di Montecitorio
The square's obelisk was once part of the Augustus's giant sundial, which used to be flanked by the Ara Pacis *(see p91)*. ◈ *Map M1*

7 Palazzo Borghese
The oddly shaped "harpsichord of Rome", begun by Vignola in 1560, was finished with a Tiber terrace by Flaminio Ponzio. ◈ *Via Borghese & Via di Ripetta • Map M1 • Free*

8 Santa Maria in Via Lata
Pietro da Cortona designed the façade and vestibule (1660); Bernini the high altar (1639–43). Its 6th-century frescoes are now in the Crypta Balbi *(see p52)*. ◈ *Via del Corso 306 • Map N3*

9 Fontanella del Facchino
This small wall fountain (probably from the 1570s) is fashioned as a water-seller whose barrel forever spouts fresh water. ◈ *Via Lata, off Via del Corso • Map N3*

10 Piazza Sant'Eustachio
A lovely square, home to two cafés competing for Rome's "best *cappuccino*" title, as well as an 1196 bell tower, and an excellent view of Sant'Ivo *(see p93)*. ◈ *Map M3*

Left **Davide Cenci** Right **Il Papiro**

🔟 Shops

1 Davide Cenci
Men's and women's clothes designer since 1926. Their own slightly conservative but eminently fashionable line is sold alongside international labels such as Ralph Lauren, Church's, Brooks Brothers and Fay. ◈ *Via di Campo Marzio 1–7 • Map M2*

2 Vittorio Bagagli
Purveyor of fine houseware since 1855, including design-led Alessi kitchen gadgets and Pavoni *espresso* machines. ◈ *Via di Campo Marzio 42 • Map M2*

3 Simotti Rocchi
Specialist in Greek, Etruscan and Roman antiquities, selling everything from coins to vases to statuary at a fraction of the prices auction-goers pay (simple coins or terracotta heads start at around €75). ◈ *Largo Fontanella Borghese 76 • Map M1*

4 Mercato dell'Antiquariato
Lovely antiquarian market consisting of about 17 stalls specializing in antique prints and books. ◈ *Piazza Borghese • Map M1*

5 Città del Sole
Part of an Italian chain of high-class toy stores with the very best in educational playthings. ◈ *Via della Scrofa 65 • Map L1*

6 Pane & Company: Forno
This tiny bakery sells an array of local pastries and sweets. The delicious pistachio biscuits are a house speciality. ◈ *Via della Stelletta 2 • Map M2*

7 Il Papiro
Rome branch of the renowned Florentine chain, selling marbled paper products, souvenir pens and calligraphy tools. ◈ *Via del Pantheon 50 • Map M3*

8 Campo Marzio Design
Here they sell their own line of fountain pens, covered in silver plating, as well as other writing and calligraphy utensils. Beautiful leather-bound notebooks make great presents. ◈ *Via di Campo Marzio 41 • Map M2*

9 Maria Teresa Nitti Valentini
This lovely shop sells stunning antique jewellery from the 1800s up to the 1940s, as well as original brooches based on the design of older pieces. ◈ *Via della Stelletta 4 • Map M2*

10 Amarena Chic
Stylish women's shoe shop selling good quality boots and shoes at affordable prices. The unique designs are highly distinctive and are available in a wide selection of colours. ◈ *Via di Campo Marzio 9 • Map M2*

Left **Caffè Sant'Eustachio** Right **Gelateria della Palma**

TOP 10 Cafés, Gelaterie and Bars

1 Giolitti
This 19th-century landmark café is widely regarded as serving Rome's best ice cream *(see p70).* ✪ *Via degli Uffici del Vicario 40 • Map M2*

2 Caffè Sant'Eustachio
Another best – this time the best *cappuccino*. Not surprisingly, the recipe is a closely guarded secret *(see p70).* ✪ *Piazza Sant'Eustachio 82 • Map M3*

3 Trinity College
Ever-popular pub off the Corso, with tasty food served upstairs and standard bar downstairs. Outdoor seating *(see p78).* ✪ *Via del Collegio Romano 6 • Map N3*

4 Black Duke
A passably genuine Irish pub in a cosy basement, with pub food and, in summer, outdoor seating. ✪ *Via della Maddalena 29B • Map M2*

5 Gelateria della Palma
A wide selection of ice cream flavours, just off the Pantheon's square, and open late *(see p71).* ✪ *Via della Maddalena 20–23 • Map M2*

6 La Tazza d'Oro
Rome's "House of Coffee" since 1946. This is a die-hard locals' joint, serving what devotees swear is Rome's best coffee *(see p71).* ✪ *Via degli Orfani 84 • Map M2*

7 Enoteca al Parlamento
Atmospheric and stylish wine bar frequented by politicos from the nearby Italian parliament buildings. ✪ *Via dei Prefetti 15 • Map M1*

8 Capranica
This wine bar-cum-restaurant is just the place for a quick *aperitivo* or a more leisurely alfresco lunch. The impressively bottle-lined interior shows that this is a serious wine bar with a well-stocked cellar offering a great choice of labels.
✪ *Piazza Capranica 99 • Map M2*

9 Cremeria Monteforte
A prime tourist position (next to the Pantheon) doesn't always sound the death knell. This joint guarded by a wooden Pinocchio doorman serves the best *fragola* (strawberry) ice cream in town and interesting variations such as orange chocolate *(see p14).* ✪ *Via della Rotonda 22 • Map M3*

10 Pascucci
This is the place with the frothiest milk shakes and smoothies in town. They come in all flavours and in any combination. ✪ *Via di Torre Argentina 20 • Map M4*

Price Categories

For a three-course	**€** under €30
meal for one with half	**€€** €30–40
a bottle of wine (or	**€€€** €40–50
equivalent meal), taxes	**€€€€** €50–60
and extra charges.	**€€€€€** over €60

Above **Il Delfino**

🔟 Places to Eat

1 L'Eau Vive
Amid 16th-century frescoes, lay sisters from around the world dressed in native costume serve refined French cuisine and dishes from their own countries. Everyone sings "Ave Maria of Lourdes" before their *crêpes flambées*. Perhaps a little kitsch but all the profits do go to charity. ◈ *Via Monterone 85* • *Map M3* • *06 6880 1095* • *Closed Sun* • *€€*

2 Il Bacaro
Booking is essential at this tiny *osteria*. Although the design is contemporary inside, it feels like old Rome when sitting at an outdoor table against the ivy-covered walls. The cuisine is traditional dishes from across Italy. ◈ *Via degli Spagnoli 27* • *Map M2* • *06 687 2554* • *Closed Sun* • *€€*

3 Osteria dell'Ingegno
This popular modern wine bar also serves huge meat and cheese platters. ◈ *Piazza di Pietra 45* • *Map N2* • *06 678 0662* • *Closed Sun* • *€€€*

4 Trattoria Enoteca Corsi
This wine shop has grown into a thriving restaurant (lunch only) serving delicious traditional cuisine at affordable prices. Check the blackboard for the daily specials. ◈ *Via del Gesù 87* • *Map N3* • *06 679 0821* • *Closed Sun* • *€*

5 Maccheroni
The fans and airy rooms wrapped around an open kitchen have a Parisian bistro look. The menu is staunchly Roman though. ◈ *Piazza delle Coppelle 44* • *Map M2* • *06 6830 7895* • *€€*

6 Ristorante Boccondivino
Classy, modern restaurant with a contemporary art collection and outdoor seating. ◈ *Piazza in Campo Marzio 6* • *Map M2* • *06 6830 8626* • *€*

7 Ristorante Trattoria
The Sicilian-inspired dishes are light and pleasing at this eatery. ◈ *Via del Pozzo delle Cornacchie 25* • *Map L2* • *06 6830 1427* • *Closed Sun* • *€€€€*

8 Settimo all'Arancio
Hectic, but excellent classic Roman cuisine. ◈ *Via del Arancio 50–52* • *Map M1* • *06 687 6119* • *Closed Sun* • *€*

9 Da Gino
Visit these *trompe-l'oeil* vaults for food like *nonna* (grandma) used to make. ◈ *Vicolo Rosini 4* • *Map M1* • *06 687 3434* • *Closed Sun* • *€*

10 Il Delfino
Self-service Roman dishes at good prices and friendly staff. ◈ *Corso Vittorio Emmanuele 67* • *Map M4* • *06 686 4053* • *€*

 Note: Unless otherwise stated, all restaurants accept credit cards and serve vegetarian meals

Left **Campo de' Fiori market** Right **Campidoglio square**

Campo de' Fiori to the Capitoline

THIS WEDGE-SHAPED AREA *holds the dubious distinction of being the place where Caesar was assassinated – but it is also home to the Capitoline Hill, Rome's finest glory right up to the present day. In ancient times, the zone was full of important public monuments, but in the 14th century, when the papacy moved to France, Rome sank close to extinction and it was along this bend in the river that the remaining 15,000 citizens huddled, in abject squalor. With the popes' return, serious gentrification took place – papal palaces sprang up, long avenues were laid to connect them with the basilicas, and commerce thrived. Today, you can find clear signs of the long history of Rome's most authentic neighbourhood.*

🔟 Sights

1. Campo de' Fiori
2. Capitoline Hill
3. Largo di Torre Argentina
4. Sant'Andrea della Valle
5. Santa Maria in Cosmedin
6. Foro Boario
7. Gesù
8. Santa Maria in Aracoeli
9. Fontana delle Tartarughe
10. Theatre of Marcellus

Palazzo Senatorio

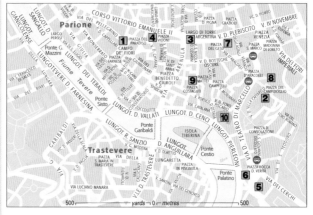

Campo de' Fiori

The "Field of Flowers" (see p46) occupies what was, in ancient times, the open space in front of the Theatre of Pompey. Since the Middle Ages, it has been one of Rome's liveliest areas, a backdrop for princes and pilgrims alike. On the darker side, it was also the locus of the Inquisition's executions, as attested to by the statue of the hooded philosopher Giordano Bruno, burned here in the Jubilee celebrations of 1600. ◈ *Map L4*

Capitoline Hill

The basic principle for comprehending Rome is that everything is built on top of something else. For example, the Capitoline (see p24) was originally two peaks: one, called the Arx, graced by the Temple of Juno, and the other, the Cavo, with the Temple of Jupiter, now mostly occupied by the Palazzo dei Conservatori (see pp26–7). The huge Tabularium (Record Office) was built between them in 78 BC, thus forming one hill, called the Capitol; and over that the Palazzo Senatorio was built in the 12th century. ◈ *Map N5*

Largo di Torre Argentina

The important ruins of four Republican temples (one dating back to the 4th century BC) were uncovered here in 1925 (see p41). On the northwest side is the pleasing façade of the 18th-century Teatro Argentina, with its

Largo di Torre Argentina

inscription to the Muses. Many operas received their debuts here in the 19th century, including Rossini's *Barber of Seville*. It was a crashing flop on its first night, but only because his enemy, Pauline Bonaparte, had paid a gaggle of hecklers. ◈ *Map M4*

Sant'Andrea della Valle

How could one of the most impressive 17th-century Baroque churches have been left with an asymmetrical façade? The answer is artistic temperament. Looking at the grandiose pile, it is quickly apparent that only one angel, on the left, supports the upper tier. Upon its completion, Pope Alexander VII dared to criticize the work, and sculptor Cosimo Fancelli refused to produce an angel for the right side. "If he wants another he can make it himself!" was his rejoinder to His Holiness (see p45). ◈ *Piazza Vidoni 6 • Map L4 • Open 7:30am–12:30pm, 4:30–7:30pm daily • Free*

Santa Maria in Cosmedin

Originally a bread distribution centre, the site became a church in the 6th century and, 200 years later, the focus of Rome's Greek exile community. The Greek epithet "in Cosmedin" means "decorated". Very little of the earliest ornamentation

Santa Maria in Cosmedin

St Ignazio chapel, Gesù

remains; most of it is from the 12th and 13th centuries, although there is a graceful altar screen characteristic of Eastern Orthodox churches. The most popular element, however, is the "*Bocca della Verità*" ("Mouth of Truth"), an ancient cistern cover. Legend has it that the mouth snaps shut on the hands of liars. ⊗ *Piazza della Bocca della Verità 18* • *Map N6* • *Open daily 9am–5pm (to 6pm in summer)* • *Free*

Foro Boario
The name refers to the ancient cattle market that was once here. Now the area is a mini-archaeological park, with two 2nd-century BC temples and a later Arch of Janus. If not for the ferocious traffic, it would be a wonderful place to linger. Dating from the reign of Constantine or later, the arch is unprepossessing, but the temples are amazingly well preserved. The rectangular shrine is to Portunus, god of rivers and ports, while the circular one is a Temple of Hercules. ⊗ *Map N6*

Gesù
A windy piazza hosts the prototype Counter-Reformation church. Enormous and ornate, it's meant to convince the wayward of the pre-eminence of the Jesuit faith. The façade is elegant, but the interior is the major dazzler – first impressions are of vibrant gold, bathed in sunlight. Then there's the vision of angels and saints being sucked into heaven through a miraculous hole in the roof. The tomb of Ignatius, the order's founder, is adorned with the world's largest chunk of lapis lazuli. ⊗ *Piazza del Gesù* • *Map N4* • *Open daily 7am–12:30pm, 4–7:45pm* • *Free*

Santa Maria in Aracoeli
The 6th-century church stands on the site of the ancient Temple of Juno Moneta (Juno the Sentinel), but it was also the Roman mint – and the origin of the word "money". Superstition claims you can win the lottery by climbing on your knees up the 14th-century staircase leading to the unfinished façade – but what you will definitely gain is a fine view. Inside, the nave's 22 columns come from

Santa Maria in Aracoeli

ancient structures; the third one on the left is inscribed "a cubiculo Augustorum" ("from the emperor's bedroom"). ◎ *Scala dell'Arce Capitolina 12* • *Map N4* • *Open 9am–12:30pm, 2:30–5:30pm (to 6:30pm in summer) daily* • *Free*

Fontana delle Tartarughe
The "Fountain of the Tortoises" is the work of three artists. First created in the late 1500s for the Mattei family, it was designed by Giacomo della Porta. The four bronze boys, however, were sculpted by Taddeo Landini. The crowning touch came almost a century later, when an unknown artist (some say Bernini) added the tortoises and gave the fountain its name *(see p47)*. ◎ *Piazza Mattei* • *Map M5*

Fontane delle Tartarughe

Theatre of Marcellus
One of three ancient theatres in this district *(see p41)*, dating back to the 1st century BC, and probably the most frequented of all Imperial theatres until the Colosseum captured the public's favour. The lower archways once housed picturesque medieval shops, until cleared away by archaeologists in the 1920s. To the right of the theatre stand three columns and a frieze fragment that belonged to a Temple of Apollo, also from the 1st century BC. ◎ *Via del Teatro di Marcello* • *Map N5* • *Open 9am–6pm (to 7pm in summer) daily*

Roman Culture, Layer upon Layer

🕐 Because of church opening times, you should take this walk (two to four hours) starting at about 10am or at 4pm. Starting with the **Theatre of Marcellus**, notice the soaring buttresses that support the palace, added in the 16th century. Heading round the next corner, in **Santa Maria in Campitelli** *(see p102)* use binoculars to espy the oak leaves depicted in the altar's tiny icon. Continuing west, as you approach the **Fontana delle Tartarughe**, listen for the sound of splashing water echoing off the medieval walls. To the north, the **Crypta Balbi Museum** *(see p53)* has fascinating displays about the neighbourhood's history. One block north is the awe-inspiring **Gesù**.

🍴 For one of the best *cappuccino-cornetto* combinations in town, stop off at Bernasconi *(Piazza Cairoli, 16)*.

At **Sant'Andrea della Valle** *(see p99)* look up at the unusual barrel-vaulted ceiling. Then head south to Via di Grotta Pinta for the remains of the **Theatre of Pompey** *(see p53)*. A block northwest, in the piazza of the **Palazzo Farnese** *(see p104)*, admire the twin fountains, composed of stone tubs from the Baths of Caracalla. Walk across **Campo de' Fiori** *(see p99)* to **Palazzo della Cancelleria** *(see p51)* to contemplate its Renaissance perfection.

🍴 End with a drink at **La Curia di Bacco** *(see p106)* set in 1st-century BC vaults of the Theatre of Pompey.

Following pages: **Campidoglio at night**

Left **Synagogue** Right **Tabernacle, Santa Maria in Campitelli**

🔟 Best of the Rest

Palazzo Farnese
One of Rome's largest palaces is graced by superlative Michelangelo creations, such as the wonderful cornice *(see p50)*. ⬧ *Piazza Farnese 167 • Map K4 • 06 688 92818 • 50-minute tours at 3, 4 & 5pm Mon & Thu. Book ahead.*

Galleria Spada
In the 17th century the brothers Bernardino and Virginio Spada amassed a fine collection of paintings. Their home now houses the Council of State and a gallery *(see p51)*. ⬧ *Piazza Capo di Ferro 13 • Map L5 • Open 8:30am–7:30pm Tue–Sun • Adm*

Il Vittoriano
The pastiche of motifs on this monument to Victor Emmanuel II inspired the Romans to nickname it "The Wedding Cake". ⬧ *Piazza Venezia • Map N4 • Open 9:30am–4:30pm (winter), to 5:30pm (summer) daily*

Palazzo Venezia
Pope Paul II, who built this palace, watched the carnival horse races from the balcony. From the same, Mussolini shouted his Fascist harangues *(see p51)*. ⬧ *Via del Plebiscito 118 • Map N4 • 06 6999 4318 • Open 8:30am–7:30pm Tue–Sun • Adm*

Portico d'Ottavia
Built in honour of Octavia, Augustus's sister, this was an entrance to the Circus Flaminius. You can view the ruins and archaeological digs from scaffolding. ⬧ *Map M5*

Museo Barracco
This palazzo houses a small but important collection of ancient sculpture *(see p53)*. ⬧ *Corso Vittorio Emanuele II 166 • Map L4 • 06 6880 6848 • Open 9am–7pm Tue–Sun • Adm*

Via Giulia
Fashionable street laid out by Bramante in the early 16th century. The ivy-hung viaduct was designed by Michelangelo, but never completed. ⬧ *Map K4*

Synagogue
This 1904 synagogue has a museum that traces the history of Rome's Jewish community *(see p100)*. ⬧ *Lungotevere dei Cenci • Map M5 • Open 9am–6pm Mon–Thu; 9am–12:30pm Fri & Sun*

Palazzo della Cancelleria
Sublime Renaissance structure, once the Papal Chancellery. ⬧ *Piazza della Cancelleria • Map L4 • Open by appt only • Adm*

Santa Maria in Campitelli
Home to one of the most lavish tabernacles in Rome. ⬧ *Piazza Campitelli 9 • Map N5 • Open 7:30am–noon, 4–7pm daily • Free*

Left **Libreria Babele** Right **Momento**

🔟 Shops

Marble and Tile Bottega
This is certainly one of the most fascinating of a nest of authentic workshops. Particularly appealing are the 18th- and 19th-century Neapolitan floor tiles. ⊗ *Vicolo Cellini 16 • Map J3*

Il Goccetto
Considered by connoisseurs to be Rome's premier wine shop, more than 500 labels are available to try by the glass. The proprietor's expertise is at your disposal when selecting which bottles to take home. ⊗ *Via dei Banchi Vecchi 14 • Map J3*

Antichitá Antonio Bacchi
One of the most appealing antiques shops on this street. An assortment of furniture and small knick-knacks at good prices.
⊗ *Via dei Banchi Vecchi 47 • Map J3*

Libreria Babele
Rome's first gay and lesbian shop has a selection of books in English, plus information concerning goings-on about town.
⊗ *Via dei Banchi Vecchi 116 • Map J3*

Sciam
This incredible shop has a Middle Eastern bazaar atmosphere. Hand-blown glass is a speciality. ⊗ *Via del Pellegrino 55 • Map K3*

Fahrenheit 451
Cinema, art and photography books galore. ⊗ *Campo de' Fiori 44 • Map L4*

Prototype
This popular store carries urbanwear for a trendy crowd, including hip sweaters, hoodies, T-shirts, trainers and jeans.
⊗ *Via dei Giubbonari 50 • Map L4*

Momento
An eclectic boutique for just about every taste, with chiffon ball gowns, floor-sweeping wool coats and tops in wild prints, as well as a collection of funky and fun accessories. ⊗ *Piazza Cairoli 9 • Map L5*

Orologeria Timeline
Looking for a nice watch that won't blow your budget? This friendly proprietor sells name brands at about 30–50 per cent below regular retail prices. Strong on Swatch watches.
⊗ *Via dei Pettinari 41 • Map L4*

Libreria Del Viaggiatore
Travellers of all ages and budgets find inspiration in this tiny, but packed bookstore. Travel-related materials, from guidebooks and maps to novels, books of photographs, globes and posters are on offer.
⊗ *Via del Pellegrino 78 • Map K4*

Left **La Vineria** Right **Rock Castle Café**

⑩ Nightspots

The Drunken Ship
Currently the top spot, with a sea of energetic carousers night after night in this jumping piazza. Mainstream rock inside. Outside you queue at the service window to get your drinks. ✪ *Campo de' Fiori 20–21 • Map L4*

Bartaruga
Local celebrities and models crowd this chic bar with ornate ceilings and furniture. In summer, the bar spills out onto the stunning piazza Mattei. Occasional live music. ✪ *Piazza Mattei 8 • Map M5*

Taverna del Campo
Occupying as it does the crucial corner position, this lively drinking and gourmet eating establishment is always a winner and perpetually jammed with merrymakers. Tables inside and out. ✪ *Campo de' Fiori 16 • Map L4*

La Vineria
This tiny wine bar has long-time regulars lounging at the outside tables. ✪ *Campo de' Fiori 15 • Map L4*

Caffè Farnese
A more chic place is hard to imagine. On a corner facing elegant Piazza Farnese, some of Rome's smartest young beautiful people sip their glasses of wine at outside tables. Yet, it's also really friendly. ✪ *Piazza Farnese 106 • Map K4*

Sciam
A taste of Arabia awaits you here. A turquoise-glazed fountain splashes gently at the entrance, and inside all is inlaid wood and tiles. Teas and sweetmeats complement the dreamy music. ✪ *Via del Pellegrino 56 • Map K4*

La Curia di Bacco
This long, narrow space is a vaulted corridor of the ancient Pompey's Theatre *(see p53).* ✪ *Via del Biscione, 79 • Map L4*

Mad Jack's
A classic Irish pub offering all the brews you can imagine, especially Guinness, along with decent light snacks. ✪ *Via Arenula 20 • Map L4*

Rock Castle Café
A medieval dungeon, with tables tucked into odd nooks. Rock music in the background, plus a dance floor. ✪ *Via Beatrice Cenci 8 • Map M5*

Shanti
An Arabian night out: hookah pipes, exotic teas, live music and belly-dancing. ✪ *Via dei Funari 21 • Map M5*

Price Categories

For a three-course meal for one with half a bottle of wine (or equivalent meal), taxes and extra charges.

€	under €30
€€	€30–40
€€€	€40–50
€€€€	€50–60
€€€€€	over €60

Above **Traditional Roman-Jewish breads**

🔟 Roman-Jewish Restaurants

1 Piperno
Roman-Jewish cuisine at its finest, in a beautiful piazza hidden away from the hubbub. Traditional dishes include *carciofi alla giudia* (Jewish-style fried artichokes). Booking is a must. ⊗ *Via Monte de'Cenci 9* • Map M5 • 06 686 1113 • Closed Sun D, Mon • €€€€

2 Da Giggetto
Famous for its first-rate cookery and grand setting, right next to the soaring columns of the Portico d'Ottavia *(see p104)*. Try chicory shoots *(puntarelle)* with anchovy dressing, a typical Roman dish. ⊗ *Via del Portico d'Ottavia 21a–22* • Map M5 • 06 686 1105 • Closed Mon • €€€

3 Vecchia Roma
One of Rome's finest institutions, noted for its historic interior, excellent service and superb wine list. ⊗ *Piazza Campitelli 18* • Map N5 • 06 686 4604 • Closed Wed, 2 weeks Aug • €€€€

4 La Taverna del Ghetto
Kosher cooking in remodelled medieval rooms, or outside on the piazza. Grilled fish is their forte. ⊗ *Via Portico d'Ottavia 8* • Map N5 • 06 6880 9771 • Closed Fri D, Sat L • €€€

5 Sora Margherita
Wonderful Jewish-Roman delicacies. No sign; look for the red streamers in the doorway. Weekday lunches only. ⊗ *Piazza delle Cinque Scole 30* • Map M4 • 06 687 4216 • Closed Sun • No credit cards • €

6 Zi Fenizia
A pizzeria and a Jewish café all rolled into one outlet. ⊗ *Via dell'Umiltà 31* • Map N3 • 349 252 5347 • Closed Fri D, Sat • No credit cards • €

7 Filetti di Baccalà
A Roman tradition, little changed for centuries. Juicy fried cod fillets, served with similar Roman standards. ⊗ *Largo dei Librari 88* • Map M4 • 06 686 4018 • Closed Sun • No credit cards • €

8 Da Sergio alle Grotte
A simple, traditional Roman dining experience: *spaghetti alla carbonara, gnocchi,* tripe and more. ⊗ *Vicolo delle Grotte, 27* • Map M4 • 06 686 4293 • Closed Sun • €

9 Osteria ar Galletto
An old favourite, tables spilling out into the piazza every summer. Good, honest cooking. ⊗ *Piazza Farnese 102* • Map K4 • 06 686 1714 • Closed Sun • €€

10 Yotvata
Kosher cuisine in a historic palazzo. Good for pizza, fresh fish and hearty pasta dishes. Excellent desserts. ⊗ *Piazza Cenci 70* • Map L5 • 06 6813 4481 • Closed Sat L, Fri D • €€

Left **Piazza del Popolo** Right **Pinturicchio fresco, Santa Maria del Popolo**

The Spanish Steps and Villa Borghese

HERE IS ROME AT ITS MOST ORDERLY AND ELEGANT, *carefully laid out under 16th-century papal urban planning schemes. Baroque popes such as Leo X and Sixtus V redeveloped the all but abandoned area around the Corso, the extension of the ancient Via Flaminia from northern Italy, for their rapidly growing city. Romans now call it the Tridente after the trident of streets – Corso, Ripetta and Babuino – diverging from Piazza del Popolo. It's an area stamped by a love of theatricality: the beautifully symmetrical Piazza del Popolo; long vistas that stretch down arrow-straight roads; the carefully*
landscaped Pincio gardens and the lush expanse of *Villa Borghese; the stage-set backdrop of the Spanish Steps; the oversized and overwrought Trevi Fountain. It's also Rome's most stylishly self-conscious district, famous for its boutiques hawking frighteningly expensive high fashion. Artists have long made their home along Via Margutta, as numerous galleries and antiques shops attest, and Rome's most elegant passeggiata (the traditional early evening see-and-be-seen stroll) unfolds down the length of Via del Corso.*

Bust, Keats-Shelley Memorial

🔟 Sights

1. Galleria Borghese
2. Santa Maria del Popolo
3. The Spanish Steps and Piazza di Spagna
4. Trevi Fountain
5. Keats-Shelley Memorial
6. La Barcaccia
7. Piazza del Popolo
8. Trinità dei Monti
9. Villa Borghese
10. Via dei Condotti

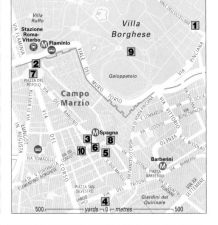

The Spanish Steps and Piazza di Spagna

Galleria Borghese

One of Europe's greatest small museums, worth seeing for its setting alone, is home to Rome's best collection of early Bernini sculptures *(see pp20–21)*.

Santa Maria del Popolo

A priceless lesson in Renaissance and Baroque art, architecture and sculpture can be found in this spectacular church *(see pp32–3)*.

The Spanish Steps and Piazza di Spagna

This elegant, off-centre sweep of a staircase is Rome's most beloved Rococo monument. It is at its most memorable in May, when it is covered in azaleas, but all year round it is littered with people drinking in *la dolce vita* (sweet life) and musicians strumming guitars until late into the night. Francesco De Sanctis designed the steps in 1723–6 for King Louis XV, and their true name in Italian is Scalinata della Trinità dei Monti, after the church at the top. The hourglass-shaped Piazza di Spagna, with its Bernini Barcaccia fountain and milling tourists, was named after the Spanish Embassy to the Vatican located nearby. ⊗ *Map D2*

Trevi Fountain

Anita Ekberg bathed in it in *La Dolce Vita; Three Coins in a Fountain* taught us to throw coins backwards over our shoulder to ensure a return visit to Rome (healthier than the original tradition of drinking the water for luck) – thanks to the world of cinema this beautiful fountain is one of the most familiar sights of Rome. The right relief shows a virgin discovering the spring from which Augustus (left relief) built the Acqua Vergine aqueduct, which still feeds the fountain. Nicola Salvi paid homage to these ancient origins by grafting his exuberant Baroque confection onto the Classical architectural framework of a triumphal arch *(see p46)*. ⊗ *Piazza di Trevi • Map P2*

Keats-Shelley Memorial

The pink-stuccoed apartment overlooking the Spanish Steps, where 25-year-old John Keats breathed his last, consumptive breath in 1821, has been turned into a modest little museum dedicated to the Romantic-era British poets who lived part of their lives in Rome *(see p56)*. Main displays include documents, letters, copies of publications and Keats' death mask. Companion Joseph Severn cradled Keats' head as he died; his resultant drawing of *Keats on his Deathbed* is also on exhibit. ⊗ *Piazza di Spagna 26 • Map D2 • 06 678 4235 • Open 10am–1pm, 2–8pm Mon–Fri, 11am–2pm, 3–6pm Sat • Adm*

La Barcaccia

Bernini's father Pietro possibly helped train his son in making this tongue-in-cheek 1629 fountain of a sinking boat. The design ingeniously solved the low water pressure problem by having a boat sprouting leaks rather than jets and sprays.
Ⓢ *Piazza di Spagna • Map D2*

Piazza del Popolo

Rome's elegant public living room started as a trapezoidal piazza in 1538. In 1589, Sixtus V had Domenico Fontana build a fountain crowned with a 3,200-year-old obelisk – the 25-m (82-ft) megalith from Heliopolis, honouring Ramses II, was brought to Rome by Augustus. Napoleon's man in Rome hired Giuseppe Valadier to overhaul the piazza to its current Neo-Classical look in 1811–24, a giant oval that grades up the steep slope of the Pincio via a winding road. Valadier also added the fountain's Egyptian-style lions *(see p46)*. Map D2

Trinità dei Monti

This church, crowning the French-commissioned Spanish Steps, was part of a convent founded by Louis XII in 1503. The twin-towered façade (1584) is by Giacomo della Porta; the double staircase (1587) by Domenico Fontana. The Baroque interior has three chapels. Daniele da Volterra frescoed the third chapel on the right and painted the *Assumption* altarpiece (which includes a portrait of his teacher Michelangelo as the far right figure), as well as the *Deposition* in the second chapel on the left. The nearby 16th-century Villa Medici (open for special exhibits) has housed the French Academy since 1803.
Ⓢ *Piazza Trinità dei Monti • Map D2*
• *Open 7am–1pm, 3–7pm Tue–Sun • Free*

Villa Borghese

Rome's largest green space is made up of 688 ha (1,700 acres) of public park, landscaped gardens, statuary, fountains, groves, pathways, pavilions and a water clock. There are also three world-class museums: Renaissance and Baroque art at Galleria Borghese *(see pp20–21)*, ancient Etruscan artifacts at Villa Giulia *(see p51)* and modern art at the Galleria Nazionale d'Arte Moderna *(see p43)*. In addition, the Museo Carlo Bilotti *(see p112)*, which

Trinità dei Monti

Via dei Condotti

opened in 2006, houses a permanent collection of contemporary works by the Italian artist Giorgio de Chirico (1888–1978). It's all thanks to Cardinal Scipione Borghese, who in 1608 turned these vast family lands just outside the Aurelian walls into a private pleasure park, opened to the public in 1901. In 1809–14, Giuseppe Valadier had turned the adjacent space within the city walls into the terraced Pincio gardens, a favourite *passeggiata* destination studded with statues of great Italians *(see p62)*. There's an elaborate tea house and an obelisk commissioned by Hadrian to honour his lover.
⊗ *Entrances on Piazza Flaminio, Piazza del Popolo, Via Trinità dei Monti and Corso Italia • Map D2*

Via dei Condotti
10 The "Fifth Avenue" of Rome, lined with chic shops and fashion boutiques of top-name designers. After flirting with high street retail chains in the 1990s, the street has been re-conquered by the *haute couture* that made it famous *(see p68)*. ⊗ *Map D2*

An Afternoon Roman Passeggiata

⏱ Begin in Piazza SS Apostoli to see its namesake church *(see p112)* and the 2nd-century AD relief of an Imperial eagle against the portico's right wall. Then continue straight across Via dell'Umiltà and through the elaborate iron, glass, and frescoed 1880s pedestrian passage. Turn right on Via di Muratte to the **Trevi Fountain** *(see p109)*. Your three coins tossed over your shoulder should ensure a return trip. Leave the square on Via di Lavoratore and turn left on Via di Panetteria for some of Rome's best *gelato* at **San Crispino** *(see p70)*.

Turn right up Via del Tritone and left on Via Francesco Crispi for the **Galleria Comunale d'Arte Moderna** to enjoy a rare glimpse in Rome of contemporary art *(see p43)*. Walk down Via Capo le Case and right on Via Due Macelli into **Piazza di Spagna** and the **Spanish Steps** *(see p109)*. Spend as long as you like window-shopping along the grid of streets west of the piazza, but try to finish up by 5pm so you can work your way north, weaving between Via del Babuino and Via Margutta to see the art and antiques shops *(see p113)*, to **Piazza del Popolo**.

🍵 Pause for a *cappuccino* at **Caffè Canova** *(see p116)*, then cross to **Santa Maria del Popolo** *(see pp32–3)*, with its works by Caravaggio, Raphael and Bernini. Try to get to **Santa Maria in Montesanto** *(see p112)* around 7pm to hear the Gregorian chant, before heading off for a special dinner at **Dal Bolognese** *(see p117)*.

111

Left **German author Goethe lived in Via del Corso** Right **SS Ambrogio e Carlo al Corso**

Best of the Rest

Villa Giulia

Contains Italy's top Etruscan collection, celebrating the peninsula's first great civilization (8th to 3rd centuries BC). ◎ *Piazzale di Villa Giulia 9 • Map D1 • Open 8:30am–7:30pm Tue–Sun • Adm • DA*

Galleria Nazionale d'Arte Moderna

The national modern art museum covers 19th- and 20th-century works. Strongest in Italian art, although foreigners feature too. ◎ *Viale delle Belle Arti 131 • Map D1 • 06 323 4000 • Open 8:30am–7:30pm Tue–Sun • Adm • DA*

Museo Carlo Bilotti

A small art collection with works by De Chirico, Warhol and others. ◎ *Viale Fiorello la Guardia (Villa Borghese) • Map D2 • Open 9am–7pm Tue–Sun • Adm • DA*

SS Ambrogio e Carlo al Corso

Roman Baroque church (1669) by Pietro da Cortona, who designed the tribune, cupola and stuccoes. ◎ *Via del Corso 437 • Map N1 • Open 7am–7pm daily • Free*

Santa Maria dei Miracoli and in Montesanto

Carlo Fontana was responsible for these late 17th-century "twin" churches, although Bernini guided him in the decoration of the more elaborate Montesanto. ◎ *Miracoli: Via del Corso 528; open 8am–1pm, 5–7pm daily. Montesanto: Via del Babuino 197; open 4–8:30pm Mon–Sat, 11am–1pm Sun • Free*

Canova's Studio

The artist's studio walls are embedded with fragments of statuary. ◎ *Via del Babuino 150a • Map D2 • Open 8am–8pm Mon–Sat • Free*

Palazzo Colonna

The gallery features work by Tintoretto, Lotto and Veronese. ◎ *Via della Pilotta 17 • Map N2 • Open 8am–8pm Mon–Sat • Closed Aug • Adm*

Porta del Popolo

Michelangelo used the Arch of Titus as the model for this gateway. ◎ *Piazza del Popolo • Map D2*

Casa di Goethe

German author Goethe lived here from 1786 to 1788 *(see p56)*, and his letters are on display. ◎ *Via del Corso 18 • Map D2 • Open 10am–6pm daily (guided tours available on request) • Adm*

Santissimi Apostoli

This 6th-century church, restructured in 1702–8, has a *trompe-l'oeil* vault above the altar. ◎ *Piazza SS Apostoli • Map N2 • Open 7am–noon, 4–7pm • Free*

Left **Galleria Veneziani** Right **Dott. Cesare Lampronti**

🔟 Art and Antiques Shops

Dott. Cesare Lampronti
Although it resembles an art museum, you can buy the work on show here: still lifes, religious paintings, mythological compositions, scenes of Roman life and Neo-Classical statues, variously dating from the 16th to 19th centuries. ✎ *Via del Babuino 174–5* • *Map D2*

Benucci
Heavy duty art and antiques of the type more usually found in museums – 15th-century Roman and Florentine Virgin and Childs, works by artists such as Luca Giordano or Fra' Bartolomeo – plus beautiful furnishings inlaid in mother-of-pearl and hardwoods.
✎ *Via del Babuino 151–3* • *Map D2*

Galleria Veneziani
A large gallery selling a wide range of high-quality antiques, from furnishings and old oil paintings to statuary, vases and various *objets d'art*. Definitely worth a browse.
✎ *Via Margutta 41* • *Map D2*

Maurizio Grossi
Maurizio Grossi is a specialist in marble. This is just the place to buy a reproduction Roman bust or an astoundingly life-like sculpted fruit.
✎ *Via Margutta 109* • *Map D2*

Alberto di Castro
Etchings, lithographs and other prints from the 1660s to the 1920s are on sale in this lovely shop. ✎ *Via del Babuino 71* • *Map D2*

Libreria Il Mare
All the books and posters in this shop are about the ocean. They also have charts and a small selection of navigation instruments, including sextants. ✎ *Via di Ripetta 239* • *Map D2*

Galleria Antiquaria
A small selection of artworks, mostly sculpture, paintings and *objets d'art*. ✎ *Via Margutta 67* • *Map D2*

Nomades
This eclectic, funky gallery housed in a former convent sells wood, stone and ceramic *objets d'art* from around the globe.
✎ *Via di Ripetta 224* • *Map D2*

Danon
Mostly 18th- to early 20th-century Oriental carpets and prayer rugs, from Persia and India, Tibet and China. ✎ *Via Margutta 36–37* • *Map D2*

La Bottega del Marmoraro
Homespun Italian homilies carved into scraps of marble are hung around a characteristic old workshop. ✎ *Via Margutta 53B* • *Map D2*

Share your travel recommendations on traveldk.com

Left **Gucci** Right **Giorgio Armani**

🔟 High Fashion Boutiques

1 Giorgio Armani
Stylishly cool service for one of Italy's top names. Emporio Armani branch (Via del Babuino 140) sells the designer's couture line at lower prices. The lowest-end line, Armani Jeans, is at Via del Babuino 70A. ◈ *Via dei Condotti 77 • Map D2*

2 Prada
The most highly priced of the top Italian designers. A Milan fashion house making minimalist, slightly retro clothing. ◈ *Via dei Condotti 92–5 • Map D2*

3 Gucci
The Florentine saddle-maker turned his leather-working skills into one of Italy's early fashion successes. The era of ostentatious interlocking "G's" on everything is over, but the accessories are still top notch. ◈ *Via dei Condotti 8 • Map D2*

4 Valentino
Boutique for the *prêt-à-porter* collection of this native Roman designer in the top echelon of fashion since Jackie Kennedy and Audrey Hepburn donned his clothes in the 1960s. ◈ *Via del Babuino 61 • Map D2*

5 Ferragamo
The shoemaker to the stars during Hollywood's Golden Age of the 1950s hasn't lost its touch, but it now mass-produces styles rather than creating unique works. ◈ *Via dei Condotti 73–4 • Map D2*

6 Gianni Versace
The house of the late fashion designer never compromises the clothing's flamboyant cuts and garish use of colour. ◈ *Via Bocca di Leone 27 • Map D2*

7 Fausto Santini
Gorgeous, classically styled shoes at stratospheric prices. ◈ *Via Frattina 120 • Map D2*

8 Fendi
Five sisters founded this Roman fashion empire from their parents' workshop and reign over Italy's rage for furs. ◈ *Largo Goldoni 420 • Map D2*

9 Philosophy di Alberta Ferretti
Well-cut women's clothing that is feminine yet powerful and modern. ◈ *Via Condotti 34 • Map D2*

10 Laura Biagiotti
Designer who has made stylish fashions for women since 1972. In menswear, she uses the soft wool that has earned her the moniker "Queen of Cashmere". ◈ *Via Borgognona 43–4 • Map D2*

Left **Messaggerie Musicali** Right **Profumum Durante**

🔟 Discount and Specialist Shops

Il Discount dell'Alta Moda
This stock house sells mostly men's and women's clothing, plus accessories. The staff are genuinely helpful. There are discounts of up to 50 per cent on Versace, Donna Karan, Armani, Dolce & Gabbana and more. ◈ Via di Gesù e Maria 14–16A • Map D2

Profumum Durante
The fragrances created by this Roman luxury perfume brand include Sugar, Sea Water and Amber. Be prepared to empty your wallet. ◈ Via di Ripetta 10 • Map D2

Buccone
Historic wine shop with a vast selection and excellent prices. Speciality Italian foods are on sale as well. ◈ Via di Ripetta 19–20 • Map D2

Enigma
Owned by Bulgari, this intriguing shop sells a highly exclusive line of watches and jewellery. ◈ Via Margutta 61 • Map D2

Vertecchi
The queen of Rome's stationery stores, with hundreds of types of pens (the fancier ones are sold next door at No. 72), thousands of notebooks and the very best in art supplies. ◈ Via della Croce 70 • Map D2

C.U.C.I.N.A.
The motto of this shop, carrying the best in minimalist kitchenware, is "How a kitchen inspires new appetites". ◈ Via Mario de' Fiori 65 • Map D2

Messaggerie Musicali
Huge, ultra-modern music store with dozens of listening stations so you can better select your choice of cassettes and CDs. Tastes range from Italian pop to classic opera. ◈ Via del Corso 473 • Map D2

Tebro
Founded in 1867, this department store specialises in luxury bed linens, towels and lingerie. A made-to-measure service is also available. ◈ Via dei Prefetti 46–54 • Map M1

Remainders
Does exactly what the name says: sells overstock books at up to 50 per cent off their original price, including lots of luxurious art catalogues and coffee table tomes. ◈ Piazza S Silvestro 27–8 • Map D2

Cravatterie Nazionali
Beautiful ties from Valentino, Gigli, Givenchy, Zenga, Gucci and Les Copains at reasonable (for designer) prices and all in one spot. ◈ Via Vittoria 62 • Map D2

Left **Caffè Rosati** Right **Babington's Tea Rooms**

🔟 Pubs, Cafés and Bars

1 Enoteca Antica
Delicious antipasti and wine by the glass, are served in this old-fashioned lively establishment. ⊗ *Via della Croce 76b • Map D2*

2 Gilda
Rome's most central disco has remained popular for years, with a pizzeria in the evening and dance music cranking up at midnight. High cover charge on weekends, but always an A-list crowd. ⊗ *Via Mario de' Fiori 97 • Map D2*

3 Antico Caffè Greco
Rome's premier literary café since 1760, best known for its popularity with the 19th-century English Romantic poets *(see p70).* ⊗ *Via Condotti 86 • Map D2*

4 Fleur Luxury Living
Owned by a family of tea traders since 1890, this tranquil, Oriental-style tea-house stocks over two hundred types of tea. Home-made cakes and light meals are also available. ⊗ *Via Bocca Leone 46 • Map D2*

5 Cinecafé Casina delle Rose
Located in the grounds of Villa Borghese, this café serves drinks and light lunches including salads, sandwiches and some seafood. ⊗ *Largo Marcello Mastroianni 1 • Map E2*

6 Ciampini al Café du Jardin
Enjoy a drink while watching the sunset at this enchanting café. ⊗ *Viale Trinità dei Monti • Map D2 • 06 678 5678 • Closed Nov–Feb*

7 Caffè Rosati
Art Nouveau rival to the right-wing Canova across the piazza, this café has long been the haunt of left-wing intellectuals *(see p71).* ⊗ *Piazza del Popolo 4–5 • Map D2*

8 Caffè Canova
The right-wing bastion in the long-standing Piazza del Popolo café war, with cheaper *espresso*, better ice cream and a restaurant upstairs (the Rosati is more stylish though). ⊗ *Piazza del Popolo 16–17 • Map D2*

9 Shaki
Post-Modern wine bar serving salads and sandwiches with a few tables outside. They also have a very good speciality foods store at Piazza di Spagna 65. ⊗ *Via Mario de' Fiori 29A • Map D2*

🔟 Babington's Tea Rooms
Good for a very pricey spot of tea and other daintily British edibles. Opened in 1893 by a Derbyshire lady, it was the expat hub of the later Grand Tour era. ⊗ *Piazza di Spagna 23 • Map D2*

For Rome's Top 10 Pubs, Bars and Music Clubs **See pp78–9**

Price Categories

For a three-course meal for one with half a bottle of wine (or equivalent meal), taxes and extra charges.

€	under €30
€€	€30–40
€€€	€40–50
€€€€	€50–60
€€€€€	over €60

Above '**Gusto**

TOP 10 Places to Eat

1 Fiaschetteria Beltramme (da Cesaretto)

Regulars and tourists are fitted around communal tables at this ultra-traditional *trattoria* just down the block from the Spanish Steps. ◊ *Via della Croce 39 • Map D2 • Closed Sun • No credit cards • €€*

2 Edy

Some of the best food and lowest prices in this high-rent neighbourhood. Mix of seafood and Roman dishes. The candlelit tables out front are a nice touch. ◊ *Vicolo del Babuino 4 • Map D2 • 06 3600 1738 • Closed Sun • €€*

3 'Gusto

Trendiest thing going: combo restaurant, pizzeria and Thai wine bar *(see p75)*. ◊ *Piazza Augusto Imperatore 9 • Map D2 • 06 322 6273 • €€€*

4 Antica Birreria Peroni

Beer hall with excellent, cheap food sponsored by Italy's premier brewery – try their "Blue Ribbon" Nastro Azzurro label *(see p75)*. ◊ *Via San Marcello 19/ Piazza SS Apostoli • Map N3 • 06 679 5310 • Closed Sun • €*

5 Dal Bolognese

This restaurant's popularity rollercoaster is currently on the upswing, with international celebrities again gracing its tables on Piazza del Popolo for classic Roman cuisine in view of the Ferraris parked out front. ◊ *Piazza del Popolo 1 • Map D2 • 06 361 1426 • Closed Mon • €€€€*

6 Abruzzi

The cuisine here hails from the owners' home in the nearby Abruzzi mountains, as the name suggests. ◊ *Via del Vaccaro 1 • Map D2 • 06 679 3897 • Closed Sat • €*

7 Hosteria St Ana

Warren of basement rooms plastered with photos of famous patrons. Classic Roman cookery. ◊ *Via della Penna 68–9 • Map D2 • 06 361 0291 • Closed Sat L, Sun • €€*

8 Al 34

Excellently priced menus featuring inventive Italian cooking. ◊ *Via Mario de' Fiori 34 • Map D2 • 06 679 5091 • Closed Mon • €*

9 Il Brillo Parlante

Popular basement eatery packed with locals enjoying huge plates of salad and delicious pizzas. ◊ *Via della Fontanella 12 • Map D2 • 06 324 3334 • €*

10 L'Archetto

The cast from nearby Teatro Quirino head here for more than 100 pasta sauces. ◊ *Via dell'Archetto 26 • Map D2 • 06 678 9064 • €*

Note: Unless otherwise stated, all restaurants accept credit cards and serve vegetarian meals

Left and right **San Teodoro**

Ancient Rome

THIS AREA HAS ALWAYS BEEN A CONTRASTING MIX *of the highest and the lowest, from the most extravagant luxury to the toughest work-a-day world. In ancient times, the emperor's lavish palaces were built on the Palatine, but they weren't far from the docks, where roustabouts heaved the tons of goods that were imported to the wealthy city from around the world. There are three hills in the zone: the Palatine and the Aventine are two of the original seven, but Monte Testaccio is entirely man-made. Legend has it that the Aventine was where Remus formed a populist settlement, to rival his twin brother Romulus's dictatorial encampment (see p38). Over the centuries it has been an area inhabited by poor workers and religious institutions. Today, it has returned to being an enclave of greenery and smart dwellings, studded with hidden art treasures and some of the world's finest ancient monuments and priceless archaeological finds.*

Capital, Baths of Caracalla

🔟 Sights

1. Roman Forum and Palatine Hill
2. Colosseum and Imperial Fora
3. Musei Capitolini
4. Santa Sabina
5. Baths of Caracalla
6. Piazza of the Knights of Malta
7. San Saba
8. Pyramid of Caius Cestius
9. San Teodoro
10. Protestant Cemetery

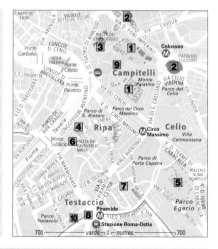

Roman Forum and Palatine Hill

Once the heart of the Roman empire, this mass of ruins is an eerie landscape that seems gripped by the ghosts of an ancient civilization *(see pp16–19)*.

Colosseum and Imperial Fora

These monuments memorialize Imperial supremacy. The Forum of Trajan was declared a Wonder of the World by contemporaries; the only remnant is Trajan's Column, considered to represent Roman sculptural art at its peak. The Colosseum embodies the Romans' passion for brutal entertainment *(see pp22–3)*.

Musei Capitolini

Notwithstanding their great beauty, the original motivation for these museums was purely political. When the popes started the first museum here in 1471, it laid claim to Rome's hopes for civic autonomy – the Palazzo dei Conservatori was the seat of hated papal counsellors, who ran the city by "advising" the Senators. Today the museums are home to a spectacular collection of art *(see pp24–7)*.

Santa Sabina

This church was built over the Temple of Juno Regina in about 425 to honour a martyred

Santa Sabina

Roman matron. In 1936–8 it was restored almost to its original condition, while retaining 9th-century additions such as the Cosmatesque work and the bell tower. Twenty-four perfectly matched Corinthian columns are surmounted by arcades with marble friezes and light filters through the selenite window panes. The doors are 5th-century carved cypress, with 18 panels of biblical scenes, including the earliest known Crucifixion – strangely without any crosses.
◈ *Piazza Pietro d'Illiria 1 • Map D5*
• Open 6:30am–1pm, 3–7pm daily
• Free • DA

Baths of Caracalla

Inaugurated in 217 and used until 546, when invading Goths destroyed the aqueducts. Up to 2,000 people at a time could use these luxurious *thermae*. In general, Roman baths included

Gymnasia, Baths of Caracalla

> Carry a bottle of water with you, which you can refill at little fountains around the area

social centres, art galleries, libraries, brothels and *palestrae* (exercise areas). Bathing involved taking a sweat bath, a steam bath, a cooldown, then a cold plunge. The Farnese family's ancient sculpture collection was found here, including *Hercules*, a signed Greek original. Today, ruins of individual rooms can be seen. ◎ *Via delle Terme di Caracalla 52 • Map E6 • Open 9am–2pm Mon, 9am–1 hr before sunset Tue–Sun • Adm • DA*

Pyramid of Caius Cestius

Piazza of the Knights of Malta

Everyone comes here for the famous bronze keyhole view of St Peter's Basilica, ideally framed by an arbour of perfect trees *(see p53)*. However, it's also worth a look for the piazza's wonderful 18th-century decoration by Giambattista Piranesi, otherwise renowned for his powerful engravings of fantasy-antiquity scenes. To honour the ancient order of crusading knights (founded in 1080), the architect chose to adorn the walls with dwarf obelisks and trophy armour, in the ancient style. Originally based on the island of Rhodes, then Malta, the knights are now centred in Rome. ◎ *Map D5*

San Saba

Originally a 7th-century oratory for Palestinian monks fleeing their homeland, the present church is a 10th-century renovation, with many additions. The portico of the beautiful 15th-century loggia houses a wealth of archaeological fragments. Greek style in floorplan, with three apses, the interior decoration is mostly Cosmatesque *(see p35)*. The greatest oddity is a 13th-century fresco showing St Nicholas about to toss a bag of gold to three naked girls lying on a bed, thus saving them from prostitution. ◎ *Piazza Gian Lorenzo Bernini 20 • Map E6 • Open 8am–noon, 4–7pm Mon–Sat, 9:30am–1pm, 4–7:30pm Sun • Free*

Class Divisions and Power Struggles

The ceaseless struggle between the governing and the working classes is typified by the history of this area. Romulus on the Palatine versus Remus on the Aventine gave rise to patricians and plebeians respectively. The contrast still exists, between wealthy Aventine and down-to-earth Testaccio.

Portico carving, San Saba

Take a torch (flashlight) and binoculars when visiting churches to see the architectural details close up

8 Pyramid of Caius Cestius

This 12 BC edifice remains a truly imposing monument to the wealthy Tribune of the People for whom it was built. It stands 36 m (118 ft) high and took 330 days to erect, according to an inscription carved into its stones. Unlike Egyptian originals, however, it was built of brick then covered with marble, which was the typically pragmatic, Roman way of doing things. ◈ *Piazzale Ostiense • Map D6*

9 San Teodoro

At the foot of the Palatine, this small, circular, 6th-century Greek Orthodox church is one of Rome's hidden treasures. St Theodore was martyred on this spot, and was church built into the ruins of a great *horrea* (grain warehouse) that stood here. The

Keats' tombstone

apse mosaic showing Christ seated upon an orb is original, but the Florentine cupola (1454) and other treatments are mostly 15th-century restorations ordered by Pope Nicholas V. The courtyard was designed by Carlo Fontana in 1705.
◈ *Via di San Teodoro • Open 9:30am–12:30pm daily • Map P6*

10 Protestant Cemetery

Also called the Acattolica (Non-Catholic) Cemetery, people of many faiths have been sepulchred here since 1738. The most famous denizens are the English poets Keats and Shelley *(see pp56–7)*. Until 1870, crosses and references to salvation were forbidden. ◈ *Via Caio Cestio 6 • Map D6 • Open 9am–4:30pm Tue–Sat, 9am–1pm Sun • Donation*

A Morning Parkland Stroll

🕐 The parkland on the other side of the Circus Maximus from the Palatine Hill conceals exquisite early churches and other gems. Start on the south side of the Circus Maximus, now a sunken patch of dust and weeds, but once a majestic racecourse until the popes plundered its stones to build their palaces. Head up the hill to the **Rose Garden** *(see p60)*. In spring and summer few places in Rome radiate such beauty. Continue along the old wall and enter Parco Savello's **Orange Garden** *(see p60)* to take in the view from the parapet. Next door is **Santa Sabina** *(see p119)*. Use a torch and binoculars to scrutinize carved wooden doors and the Crucifixion scene. Stop next at Piranesi's **Piazza of the Knights of Malta** and peer through the celebrated keyhole.

Wind down Via di Sant' Alessio until Viale Aventino and **San Saba**. Take time to appreciate the notorious St Nicholas fresco on the left wall. In the **Parco della Resistenza dell'8 Settembre** *(see p63)* you can get a *gelato* in the park's café and gaze at length on the 3rd-century **Aurelian Wall** *(see p152)*.

Cross over to the lovely **Protestant Cemetery**, pay your respects at the graves of Shelley, Keats and friends, pause to reflect on the splendid **Pyramid of Caius Cestius** and leave your donation in the box as you exit.

🍴 Volpetti *(see p125)* is a fabulous choice for lunch with a made-to-order gourmet sandwich.

▷ *Following pages* **Palatine Hill**

Left **Alpheus** Right **L'Alibi**

🔟 Rome's Trendiest Nightlife

1 Alpheus
Alpheus contains three individual discos, each of which plays different music, plus a garden. It holds special shows too, plus theme nights and the occasional live concert. The entrance ticket includes one free drink. ✪ *Via del Commercio 36* • *Map D6* • *DA*

2 Nazca
This is the place where Rome's bright young things sip a well-mixed cocktail or two before sampling the other delights of the Testaccio-Ostiense area. It has a good sound system and an equally trendy restaurant. ✪ *Via del Gazometro 42* • *Map D6*

3 Radio Londra
One of Rome's perennial favourites for an energetic night out. This is a noisy, buzzing rock-and-roll venue with an air-force theme and occasional up-and-coming live bands. Food is also available. ✪ *Via di Monte Testaccio 65B* • *Map D6* • *DA*

4 L'Alibi
This is Rome's largest and most famous gay disco, with several dance floors, lounges and a huge terrace garden to cool off in in summer. ✪ *Via di Monte Testaccio 44* • *Map D6*

5 Villaggio Globale
Occupying part of an old slaughterhouse, the "Global Village" offers great world music, plus ethnic snacks. Winter only. ✪ *Via di Monte Testaccio 22* • *Map C6*

6 Akab
Cinema, art exhibitions and varied music keep all ages partying here. ✪ *Via di Monte Testaccio 68* • *Map D6* • *06 5725 0585* • *Closed Sun, Mon*

7 Café de Oriente/Caruso
Occasional Brazilian bands rock the samba, while the rest of the time Latin-tinged disco gets you going. ✪ *Via di Monte Testaccio 36* • *Map D6* • *DA*

8 Four XXXX Pub
This popular English-style pub features South American-inspired food. Jazz and Latin music on occasion. ✪ *Via Galvani 29* • *Map D6* • *DA*

9 Joia
Joia comprises a restaurant, wine bar, piano lounge, disco and a terrace on the top floor. ✪ *Via Galvani 20* • *Map C6* • *06 5740 8062* • *Closed Sun, Mon*

10 Caffè Emporio
This pub projects a genuine English atmosphere with a zippy Italian twist. Guinness is on offer, along with snacks. ✪ *Piazza dell'Emporio 2* • *Map D5* • *DA*

Above **Checchino dal 1887**

Price Categories

For a three-course meal for one with half a bottle of wine (or equivalent meal), taxes and extra charges.	
€	under €30
€€	€30–40
€€€	€40–50
€€€€	€50–60
€€€€€	over €60

🔟 Traditional Roman Restaurants

1 Checchino dal 1887
Among the great Roman restaurants *(see p74)*, the menu offers offal-based delicacies such as *rigatoni alla pajata* (pasta with calf intestine). 🏷 *Via di Monte Testaccio 30 • Map D6 • 06 574 6318 • Closed Sun, Mon • €€€*

2 Agustarello
Roman-style, heavy-duty dishes are the standard here. Sample tripe, *coda alla vaccinara* (oxtail), *lingua* (tongue) and other peasant fare *(see pp76–7)*. 🏷 *Via G Branca 100 • Map D6 • 06 574 6585 • Closed Sun • No credit cards • €€*

3 Da Remo
One of Rome's quintessential pizzerias. Authentic, cheap and always packed. 🏷 *Piazza S Maria Liberatrice 44 • Map D6 • 06 574 6270 • Closed Sun • €*

4 Volpetti
Rome's premier delicatessen and the ideal place to have a lunchtime sandwich or a whole picnic made to order. 🏷 *Via Marmorata 47 • Map D6 • 06 574 4306 • Closed Sun • €*

5 Felice
This simple *trattoria* is one of the best places in the city to try the traditional *carciofi alla romana (see p76)*. 🏷 *Via Mastro Giorgio 29 • Map D6 • 06 574 6800 • Closed Sun D • €€*

6 Osteria Degli Amici
A traditional osteria created by two gourmet friends. Roman specialities are served in a friendly setting. 🏷 *Via Zabaglia 25 • Map D6 • 06 578 1466 • Closed Tue • DA • €€*

7 Da Bucatino.
This old-school trattoria has wood-panelled walls and wooden tables. Da Bucatino's speciality is *Bucatini All'Amatriciana (see p76)*. Service is loud and quick – the way the Romans like it. 🏷 *Via della Robbia 84–86 • Map D6 • 06 574 6886 • Closed Mon • DA • €*

8 Acqua e Farina?
At "Water and Flour?" practically everything on the menu, from savouries to sweets, is pastry-based and made to an original recipe. 🏷 *Piazza O Giustiniani 2 • Map C6 • 06 574 1382 • €*

9 Il Seme e la Foglia
Great for large salads and inventive sandwiches, such as goats' cheese, radicchio and olive spread. 🏷 *Via Galvani 18 • Map D6 • 06 574 3008 • Closed Sun • No credit cards • €*

10 Né Arte ne Parte
Run by two Italian TV actors, the menu features such Roman classics as carbonara and roast lamb. 🏷 *Via Luca della Robbia 15–17 • Map D6 • 06 575 0279 • Closed Sun • €€*

Note: *Unless otherwise stated, all restaurants accept credit cards and serve vegetarian meals*

Left **Mosaic, Santa Prassede** Right **Nave, Santi Giovanni e Paolo**

The Esquiline and Lateran

IN ANCIENT TIMES THE LARGEST OF ROME'S SEVEN HILLS *was almost entirely residential, consisting mostly of upper-class villas. The western* slope of the quarter, just behind the Imperial Fora (see pp22–3) *was considered rather unhealthy as it was densely populated – the massive wall at the back of the Fora was intended to keep the squalid slum out. However, in the 4th century, this zone became central to the development of Christianity. In setting up the religion as the official faith, Constantine did not dare step on too many pagan toes, so he established Christian centres outside of town, on the sites of holy tombs. The main one was what is now San Giovanni in Laterano (Saint John in Lateran). Other churches quickly followed, culminating in the striking Santa Maria Maggiore, built in the 5th century. The district remains steeped in history and religious mystique.*

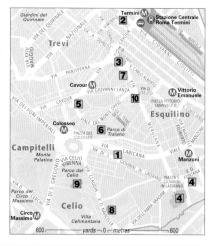

Statue, San Giovanni in Laterano

🔟 Sights

1. San Clemente
2. Palazzo Massimo alle Terme
3. Santa Maria Maggiore
4. San Giovanni in Laterano & Scala Santa
5. San Pietro in Vincoli
6. Nero's Golden House
7. Santa Prassede
8. Santo Stefano Rotondo
9. Santi Giovanni e Paolo
10. Oriental Art Museum

San Clemente

Architectural layers of this church unravel Rome's history, from the 2nd century BC to the 15th century AD *(see pp34–5)*.

Palazzo Massimo alle Terme

Housing an extraordinary collection of ancient frescoes, mosaics and sculpture, this branch of the Museo Nazionale Romano is perhaps the most inspiring. The building itself was erected by the Massimo family at the end of the 19th century and later served as a Jesuit college *(see pp28–9)*.

Santa Maria Maggiore

This church is a unique blend of architectural styles. The nave and its mosaics are original 5th-century; the Cosmatesque work, the apse mosaics and the Romanesque bell tower are medieval; the coffered ceiling (of New-World gold) is Renaissance; and the twin domes and front and back façades are Baroque. Pope Sixtus V erected the Egyptian obelisk in 1587 as part of his overall town-planning, to provide landmarks for pilgrims. The column in front was taken from the Basilica of Maxentius and Constantine in 1615 *(see p44)*. ◎ Piazza di S Maria Maggiore • Map F3 • Open 7am–7pm daily • Free

Catacomb, San Clemente

San Giovanni in Laterano and Scala Santa

Besides its grandiose Baroque bulk, this former papal complex boasts the world's first baptistry, its octagonal shape the model for all those to come. A building on the piazza houses the Scala Santa, claimed to be the staircase from Pontius Pilate's house that Jesus ascended to face his trial – the devout climb the 28 steps on their knees. Tradition says that the stairs were brought from Jerusalem by St Helena, mother of Emperor Constantine *(see p45)*. ◎ Piazza di S Giovanni in Laterano • Map F5 • Open 7am–7pm daily (cloisters 9am–6pm; baptistry 7am–12:30pm, 3–6:30pm); Scala Santa 6:15am–noon, 3–6pm daily • Adm to cloisters

San Pietro in Vincoli

Michelangelo's *Moses* is the unmissable experience here. Weirdly horned and glaring, the

Façade, Santa Maria Maggiore

Sign up for DK's email newsletter on traveldk.com

righteously indignant patriarch is about to smash the tablets down in outrage at his people's idolatry. This powerful sculpture was just one of 40 the artist planned, but never finished, for the tomb of Pope Julius II *(see p49)*. The original shrine was built in the 4th century to house the chains supposedly used to bind St Peter in prison. It has been rebuilt since, first in the 8th century and again in the 15th century. ◈ *Piazza di S Pietro in Vincoli 4A • Map R4 • Open 8am–12:30pm, 3:30–7pm daily (to 6pm Oct–May) • Free • DA*

Statuary, San Pietro in Vincoli

Nero's Golden House
Subsequent emperors were so embarrassed by Nero's gargantuan profligacy that they went to great lengths to undo as much of it as they could. One way was to give some of the land Nero took for himself back to the use of the Roman people. The Flavians drained his lake and built the Colosseum *(see p22)* to provide the citizenry with a suitable place for their gladiatorial spectacles. Then Trajan built Rome's first great bath complex by cutting through Nero's original house and building right over it *(see p41)*. ◈ *Via della Domus Aurea • Map E4 • This sight is temporarily closed for restoration • Adm • DA*

Santa Prassede
Built in the 9th century over a 2nd-century oratory, the original design is still discernible despite restorations. In the central nave, a stone slab covers the well where St Prassede is said to have buried 2,000 martyrs. Byzantine artists decorated the apse with mosaics depicting saints, lambs, palm trees and poppies. The walls and vaults of the Chapel of St Zeno also have mosaics from the same period, and there is a fragment of the column Christ was bound to when he was flogged. ◈ *Via S Prassede 9A • Map F4 • Open 7:30am–noon, 4–6:30pm daily (from 8am in winter) • Free • DA*

Santo Stefano Rotondo
The unusual shape of this early church (468–83) may mean it was built over Nero's round *Macellum Magnum* (meat market). Or perhaps its form was inspired by Jerusalem's Church of the Holy Sepulchre. Whatever the case, recent digs have found a Mithraeum underneath *(see p53)*. The structure is a peaceful, delightful sanctuary, situated far from urban uproar, although

Establishment of the Church
This area played a central role in early Christianity. Although Constantine himself was not a convinced convert, his mother, St Helena, was indefatigable in her promotion of the new religion. She convinced her son to found the official seat of the Bishop of Rome on the site of the ancient Laterani family villa, which his wife Fausta had inherited.

16th-century frescoes by Niccolò Pomarancio depict martyrdoms in sadistic fashion. ◈ *Via di S Stefano Rotondo 7 • Map F5 • Open 9:30am–12:30pm, 2–6pm Tue–Sat (to 5pm in winter); 9:30am–12:30pm Sun • Free*

Santi Giovanni e Paolo

The eponymous saints were 4th-century martyrs and their home is still seen under the 5th-century structure. They were beheaded here in 361 on orders from Emperor Julian. Except for the Late Baroque interior, much of the church is pure medieval. The base of the bell tower is that of the 1st-century Temple of Claudius that once stood here. ◈ *Piazza SS Giovanni e Paolo 13 • Map E5 • Open 8:30am–noon, 3:30–6pm daily • Free*

Oriental Art Museum

A fine, though small, collection of Middle and Far Eastern art, ranging from prehistoric Persian ceramics to 18th-century Tibetan paintings. The most fascinating works are the Ghandharan. These 3rd-century BC to 10th-century AD Indian Buddhist works display both Asian and Greek influences, due to the conquest of the area that is now Pakistan by Alexander the Great. ◈ *Via Merulana 248 • Map F4 • Open 9am–2pm Tue, Wed, Fri; 9am–7:30pm Thu, Sat, Sun • Adm • DA*

Santo Stefano Rotondo

Exploring Rome's Early Churches

Morning

🕐 Start with **San Clemente** *(see pp34–5)*, with its fascinating layers. At the lowest level use a torch (flashlight) to appreciate the beautiful fresco of the head of a bearded man.

Walk one block over to the **Via dei Santi Quattro Coronati** to glimpse the produce market *(see p69)*; turn left and walk up the hill to Santi Quattro Coronati, a rich and little visited 4th-century church with remarkable frescoes in the chapel (1246). Continue on until you reach **San Giovanni in Laterano** *(see p127)*. The cloisters with gorgeously twisted columns and mosaic inlays will make your visit truly memorable.

🍴 For an equally memorable lunch, head to **Cannavota** *(see p131)*.

Afternoon

After lunch, it's time for another of the great basilicas, **Santa Maria Maggiore** *(see p127)*. Check out the ancient column in front and inside use binoculars to examine the 5th-century mosaics lining the upper reaches of the nave. Finally, cut over to **Santa Prassede,** where you can take in some of Rome's most radiant Byzantine mosaics and a powerful painting of the Flagellation in the sacristy.

For sustenance after your spiritual journey, continue down the hill, past Santa Maria Maggiore's grand staircase and enjoy a drink at **L'Angolo di Napoli** *(see p131)*, or stay for a dinner of Neapolitan-style pizza.

Left **Via Mamiani Market** Right **Via Sannio Market**

🔟 Clothing and Discount Shops

Via Sannio Market
The market is a good bet for new leather jackets at great savings. Otherwise there is a lot of quite junky fakes, good-condition second-hand clothing, and other miscellaneous items *(see p69).* 🏵 *Map G5*

Via Mamiani Market
Exotic foodstuffs, spices, flowers, clothing, luggage, leather goods and wine – you can find all that and more around this huge covered market square *(see p69).* 🏵 *Map F4*

Oviesse
Fairly well-made clothing at bargain prices, plus a large selection of cosmetics and toiletries. This is the largest of several branches of Oviesse in Rome. 🏵 *Piazza Vittorio Emanuele 108–10 • Map F4*

Coin
A fashionable department store, with reasonable prices. It's mostly clothing, shoes and accessories, but they also carry kitchenware and more general furnishings. 🏵 *Piazzale Appio 7 • Map G5*

MAS
MAS stands for *"Magazzini allo Statuto"*. Shopping here is like one vast rummage sale. There's tons of merchandise piled up in bins, but the prices are ludicrously low. Check out the homeware department downstairs. 🏵 *Via dello Statuto 11 • Map F4*

Barrita Boutique
The lovely, handmade leather shoes are good value for money. Stock includes boots, shoes and leather bags. A boot-stretching service is also available. 🏵 *Via Appia Nuova 41 • Map G5*

UPIM
A mid- to low-range department store that carries clothing, toiletries and practical items for the home. 🏵 *Via Gioberti 64 • Map F3*

Leam
An extremely trendy clothing emporium with a factory outlet on the top floor selling Prada and D&G. 🏵 *Via Appia Nuova 26 • Map G5*

Exotic Foods
One of the few places in the city where you can find Chinese, Thai and Indian spices and cooking pastes. 🏵 *Via Napoleone III 95 • Map F3*

Firmastock
Small, eclectic collection of designer men's and women's suits, dresses, coats and shoes with up to 50–70 per cent off the usual retail prices. 🏵 *Via Appia Nuova 391 • Map G6*

Price Categories

For a three-course meal for one with half a bottle of wine (or equivalent meal), taxes and extra charges.

€	under €30
€€	€30–40
€€€	€40–50
€€€€	€50–60
€€€€€	over €60

Above **Agata e Romeo**

🔟 Places to Eat

Agata e Romeo
The eponymous couple divide the labour expertly, she as chef and he as *maître d'*. Try the *menu degustazione* for a sampling of each day's masterworks. Reservations a must *(see p74)*. ◈ *Via Carlo Alberto 45 • Map F3 • 06 446 6115 • Closed Sat, Sun, 2 weeks Jan & Aug • DA • €€€€€*

Baia Chia
Cuisine from Sardinia, which adds up to lots of fish and lots of flavour. ◈ *Via Machiavelli 5 • Map F3 • 06 7045 3452 • Closed Sun • DA • €€*

Cannavota
A traditional neighbourhood restaurant. Try *risotto alla pescatore* (seafood risotto). ◈ *Piazza S Giovanni in Laterano 20 • Map F5 • 06 7720 5007 • Closed Wed, Aug • DA • €€*

Trattoria Monti
This friendly, intimate restaurant serves creative dishes from the Marche region. The *tagliatelle con ragù* is excellent, and the house Verdicchio wine is above average. Booking in advance is advised. ◈ *Via di San Vito 13A • Map F4 • 06 446 6573 • Closed Mon, Sun D, Aug • €€*

F.I.S.H.
Seafood and fusion cuisine served by a bilingual staff. ◈ *Via dei Serpenti 16 • Map Q3 • 06 478 24 962 • Closed Aug, Mon • €€€€*

Al Maharajaha
Tandoori dishes are the speciality at this elegant Indian restaurant. Fixed menus are available. ◈ *Via dei Serpenti 12 • Map Q4 • 06 474 7144 • DA • €€*

Hang Zhou
Quite possibly the best Chinese food in town, and recommended by the gourmet guide *Gambero Rosso*. The rooms are small and the queue outside is long, so book ahead. ◈ *Via San Martino Ai Monti 33C • Map F4 • 06 487 2732 • DA • €*

Enoteca Cavour 313
A clubby old wine bar. Bottles from around the world to choose from, as well as a decent menu of salads, pastas, sandwiches and more. ◈ *Via Cavour 313 • Map R4 • 06 678 5496 • €*

L'Angolo di Napoli
Head here for lunch in this light and airy establishment with cafeteria-style service. Great hot or cold buffet selections. ◈ *Via Agostino Depretis 77A • Map E3 • 06 474 6866 • Closed Sun L • €€*

Il Guru
Elegant Indian restaurant, a cut above the rest. The food is superbly prepared in north-Indian style. ◈ *Via Cimarra 4/6 • Map R4 • 06 474 4110 • €*

> **Note:** Unless otherwise stated, all restaurants accept credit cards and serve vegetarian meals

Left **Palazzo del Quirinale** Right **Via Veneto**

The Quirinal and Via Veneto

THE ORIGINAL HILL OF ROME, *the Quirinal was mainly residential in Imperial times, noted for its grand baths and temples. In the Middle Ages, it reverted to open countryside and it wasn't until the 16th century that it again became important, when the crest of the hill was claimed for the pope's new palace. Following that, important papal families built their large estates all around the area, including the Barberini, the Corsini and the Ludovisi. The Quirinal Palace has passed through many metamorphoses but the biggest change to the area came after 1870. The Ludovisi sold off their huge villa to developers, and Via Veneto and the smart area around it became an instant success with the wealthy classes of the newly unified country. This quarter speaks of elegance and power throughout all its ages.*

🔟 Sights

1. Baths of Diocletian & Aula Ottagona
2. Santa Maria degli Angeli
3. Santa Maria della Vittoria
4. Palazzo Barbarini
5. Piazza Barbarini
6. Via Veneto
7. Capuchin Crypt
8. Palazzo del Quirinale
9. Sant'Andrea al Quirinale
10. San Carlo alle Quattro Fontane

Baths of Diocletian

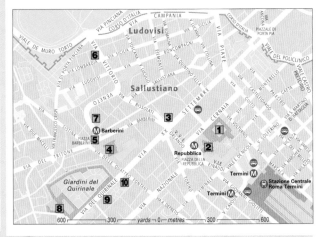

Baths of Diocletian and Aula Ottagona

The main collection of this museum is dedicated to rather academic holdings, principally inscriptions and *stele* (funeral stones). The Aula Ottagona features two 2nd-century BC bronze sculptures of great beauty, which were discovered lovingly hidden in a trench 6 m (20 ft) below the concrete floor of the Temple of the Sun, on the steep hillside of the Quirinal *(see p40)*. 🔖 *Baths of Diocletian: Viale Enrico de Nicola 78 • Map F3 • Open 9am–7:45pm Tue–Sun • Adm • Aula Ottagona: via Romita, Piazza della Repubblica • Map F3 • 06 477 881 • Currently closed to the public*

Santa Maria degli Angeli

In 1561 the pope commissioned Michelangelo to transform the central hall of Diocletian's Baths, the *frigidarium* (cold plunge room), into a church. The result is this overwhelming space, which gives a clearer idea than anywhere else in Rome of how vast these public bathing palaces were. Even then, the finished church takes up only half of the original. Michelangelo had to raise the floor 2 m (6 ft) in order to use the ancient 15-m (50-ft) rose-red granite columns the way he wanted to. 🔖 *Piazza della Repubblica • Map F3 • Open 7am–6:30pm daily • Free • DA*

Santa Maria della Vittoria

This 17th-century Baroque extravaganza has perhaps Rome's most ornate decor, most of it executed by Bernini and his students. The most indulgent corner is the Cornaro Chapel to the left of the altar, home to Bernini's shocking *Ecstacy of St Teresa (see p49)*. 🔖 *Via XX Settembre 17 • Map E2 • Open 9am–noon, 3:30–6:30pm daily • Free • DA*

Santa Maria della Vittoria

Palazzo Barberini

The Barberini sold their palace to the Italian State in 1949 to house part of the National Gallery, which was founded in 1893 with the purchase of the Corsini Palace. The number of pictures in the collection now exceeds 1,700 and has been added to through the acquisition of collections from Rome's noble families over the ensuing years. Among the most famous works are Filippo Lippi's *Madonna and Child*, the controversial *La Fornarina* (supposedly Raphael's mistress, probably painted by Giulio Romano, his favourite pupil), and Caravaggio's *Judith and Holofernes (see p51)*. 🔖 *Via delle Quattro Fontane 13 • Map Q1 • 06 32810 • Open 8:30am–7:30pm Tue–Sun • Adm • DA*

Palazzo Barberini

Power and Elegance

Since the 16th century, the Quirinal Hill has been the elemental expression of temporal power and dominion in Rome: first the popes, then the kings, and now the Presidents of the Republic. Since the late 1800s, Via Veneto has complemented that raw clout with the charisma and glamour of great wealth and all that money can buy.

Piazza Barberini

This could be called the "piazza of the bees", the Barberini family symbol (judiciously upgraded from horseflies when their fortunes improved). Both of the piazza's fountains by Bernini have large, mutant-like versions of the busy insects carved onto them, to let everyone know who sponsored their creation. The central figure of a triton blowing his conch is one of Rome's most appealing and memorable, made of travertine that takes on a warm honey colour. The other fountain is a simple scallop shell (see p47). ◈ Map Q1

Via Veneto

This lazy curve of a street sports a number of belle époque grand hotels and canopied pavement cafés. It enjoyed its famous dolce vita (sweet life) heyday in the 1950–60s, when movie stars supped, sipped and simpered here for the paparazzi. Today, the allure is sadly limited for anybody other than tourists, but every visitor to Rome should come at least once to take a stroll here. ◈ Map E2

Fountain, Piazza Barberini

Capuchin Crypt

A taste for the macabre may be all you need to enjoy this place. A cast-iron stomach doesn't hurt, either. Perhaps the most fascinating thing about this intense memento mori is its position, at the bottom of what was the most sophisticated of streets when la dolce vita was in full swing (see p64). ◈ Via Veneto 27 • Map E2 • Open 7am–noon, 3–6pm daily • Donation

Palazzo del Quirinale

The highest of the original seven hills, the Quirinal was also the enclave of the ancient Sabines (see p38) in Rome's earliest days. Today, it is graced by 5.5-m (18-ft) Roman copies of 5th-century BC Greek originals of the Dioscuri and their prancing horses. The hill's stark, imposing palace, Rome's largest, was built in 1574 as a summer papal-residence, to escape the endemic malaria around the Vatican. In 1870 it became the residence of the kings of Italy and, since 1947, Italy's presidents have resided and held official functions here. ◈ Piazza del Quirinale • Map P2 • Open 13 Jan–15 Dec 8:30am–noon Sun (gardens open to the public on 2 Jun, Italian Republic Day) • Adm • DA

Sant'Andrea al Quirinale

This may represent Bernini's architectural peak, built between 1658 and 1670, the only construction over which he was able to exercise total artistic control. The wide, shallow space needed an oval plan, counterpoised in the concave curving entrance. The eye is masterfully drawn around the elliptical interior, where canonical elements are blended

Sant'Andrea al Quirinale

with sculptural decoration to produce an elegant harmony. For so small a church, the impact is surprisingly grand, made richer by the columns of red marble from Sicily. ✪ *Via del Quirinale 29 • Map Q2 • Open 8:30am–noon, 3:30–7pm Mon–Sat, 9am–noon, 4–7pm Sun • Donation • DA*

10 San Carlo alle Quattro Fontane

Borromini's masterpiece appears about as radically freeform as architecture could be in the 17th century. He filled this small space with fluid undulations, which have complex geometrical relationships. Borromini succeeded in blurring the line between architecture and sculpture, resulting in a homogeneous interior topped by an oval dome. ✪ *Via del Quirinale 23 • Map R2 • Open 10am–1pm daily; 3–6pm Mon–Fri, 10am–1pm Sat & Sun. Mornings only in July • Free • DA*

One of the Quattro Fontane statues

Exploring the Quirinal

Morning

🕐 Start on Quirinal Hill (or Monte Cavallo after the horse sculptures). The **Palazzo del Quirinale** is uninspiring. Walk across the Piazza to the Scuderie del Quirinale, for important exhibitions. Walk halfway down Via del Quirinale and, across from a gate, find Bernini's architectural tour de force, **Sant'Andrea al Quirinale**. Inside, note the maritime motifs, symbolic of Andrew the fisherman.

Continue on to Borromini's **San Carlo alle Quattro Fontane**. Don't miss the masterful crypt and the exquisite cloister. Two blocks along, take a right to the **Aula Ottagona** *(see p133)*. The ancient bronzes of the Prince and the Boxer are amazing expressions of controlled power.

Take Via Bissolati to **Via Veneto**. Check out the cafés, shops and hotels before enjoying lunch at the elegant **Gran Caffè Doney** *(see p136)*.

Afternoon

After lunch, admire the *belle époque* **Excelsior Hotel** *(see p171)* for its appealing architecture, especially its cupola and sexually ambiguous caryatids. And don't miss the public rooms of the sublime **Regina Baglioni** *(see p170)*, which positively reek of luxury.

Finally, after soaking up all the opulence, walk down to visit the eerie **Capuchin Crypt** to put things back in perspective. Round off your tour with a stop at **Piazza Barberini** and Bernini's marvellously lifeaffirming Triton Fountain.

Left **Pavement café, Via Veneto** Right **Café de Paris**

La Dolce Vita Venues

Gran Caffè Doney
One of the best spots in the world to sit under the magnolias, sip *cappuccino* and watch passers-by – although they're mostly tourists now not the celebrities of old *(see pp70–71)*. ✎ *Via Veneto 145 • Map E2 • DA*

Café de Paris
This café has always been the landmark of *dolce vita* life-style along this glossy strip. It's still a magical place to sip an *espresso* or partake of a light snack. ✎ *Via Veneto 90 • Map E2 • DA*

Harry's Bar
Noted for its clubby American style – a dry Martini, tuxedo and cigar sort of place, featuring a piano bar, a restaurant with gourmet cuisine and a café with tables outside. Be prepared to spend lavishly. ✎ *Via Veneto 150 • Map E2*

La Terrazza dell'Eden
At the top of the erstwhile premier celebrity hotel, this bar-restaurant has perhaps the best views in Rome. It's perfect for a romantic tête-à-tête or any special do *(see p170)*. ✎ *Via Ludovisi 49 • Map E2*

Gran Caffè Roma
Located in an elegant curve of the street, with outdoor tables at the bottom of a broad staircase. A great spot to linger over your *cappuccino* and newspaper. ✎ *Via Veneto 32 • Map E2 • DA*

R & Co
Nothing short of fabulous is this collection of designer shoes, leather goods and other fashions. ✎ *Via Veneto 104 • Map E2 • DA*

Brioni
This legendary Italian tailor was established in 1945. The beautifully cut suits have been used in James Bond films. ✎ *Via Veneto 129 • Map E2 • DA*

Jackie O'
As the name implies, this was a leading watering-hole and club in the 1960s. It still attracts international stars. Call ahead if you are not world-famous. ✎ *Via Boncompagni 11 • Map E2 • DA*

Hard Rock Café
It was inevitable that this international chain would choose Via Veneto for its Roman home. Serves standard American fare. ✎ *Via Veneto 62/A/B • Map E2 • DA*

Arion
Independent bookstore specializing in exquisite art books. It stays open until 10pm on Sundays. ✎ *Via Veneto 42 • Map E2 • DA*

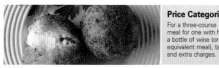

Price Categories

For a three-course meal for one with half a bottle of wine (or equivalent meal), taxes and extra charges.

€	under €30
€€	€30–40
€€€	€40–50
€€€€	€50–60
€€€€€	over €60

Above **Supplí, Andrea**

🔟 Places to Eat

1 Café Veneto
Right in the heart of the famous street, habitués find elegance and carefully prepared fare. Specialities include game and truffles. ⊗ *Via Veneto 120* • *Map E2* • *06 482 7107* • *Closed Mon* • *DA* • *€€€€€*

2 La Scala
A most inviting setting, with wood panelling and stained-glass skylights, situated at the top of a grand staircase. Unusual dishes such as *bombolotti spada e melanzane* – pasta tubes with swordfish and aubergine (eggplant). Dinner only; reserve. ⊗ *Via di S Isidoro 5* • *Map E2* • *06 481 9264* • *Closed Tue* • *€€€*

3 La Giara
A traditional *trattoria* with an unpretentious charm. The menu includes mussels with port and curry. ⊗ *Via Toscana 46, at Via Sardegna* • *Map E2* • *06 4274 5421* • *Closed Sun* • *DA* • *€€*

4 Colline Emiliane
The speciality here is Emilia-Romagna cuisine, which highlights a variety of *prosciutto* (ham) dishes and *tortellini in brodo* (meat-filled pasta in broth). ⊗ *Via degli Avignonesi 22* • *Map E2* • *06 481 7538* • *Closed Sun D, Mon* • *DA* • *€€*

5 Andrea
Very congenial and featuring a wide-ranging menu. The *supplì* (rice croquette) is a classic starter. ⊗ *Via Sardegna 28* • *Map E2* • *06 482 1819/474 0557* • *Closed Sat L, Sun* • *DA* • *€€€€€*

6 Trimani
A classy wine bar with a full menu of soups, pastas, cheeses and cured meats. ⊗ *Via Cernaia 37/B* • *Map F2* • *06 446 9630* • *Closed Sun* • *DA* • *€*

7 La Gallina Bianca
Close to Roma Termini, this pizzeria serves thick-crusted Neapolitan pizza. The dough is slow-risen, and therefore very light. ⊗ *Via a Rosmini 9* • *Map F3* • *06 474 3777* • *DA* • *Open daily* • *€*

8 Dagnino
Rome's favourite spot for sampling Sicilian pastries, like *cassata* (iced cake). ⊗ *Via Vittorio Emanuele Orlando 75 & Via Torino 95* • *Map E3* • *06 481 8660* • *DA* • *€*

9 Mariano
A pleasant setting with fine roasted game or *abbacchio* (lamb). ⊗ *Via Piemonte 79* • *Map E2* • *06 474 5256* • *Closed Sat L, Sun* • *DA* • *€€*

10 Africa
Scoop up spicy vegetables and meats with spongy bread. ⊗ *Via Gaeta 26* • *Map F2* • *06 494 1077* • *Closed Mon* • *DA* • *€*

Note: *Unless otherwise stated, all restaurants accept credit cards and serve vegetarian meals*

Left **Fresco, Castel Sant'Angelo** Right **Mosaic, Santa Maria in Trastevere**

Trastevere and Prati

TRASTEVERE, WHICH LITERALLY MEANS "ACROSS THE TIBER", *is Rome's left bank and Bohemian neighbourhood. The former working-class ghetto* has retained its medieval character better than any other part of Rome, despite having become one of the most restaurant- and nightlife-packed zones of the city. The Borgo is Vatican turf, a largely uninspired grid of streets strung with kitsch religious souvenir shops and bad, tourist-orientated restaurants. Its medieval character was ruined when Mussolini laid out the grand Via della Conciliazione leading to St Peter's. North of the Borgo however stretches Prati, developed in the 19th century and one of Rome's most genuine, non-touristy, middle-class neighbourhoods. Its widest boulevards, Via Cola di Rienzo, Viale Giulio Cesare and Viale delle Milizie, are where Romans shop for everything from sporting goods to CDs to imported foods and the best fresh-baked calzone in town.

Statue, Ponte Sant'Angelo

🔟 Sights

1. Vatican City
2. St Peter's Basilica
3. Villa Farnesina
4. Santa Maria in Trastevere
5. Santa Cecilia in Trastevere
6. Vatican Gardens
7. Castel Sant'Angelo
8. San Francesco a Ripa
9. Gianicolo
10. Ponte Sant'Angelo

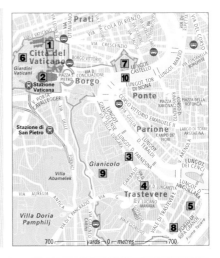

Vatican City

One of the great museum complexes of the world includes Michelangelo's Sistine Chapel and the extensive Raphael Rooms *(see pp8–11)*.

St Peter's Basilica

The capital of Christendom is packed with works by Bernini, statues by Michelangelo and panoramic views from the dome *(see pp12–13)*.

Villa Farnesina

Peruzzi's sumptuous villa (1508–11) was built for papal banker Agostino Chigi, whose parties were legendary – he would toss silver platters into the Tiber after each course. In a down-stairs room, Peruzzi painted Chigi's horoscope on the ceiling, Sebastiano del Piombo painted scenes from Ovid's *Metamorphoses*, and Raphael painted the sensual *Galatea*. Peruzzi's up-stairs hall features a *trompe-l'oeil* balustrade overlooking hills. The 1527 graffiti by Charles V's troops is now historic vandalism, protected under glass. The bedroom contains Sodoma's *Wedding Night of Alexander the Great* (1517) *(see p50)*. ◈ *Via della Lungara 230 • Map J5 • Open 9am–1pm Mon–Sat & afternoons by appt • Adm*

Dome, St Peter's Basilica

Santa Maria in Trastevere

Rome's oldest church dedicated to the Virgin was founded in 337 on the site where a miraculous font of oil spouted the day Christ was born. The miracle is depicted in the stupendous *Life of the Virgin* mosaics (1291) by Pietro Cavallini, covering the lower half of the apse. The current 12th-century church has 13th-century mosaics, 22 mismatched ancient columns and a Cosmatesque pavement. There's also a rare 7th-century panel painting of the *Madonna della Clemenza* in the chapel left of the altar *(see p45)*. ◈ *Piazza S Maria in Trastevere • Map K6 • Open 7:30am–8pm daily • Free*

St Cecilia statue, Santa Cecilia in Trastevere

View of the Tiber from Castel Sant'Angelo

Santa Cecilia in Trastevere

Built atop the saint's house, some of which is visible in the crypt excavations. A Guido Reni painting of Cecilia's decapitation sits off a right-hand corridor of the nave. Under the apse's glittering 9th-century mosaics rests a *baldacchino* (1293) by Arnolfo di Cambio and Carlo Maderno's 1600 statue of the saint (he saw her incorrupt body when her tomb was opened in 1599). Ring the bell on the left aisle to see the top half of Pietro Cavallini's *Last Judgment* (1289–93), his only remaining fresco in Rome.
- Piazza di S Cecilia 22 • Map D5
- Open 9:30am–1pm, 4–6:30pm daily (summer 4:15–6pm) • Adm for crypt

Vatican Gardens

Typical 16th-century Italianate gardens of lawns, woods, grottoes and fountains. Structures include the first Vatican radio tower, designed by Marconi in 1931, Pier Luigi Nervi's shell-shaped audience hall (1971) and the Mannerist Casina of Pius IV (1558–61), home to the Pontifical Academy of Sciences. • Viale Vaticano
- Map A2 • Tours 11am Mon, Tue, Thu, Fri, Sat (06 6988 4676 or www.vatican.va)
- Adm €30 • DA

Castel Sant'Angelo

Hadrian designed his massive circular tomb in 123–39. Aurelian fortified it in 271 as part of his city walls *(see p152)*. It was the papal castle for 1,000 years – a viaduct from the Vatican let the popes scurry here in times of crisis. Gregory the Great named it in 590 after a vision of St Michael announced the end of a plague from its tower, commemorated by the bronze statue of a sword-bearing archangel. There are frescoed Renaissance papal apartments and a small arms and armour collection (Etruscan through to the 1900s), plus stunning panoramas from the ramparts.
- Lungotevere Castello 50 • Map J1 • Open 9am–7:30pm Tue–Sun • Adm

San Francesco a Ripa

Though altered during the Renaissance and Baroque eras, the church was built just 12 years after St Francis stayed at this hospice in 1219. Ask the

St Cecilia

Cecilia was a Roman patrician and secret Christian. In 230 she was locked in steam baths for three days by political enemies. She came out singing (hence becoming patron saint of music), so they tried to behead her, but the requisite three strokes initially failed and Cecilia lingered for three days, converting hundreds to their faith.

sacristan's permission to visit the cell in which St Francis stayed, bearing a copy of his portrait by Margaritone d'Arezzo. The last chapel on the left houses Bernini's *Beata Ludovica Albertoni* (1671–4), in a state of religious ecstasy bordering scandalously on the sexual. ® Piazza di S Francesco d'Assisi 88 • Map C5 • Open 7am–noon, 4–7:30pm daily • Free

Gianicolo

This long ridge separating Trastevere from the Vatican offers some of the best views of Rome *(see p60)*. Its two equestrian monuments celebrate Garibaldi and his wife Anita, who is buried underneath. ® Map B4

Ponte Sant'Angelo

Hadrian built this bridge in 133–4 to access his mausoleum, but only the three central arches of that span remain. Clement VII had the statues of St Peter (by Lorenzetto) and St Paul (by Paolo Taccone) installed in 1534. Clement IX hired Bernini in 1688 to design the statues of 10 angels holding symbols of the Passion. ® Map J2

Bernini sculpture, San Francesco a Ripa

A Tour of Trastevere

Morning

Begin at **San Crisogno** *(see p142)*; ask the custodian to let you into the excavations downstairs. By 10am be at **San Francesco a Ripa** for the five minutes it takes to see Bernini's stunning sculpture. Head down Via Anicia Antica, right on Via Madonna dell'Orto, and left on Via di S Michele to reach **Santa Cecilia**. Explore the crypt and pay the nuns a small donation to get up to see the Cavallini frescoes. Head out of the courtyard left onto Via di Genovesi, which leads to Viale Trastevere.

Crossing Piazza S Maria in Trastevere, bear right into Piazza S Egidio and fork left onto Via della Scala. Continue past Santa Maria della Scala and up Via della Lungara to **Villa Farnesina** *(see p139)*. You'll be here before noon, time enough to spend 30 minutes admiring the frescoes. Take a breather amid the greenery of the **Orto Botanico** *(see p142)*, then return to the heart of Trastevere to enjoy a pizza at **Dar Poeta** *(see p148)*.

Afternoon

After lunch, peruse the collections of the **Museo di Roma** *(see p142)*, visit the marvellous medieval church of **Santa Maria in Trastevere** *(see p139)* and walk up Via Garibaldi to peek through the grille at Bramante's Tempietto in the courtyard of **San Pietro in Montorio** *(see p142)*. Or simply spend the afternoon wandering the medieval streets shrouded by washing lines, awaiting the dinner hour when Trastevere comes to life.

Left **Palazzo Corsini** Right **Ponte Rotto**

🔟 Best of the Rest

1 San Pietro in Montorio
Bramante designed the mini-temple in the courtyard to mark the spot where St Peter was supposedly crucified. ◈ *Piazza San Pietro in Montorio 2 • Map C4 • Open 8:30am–noon, 3–4pm Mon–Fri, 8:30am–noon Sat, Sun • Free*

2 Palazzo Corsini
Small painting collection, featuring works by Fra' Angelico, Van Dyck, Titian, Rubens and Caravaggio. ◈ *Via della Lungara 10 • Map J5 • Open 8:30am–7:30pm Tue–Sun • Adm*

3 Tiber Island
It is said that the serpent of medical god Aesculapius jumped ship and swam ashore here in 293 BC. Rome's maternity hospital is still here. ◈ *Map M6*

4 Orto Botanico
Palazzo Corsini's beautiful gardens are now the University of Rome's botanical museum. ◈ *Largo Cristina di Svezia 24 • Map J5 • Open Apr–Oct: 9:30am–6pm; Nov–Mar: 9:30am–5:30pm Mon–Sat • Adm • DA*

5 Ponte Rotto
Rome's first stone bridge (181–142 BC) was ruined in 1598. It retained three arches until 1886, when two were destroyed to make room for Ponte Palatino (*Rotto* means broken in Italian). ◈ *Map N6*

6 Santa Maria della Scala
A charming Renaissance church, whose claim to fame is a *Virgin and Child* by Cavalier d'Arpino (Caravaggio's teacher). ◈ *Piazza S Maria della Scala 23 • Map K6 • Open 9am–noon, 3:30–6pm daily • Free*

7 Fontana Paola
This wide basin at the end of the Paola aqueduct is a favourite backdrop for wedding photos *(see p60)*. ◈ *Map B5*

8 Villa Doria Pamphilj
Rome's largest public park was established in 1644–52 by Camillo Pamphilj. A great place for picnics. ◈ *Via di S Pancrazio • Map B5 • Open sunrise–sunset daily • Free • DA*

9 Museo di Roma in Trastevere
Housed in a beautifully restored ex-convent, this museum includes life-size dioramas of Ancient Roman rooms and shops. ◈ *Piazza di S Egidio 1b • Map K6 • Open 10am–8pm Tue–Sun • Adm*

10 San Crisogono
The 1626 façade copies the medieval one. Inside are 22 ancient columns and excavations of the 5th-century basilica. ◈ *Piazza S Sonnino 44 • Map L6 • Open 7:30–11:30am, 4–7:30pm Mon–Sat, 8am–1pm, 4–7:30pm Sun • Adm*

Left **COIN** Right **Polvere di Tempo**

🔟 Locals' Favourite Shops

COIN
This good-value department store is where real Romans shop, for back-to-school clothes, kitchen utensils, stationery, household appliances and much, much more. There's also a supermarket in the basement, which is great for buying a picnic. 🐾 *Via Cola di Rienzo 173 • Map C2*

Franchi
One of the best grocers in the city, extremely popular at lunchtime for its hot dishes and in the evening for its fried and baked *calzone* (stuffed pizza pockets). Locals start queueing up at 5pm. 🐾 *Via Cola di Rienzo 200 • Map C2*

Castroni
The gastronomic temple of Rome since 1932, this shop is piled high with packaged and prepared speciality foods from countries the world over, such as Japan, Greece, India, China and the Middle East.
🐾 *Via Cola di Rienzo 196 • Map C2*

Energie
Energie provides all that's new in the world of Italian youth fashion. Whether it's jeans, shirts or shoes you're after, all are on offer for both sexes.
🐾 *Via Cola di Rienzo 143 • Map C2*

Azi
From kitchenware to furniture, Azi gives slick ideas for the home from top Italian designers. 🐾 *Via L Manara 7 • Map C5*

New Fashion
Slightly higher prices than most but better selection and more fashionable wares at this stock house for mostly women's suits and skirts. 🐾 *Via Simone de Saint Bon 85–7 • Map B1*

Il Picchio
The gorgeous wooden creations, including toys and homewares, are all crafted by hand and painted in-store by the owner. 🐾 *Via del Moro 46 • Map K6*

Polvere di Tempo
The non-mechanical time-pieces, including hour glasses, various sundials, candle clocks and astrolabes, are all hand crafted by the Argentinian owner. 🐾 *Via del Moro 59 • Map L6*

Sabon
The scented soaps, candles and toiletries are made using Dead Sea salts. 🐾 *Via Cola di Rienzo • Map C2*

Costantini
This huge fine wine cellar has one of the best selections in Rome at reasonable prices. 🐾 *Piazza Cavour 16 • Map C2*

Stazione di San Pietro

Following pages: **St Peter's Basilica and St Peter's Square**

Left **Ombre Rosse** Right **A typical Trastevere bar**

Pubs, Cafés and Bars

1 Ombre Rosse
This laid-back pub is a staple of Trastevere nightlife. The atmosphere is always lively, with tables on the piazza in summer.
Ⓢ *Piazza S Egidio 12–13 • Map K6*

2 Freni e Frizioni
This former mechanic's garage is now a hip *aperitivo* serving a buffet in summer. The bar overflows into an outdoor courtyard overlooking the Tiber.
Ⓢ *Via del Politeama 4 • Map K5*

3 Bar San Calisto
This quiet neighbourhood bar is the antithesis of the trendy Trastevere scene. Locals come here to play cards, read papers and catch up on the day's gossip. Welcoming atmosphere and drinks at reasonable prices.
Ⓢ *Piazza San Calisto • Map K6*

4 Caffè delle Arance
Overpriced and indifferent, sullen service but a prime location smack on Trastevere's public "living room", Piazza Santa Maria. The *spremuta* (freshly squeezed orange juice) is made from a kilo of oranges.
Ⓢ *Piazza S Maria in Trastevere 2 • Map K6*

5 Big Hilda Café
A welcoming joint offering rock 'n' roll, cheap drinks and a range of sandwiches and salads. Ⓢ *Vicolo del Cinque 33–4 • Map K6*

6 Friends
The semi-circular bar and restaurant is always packed with Trastevere regulars. The menu includes inventive dishes and excellent bar sandwiches.
Ⓢ *Piazza Trilussa 34 • Map K6*

7 Enoteca Trastevere
A thriving wine bar, with pleasingly dark wood interior and plenty of seating out front on the cobblestones. Light snacks and cocktails are served too.
Ⓢ *Via della Lungaretta 86 • Map L6*

8 Roma Caput Mundi
One of Rome's most popular Irish pubs with a corner location that most locals pass through for a pint of Kilkenny or Harp during the evening. Ⓢ *Via Luciano Manara 64 • Map K6*

9 Borgo Antico
A wood-filled, classically styled 16th-century tavern, with coffered ceilings. They also offer more than 60 different wines by the glass. Typical *osteria* dishes are on offer too. Ⓢ *Borgo Pio 21 • Map B3*

10 Mr Brown
This very popular British-style bar has a vaguely old-fashioned sporting theme. It is a regular haunt for a faithful English expat clientele. Ⓢ *Vicolo del Cinque 29 • Map K6*

Around Town – Trastevere & Prati

Stazione di San Pietro

Left **Big Mama** Right **Alexanderplatz**

🔟 Live Music Venues

Alexanderplatz
A little bit off the beaten track, in Prati, but the best jazz club in Rome bar none – Winton Marsalis, Lionel Hampton, George Coleman and many other international jazz stars have played here *(see p78)*. ✆ *Via Ostia 9 • Map B1*

Big Mama
Rome's real house of blues, where the big names book and the smaller acts gig. Only open for live performances *(see p78)*. ✆ *Vicolo S Francesco a Ripa 18 • Map C5*

Stairs Club
A trendy bar with large, comfy sofas on the lower level. Cocktails and bar snacks are available every evening and live accoustic jazz combos are performed once a week. ✆ *Via della Scala 43 • Map K6*

Saxophone Pub
This warm, cosy pub, close to the Vatican, serves simple pub fare including salads and sandwiches. There is always a friendly atmosphere, with jazz and blues on the stereo and local bands that come here to jam. ✆ *Via Germanico 26 • Map B1*

Four Green Fields
Upstairs there is a vaguely British-style pub, while in the basement live music is played nightly. ✆ *Via C Morin 42 • Map B1*

Fonclea
Established in 1977, this historic music venue is located close to Piazza del Risorgimento and features a variety of live music including jazz, soul, funk and rock. Punters can either drink at the bar or eat in the buffet restaurant. ✆ *Via Crescenzio 82 • Map B2*

Birreria Trilussa
Beer and simple dishes are served until the early hours, with live music some nights. Cosy, traditional atmosphere. ✆ *Via Benedetta 19 • Map K6*

The Place
There's always live music on the main stage, be it jazz or soulful singer-songwriters. ✆ *Via Alberico II 29 • Map B2*

Caffè della Scala
A relaxed bar serving powerful cocktails and a great *grappa* selection. Live music is also on offer from time to time. ✆ *Via della Scala 4 • Map K6*

Lettere Café
The focus is on books, but a couple of nights a week are devoted to live roots music. ✆ *Via S. Francesco a Ripa 100 • Map C5*

147

Left **Insalata Ricca** Right **Pizzeria da Ivo**

🔟 Cheap Eats

Da Augusto
Die-hard Trastevere *osteria* complete with wooden tables and traditional menu. ✎ *Piazza de' Renzi 15 • Map K6 • 06 580 3798 • No credit cards • €*

Osteria Pucci
This restaurant serves a good selection of Roman specialties and traditional Italian fare. The outdoor terrace is open most of the year. ✎ *Piazza Mastai 1–4 • Map C5 • 06 581 9870 • €€*

La Tana dei Noantri
Lengthy menu promising all the best of Roman cuisine, including *penne arrabbiata* (pasta in a spicy tomato sauce). There are a few tables in the piazza against the church in summer. ✎ *Via della Paglia 1–3, off Piazza Santa Maria in Trastevere • Map K6 • 06 580 6404 • Closed Tue • €*

Pizzeria Da Ivo
A lively football theme and ever-present crowds are the features of Rome's favourite pizzeria *(see p72)*. ✎ *Via S Francesco a Ripa 158 • Map C5 • 06 581 7082 • Closed L, Tue • €*

Insalata Ricca
Part of a popular chain of restaurants serving huge salads, pizzas and other light dishes. ✎ *Piazza del Risorgimento 5–6 • Map B2 • 06 3973 0387 • €*

Pizzeria Dar Poeta
Innovative pizza is served here – Roman-style, but with a thick crust *(see p72)*. ✎ *Vicolo del Bologna 45–6 • Map K6 • 06 588 0516 • €*

Osteria dell'Angelo
Angelo prepares excellent traditional Roman cooking at equally admirable prices. Service charge is 15 per cent. Book ahead. ✎ *Via G Bettolo 24 • Map B1 • 06 372 9470 • Closed L (except Mon & Sat), Sun • €*

Pizzeria Da Vittorio
Good Neapolitan-style pizza, *antipasti* and a fan-cooled interior plastered with photos of famous patrons make this one of Rome's best pizzerias *(see p72)*. ✎ *Via S Cosimato 14A • Map K6 • 06 580 0353 • €*

Bir & Fud
More than 100 beers, delicious fried appetizers and thick-crusted pizzas made with top quality ingredients define this popular pizzeria. ✎ *Via Benedetta 23 • Map K5 • 06 589 4016 • Closed L • €*

Napul'è
Campanian cuisine and more than 40 types of pizza approved by Naples' strict "True Pizza" association. Live Neapolitan music is played most nights. ✎ *Viale Giulio Cesare 89–91 • Map C1 • 06 323 1005 • €*

Above **Il Matriciano**

Fine Dining

Sabatini
Roman cuisine and seafood in an old Fellini hang-out. Book ahead for a table out on the main square *(see p74)*. ◈ *Piazza S Maria in Trastevere 13 • Closed Wed • Map K6 • 06 581 2026 • €€€€*

Ferrara
Deservedly trendy; decoration is minimalist, with patio seating and the creative menu is based around the remarkable wine selection. ◈ *Via del Moro 1a • Map K6 • 06 580 3769 • €€€€*

Sora Lella
Low wood-beam ceilings and classic Roman cooking define this restaurant on Tiber Island (sadly, no river views). The food is delicious but the portions are small by Italian standards. ◈ *Via Ponte Quattro Capi 16 • Map M6 • 06 686 1601 • Closed Sun, Tue L • €€€*

Les Etoiles
Not only do you come here for the cuisine, but also for the *al fresco* dining and wonderful panoramas of St Peter's Basilica. ◈ *Via Vitelleschi 34, Hotel Atlante Star • Map B2 • 06 687 3233 • €€€€€*

Antico Arco
Trendy, pan-Italian, creative eatery in a lovely setting on Gianicolo hill. ◈ *Piazzale Aurelio 7 • Map B5 • 06 581 5274 • Closed L • €€€€*

Il Ciak
Excellent game dishes are among the offerings served in this typical Tuscan *trattoria*. ◈ *Vicolo del Cinque 21 • Map K6 • 06 589 4774 • €€*

La Gensola
Frequented by artists and intellectuals in the early 1900s, La Gensola has maintained its charm with a classic but informal setting. The cuisine is mainly Sicilian and based on fish. ◈ *Piazza della Gensola 15 • Map M6 • 06 581 6312 • €€€€*

Il Matriciano
Businessmen and Cinecittà film directors patronize this Prati restaurant named after the spicy bacon-and-tomato pasta sauce. Try to sit outside in summer. ◈ *Via dei Gracchi 55 • Map C2 • 06 321 3040 • Closed Wed • €€*

La Pergola
Vistas of the city and food by a top international chef – one of Rome's best dining experiences. Elegant dress code. ◈ *Rome Cavalieri Hilton Hotel, Via Cadlolo 101 • 06 3509 2211 • Closed Sun, Mon • €€€€€*

Taberna de' Gracchi
Dante Mililli's dining rooms may be large and modern, but the spirit is old-school Roman dining with a contemporary touch. ◈ *Via dei Gracchi 266–8 • Map C2 • 06 321 3126 • Closed Sun • €€€€€*

Stazione di San Pietro

Note: Unless otherwise stated, all restaurants accept credit cards and serve vegetarian meals

Left **Square Colosseum, EUR** Right **Via Appia Antica**

Beyond the City Walls

THE 3RD-CENTURY AURELIAN WALLS ARE STILL *largely intact and served as the defence of the city for 1,600 years until Italian Unification was achieved in 1870.* After that, the walls were pierced in several places so that traffic could bypass the old gates and the modern city quickly sprawled far and wide in every direction. Although it's undeniable that Rome's most dazzling sights are contained within the walls, venturing outside them can have spectacular rewards. Ancient roads and even an entire ancient town, as

well as some of Rome's oldest churches, the mystical catacombs, and even Benito Mussolini's pretentious contributions to modern architecture are all must-sees if you can draw yourself away from the city centre.

Apse mosaic, Sant'Agnese fuori le Mura

🔟 Sights

1. Ostia Antica
2. San Paolo fuori le Mura
3. EUR
4. Via Appia Antica
5. Catacombs
6. Montemartini Art Centre
7. Auditorium Parco della Musica
8. MAXXI
9. Foro Italico and Stadio dei Marmi
10. Sant'Agnese fuori le Mura and Santa Costanza

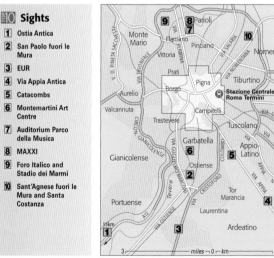

1 Ostia Antica

Ancient Rome's trading heart has a wealth of fascinating ruins that evoke the city's earliest days *(see pp36–7)*.

2 San Paolo fuori le Mura

Façade, San Paolo fuori le Mura

Rome's second largest church has had a history of violent ups and downs. It was built by Constantine in the 4th century, over the spot where St Paul was buried, and for about 400 years it was the largest church in Europe, until it was sacked by the Saracens in 846. It was rebuilt and fortified, but its position outside the walls left it mostly ignored until the mid-11th century, when it underwent a renewal. Then came the 1823 fire, which led to the reworking we see today *(see p45)*. ◉ *Via Ostiense 184 • Metro Basilica S Paolo • Open 7am–7pm daily • Free*

3 EUR

Built by Mussolini as a show-case to the world of the ideal Fascist metropolis, the EUR (l'Esposizione Universale di Roma) is disturbing to many visitors. The critic Robert Hughes described the so-called Square Colosseum as "the most frightening building in the world", yet the aesthetic inspired many postwar architects. Aside from the hard-edged archi-tecture, there's a park with a lake, and a visit to the Museo della Civiltà Romana is instructive. ◉ *Metro EUR Palasport and EUR Fermi*

Tomb statue, Via Appia Antica

4 Via Appia Antica

"The Queen of Roads" was completed in 312 BC by Appius Claudius, also the architect of Rome's first aqueduct. The most pastoral part begins at the circular Tomb of Cecilia Metella, which was made into a fortification in the Middle Ages. Starting here, you'll see more tombs and fragments of tombs, as well as grazing sheep and the private gates to fabulous modern-day villas. As you walk along, look to the east to see the arches of an ancient aqueduct marching towards the city *(see p61)*. ◉ *Buses 118, 218*

5 Catacombs

The burial tunnels of Rome's early Christians are like a honey-comb beneath the consular roads out of Rome, especially along Via Appia Antica. Grave niches stacked like shelving along dark corridors are carved into the tufa. The soft volcanic rock under Rome is highly suitable for tunnelling, as it is softer when first exposed to air, hardening afterwards. There are some precious remnants of fresco and engraved marble slabs *(see p52)*.

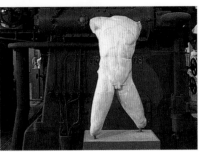

Statue in the Montemartini Art Centre

6 Montemartini Art Centre

Rome's very first power station has been transformed into a remarkable showcase for Greek and Roman statues – parts of the Musei Capitolini collection *(see pp24–7)* that, until now, were kept in storage. The effect is extraordinary, playing the monolithic might of modern technology off against the noble, human vulnerability of these ancient masterpieces. ◎ *Via Ostiense 106 • Metro Piramide, Garbatella • Open 9am–7pm Tue–Sun • Adm • DA*

7 Auditorium Parco della Musica

Italian architect Renzo Piano's "city of music" is the beating heart of the city's cultural life, with three whale-shaped concert halls hosting daily classical, rock, pop and jazz performances by important international artists. The "theatre hall" is for dance shows and electronic nights, while revolving art exhibitions adorn the complex's hallways. There is also a café, a well-stocked book-and-music store and, in winter, an ice-skating rink. ◎ *Via Pietro de Coubertin 30 • 06 802 41281 • www.auditorium.com • Closed Aug • Adm to concerts*

8 MAXXI Contemporary Art Museum

Inaugurated in May 2010, Rome's first contemporary art centre was designed by the English-Iraqi architect Zaha Hadid and is a jewel of modern architecture. The galleries are arranged in a series of long inter-twining bands. The permanent collection contains more than 350 works, and the museum is divided into two sections, one for visual arts and one for architecture. ◎ *Via Guido Reni, 4A • www.maxxi.beniculturali.it • Adm*

9 Foro Italico and Stadio dei Marmi

Originally called the Foro Mussolini, the name was understandably changed in the late 1940s, even though the 16-m

The Aurelian Wall

This ancient wall was begun by Emperor Aurelian (AD 270–75) and completed by his successor Probus (AD 276–82). It stretches 18 km (11 miles) around the city, with 18 gates and 381 towers, enclosing all seven of Rome's hills. In the 4th century, Emperor Maxentius raised it to almost twice its original height. To this day, most of the wall survives.

MAXXI Contemporary Art Museum

(55-ft) obelisk still shouts out "Mussolini Dux" ("Mussolini the Leader"). In imitation of every mad Roman emperor, there was even supposed to have been a 75-m (250-ft) statue of Il Duce posing as Hercules. The sculptures of the Stadio dei Marmi, 60 colossal nude young Fascist athletes, are worth a look. ◈ Viale del Foro Italico • Bus 280

10 Sant'Agnese fuori le Mura and Santa Costanza

These 4th-century gems are located in the same Early Christian complex. Both are decorated with sublime mosaic work, the former depicting the martyred St Agnes as she appeared in a vision eight days after her death. The ambulatory around the circular Santa Costanza has truly delightful, richly detailed scenes of an ancient Roman grape harvest.
◈ Via Nomentana 349 • Buses 36, 60, 62, 84, 90 • Open 7:30am–noon, 4–7pm daily • Free • DA

Santa Costanza

A Morning Walk on the Appia Antica

🕐 Start at the Porta San Sebastiano, the grandest city gate of them all, where you can visit the **Museo delle Mura** (see p55). Climb the stairs for great views. From here, continue straight on along the **Via Appia Antica** (see p153). One of the first sights you'll come to, on the left at a crossroads, is the small church of Domine Quo Vadis? – this marks the spot where Peter, fleeing persecution, encountered Christ and decided to return to Rome and face his martyrdom like a saint. The church contains a replica of footprints in stone, said to be those of Christ, but it is actually an ancient pagan ex voto.

Quite a bit further ahead, you'll come to the **Catacombs of San Sebastiano**. Take the guided tour, and don't miss the curious fresco of a bowl of fruit and a partridge, which, according to some ancient writers, was the most lascivious of all creatures. Continuing on, past a mobile bar where you can buy snacks and drinks, visit the Circus of Maxentius, an ancient racetrack. Note how amphorae were embedded in the bricks to lighten the construction of the upper grandstands. Last stop will be the 1st-century BC Tomb of Cecilia Metella. The frieze of bulls' skulls and garlands is beautiful and the cone-shaped sanctum is peaceful.

For lunch, walk back to the **Ristorante l'Archeologia** (see p155). After lunch, backtrack a few hundred metres to the bus stop to catch the No. 118 into town.

Left **Mosaic pavement, Hadrian's Villa** Right **Ionic columns, Hadrian's Villa**

Daytrips from Rome

Tivoli, Villa d'Este
This hilltown is renowned for its gardens and the villa of Cardinal d'Este, built in the 16th century and boasting 100 fountains.
COTRAL bus from Ponte Mammolo • Villa d'Este: piazza Trento • 07 7433 2920 • Open 8:30am–1hr before sunset Tue–Sun • Adm • DA

Hadrian's Villa
Built as the emperor's summer retreat between AD 118–34, the area was a vast open-air museum of reproductions of Hadrian's favourite buildings.
Via Tiburtina, 6 km (4 miles) southwest of Tivoli • COTRAL bus from Ponte Mammolo • 06 3996 7900 • Open 9am–1hr before sunset daily • Adm • DA

Tarquinia
A museum of Etruscan artifacts famous for its 4th-century BC terracotta horses. *Train from Termini or Ostiense or COTRAL bus from Lepanto • 07 6685 6036 • Open 8:30am–1 hr before sunset Tue–Sun • Adm*

Cerveteri
The necropolis of this 6th-century BC city is quite intact, with streets, houses and frescoes.
Train from Termini to Cerveteri-Ladispoli • 06 994 0001 • Open 8:30am–1 hr before sunset Tue–Sun • Adm

Castelli Romani
There is much to attract in this area of the Alban Hills. Swim in Lago di Albano, or visit Palazzo Chigi in Ariccia, a Baroque complex designed by Bernini in the 17th century. *Metro Anagnina, then COTRAL buses • Palazzo Chigi: 06 933 0053 • Open 10am–7pm daily – tours at 11am, 4pm, 5:30pm Mon–Fri & all day on weekends (gardens open Apr–Sep) • Adm*

Frascati
From the 16th-century Villa Aldobrandini you can take in magnificent panoramas of Rome. *Metro Anagnina, then COTRAL bus • Villa Aldobrandini: 06 678 7864 • Open 9am–1pm, 3–6pm Mon–Fri (to 5pm in winter)*

Palestrina
This town boasts the greatest Hellenistic temple in Italy. Among the treasures unearthed here is a 2nd-century BC mosaic. *Metro Anagnina, then COTRAL bus • Museum: Open 9am–8pm daily • Adm*

Rome's Beaches
The Ostia sea strip to the city's south is dotted with beach clubs and free beaches (*spiaggia libera*). *Trains depart from Porta San Paolo; ATAC bus or metro ticket required.*

Viterbo
Within this medieval town's walls, visit the Papal Palace, the Archaeological Museum and the Fontana Grande. *Most sights: Open 8:30am–7pm Tue–Sat • Adm*

Pompeii
In AD 79 the volcano Vesuvius erupted, and this city was buried and preserved forever. *Train from Termini to Naples, then "Circumvesuviana" train • Open 9am–1.5hrs before sunset daily • Adm • DA*

Above **View from La Sibilla**

Price Categories

For a three-course meal for one with half a bottle of wine (or equivalent meal), taxes and extra charges.	€ under €30
	€€ €30–40
	€€€ €40–50
	€€€€ €50–60
	€€€€€ over €60

📖 Places to Eat

1 Allo Sbarco di Enea, Ostia Antica

Kitsch, but fun. The waiters dress up in Roman gear and the decor is like a low-budget epic movie. The speciality is fish; try the *spaghetti alle vongole* (clams). ⊗ *Via dei Romagnoli 675 • Metro Piramide then local train • 06 565 0034 • Closed Mon–Thu L • €€*

2 Il Pulcino Ballerino

This lively trattoria in the heart of Rome's student neighbourhood is known for its lemon-and-cream *spaghetti al pulcino*. They also serve a meat platter on a hot stone. In summer there is a pleasant patio. Booking recommended. ⊗ *Via Degli Equi 66 • Map G4 • 06 494 1255 • Open daily • DA • €*

3 Ristorante l'Archeologia, Via Appia Antica

An elegant converted farmhouse, where you dine around the fireplace in winter and in the garden in summer. Rustic regional fare, such as roast lamb and homemade pasta. ⊗ *Via Appia Antica 139 • Bus 118 • 06 788 0494 • Closed Tue • €€*

4 La Villetta dal 1940, Piramide

The favourite hangout of 20th-century Surrealist painter Giorgio De Chirico and his crowd of passionately avant-garde artists. The food is hearty and traditional Roman fare, such as *saltimbocca alla romana* (veal and ham). ⊗ *Viale della Piramide Cestia 53 • Buses 23, 30, 75, 95, 280, 716, 719 • 06 575 0597 • €*

5 Arancia Blu

A seasonally varied menu, which includes exquisite desserts, sets this vegetarian restaurant apart. ⊗ *Via Prenestina 396a • Map H4 • 06 445 4105 • Closed L • €€€*

6 La Sibilla, Tivoli

The most spectacular spot in town, overlooking Villa Gregoriana. ⊗ *Via della Sibilla 50 • COTRAL bus from Ponte Mammolo • 0774 335 281 • Closed Mon • €€*

7 San Marco, Tarquinia

An old converted monastery. Game and *funghi selvaggi* (wild mushrooms) in season are good. ⊗ *Piazza Cavour 18 • Train from Termini or Ostiense or COTRAL bus from Cornelia • 0766 842 239 • Closed Mon L • €*

8 Pinocchio, Frascati

Pinocchio (also a hotel) specializes, as does this entire area, in the celebrated *porchetta* (pork roast). ⊗ *Piazza del Mercato 21 • Metro Anagnina, then COTRAL bus • 06 941 7883 • Closed Mon–Sat L • €*

9 Scylla, Sperlonga

On the beach and great for seafood. ⊗ *Via San Rocco 26 • Train from Termini to Fondi, then bus • 0771 549 652 • Closed Tue (winter) • €€*

10 Enoteca La Torre, Viterbo

This bar-restaurant offers local dishes, with an emphasis on fish. Great wines too. ⊗ *Via della Torre 5 • COTRAL bus from Saxa Rubra or train from Roma Ostiense • 0 761 226 467 • Closed Mon, Tue, Wed L • €*

> **Note:** Unless otherwise stated, all restaurants accept credit cards and serve vegetarian meals

STREETSMART

ROME'S TOP 10

Left **ENIT logo** Centre **Italian socket** Right **Various newspapers**

⑩ General Information

① ENIT
ENIT, Italy's national tourist office, is well-intentioned but is often of little help for specific needs. There are branches in most major capital cities. ✆ www.enit.it

② Rome Tourist Offices
Rome has three main tourist offices across the city *(see box)*. There are also 10 privately run information kiosks (PIT points) at tourist locations around the city, although their material is less detailed than at the tourist offices. A tourist infoline (06 0608) operates daily 9am–9pm.

③ The Internet
Rome's official website is www.turismoroma. it or www.060608.it; the Vatican's is www.vaticano. va. Search engines such as google and yahoo have detailed travel and regional sub-menus linking useful private websites.

④ Customs and Immigration
Citizens of the UK, Eire, USA, Canada, Australia and New Zealand need only a valid passport to visit Italy for up to 90 days. Non-EU citizens may bring into Italy personal items with the following limits: 200 cigarettes (or 250 grams of tobacco), 2 cameras, 10 rolls of film, a pair of skis, two tennis racquets and a litre of alcohol. EU citizens are allowed more.

⑤ Business Hours
Most businesses, churches and some museums open at 8 or 9am, shut for *riposo* from 12:30 or 1pm until 3 or 4pm, and close around 6 or 8pm.

⑥ Electricity
Italy is on 220V/50 cycles. To operate a 110V device you need an adaptor (most laptops and camcorders have this built-in). You will also need an adaptor if your equipment has pronged plugs rather than Europe's two round pins.

⑦ TV and Newspapers
Most 3-star hotels and above have satellite TV with CNN and BBC news. English-language newspapers such as the *International Herald Tribune*, *USA Today*, *New York Times* and magazines are sold at most newsstands. The weekly *Roma C'è* ("This is Rome") beats the tourist office's handout for events, entertainment listings, plus sightseeing information and special tours (section in English).

⑧ When to Go
Rome has a temperate climate. August heat is oppressive; February snow flurries are possible. Spring's middle ground keeps hotels booked; autumn is less crowded, but prone to downpours.

High season is Easter to July and September to October. Rome is deserted much of August as residents head to the beaches or mountains to escape the heat and most of the city's shops and restaurants are closed.

⑨ Public Holidays
Public holidays include 1 and 6 January, Easter Sunday and Monday, 25 April, 1 May, 2 and 29 June, 15 August, 1 November and 8, 25 and 26 December.

⑩ What to Pack
Italians dress well so try to bring one nice outfit. Few restaurants, however, require jacket and tie. Many churches do not allow you to enter with bare knees or shoulders (no shorts, miniskirts or vests) so make sure you have something to cover up.

Rome Tourist Offices

Information Line
• *06 0608*

Via Parigi 5
Map E3 • 06 4889 91
• *Open 9am–7pm Mon–Sat*

Termini Railway Station
Map F3
• *Ticket office: 892021*

Fiumicino Airport
06 65951

Left **Tourist horse and carriage** Right **Bus tour**

TOP 10 Tours and Specialist Holidays

Package Tours
Airlines, large travel agencies and tour companies offer discount packages combining airfare and hotels. Many, however, stick to large international hotel chains, usually in uninteresting neighbourhoods. You can often do better at a small hotel in the centre.

Standard Guided Tours
Tours, booked by your travel agent, leave the driving, hotels, language barriers and all decisions to the tour company, but they often take out much of the fun in the process. You see the company's neatly packaged idea of Rome, not the Rome you can find travelling on your own. It's also hard to meet the locals when surrounded by a large group of compatriots.

Study Holidays
Art history is so much better when the teacher can show you real paintings. History, culture, painting, cookery and language courses are all available. The following websites have more information: www.specialtytravel.com, www.shawguides.com, and www.infohub.com.

Rome Bus Tours
City-run ATAC bus No. 110 makes a three-hour circuit around 80 sights with no guide. It leaves daily from outside Termini every 25 minutes from 8:35am to 8:15pm Mon–Fri, every 20 minutes from 8:40am to 8:20pm Sat–Sun. The €19 ticket allows you to hop on and off. If you want a guide's commentary, take a ride with Green Line Tours, American Express or Carrani Tours. ℵ *ATAC bus: 800-431784, www. atac.it • Green Line Tours: via Farini 16, 06 4827480, www.greenline tours.com • American Express: Piazza di Spagna 38, 06 67641 • Carrani Tours: Via Vittorio E. Orlando 95, 06 474 2501*

Walking Tours
Enjoy Rome runs three-hour walks of Ancient Rome, Rome at Night (both daily), the Vatican and Trastevere and the Jewish Ghetto (both thrice weekly). The tourist office has also been sponsoring free guided walks, usually at weekends. ℵ *Enjoy Rome: via Marghera 8a, 06 445 1843, www.enjoyrome.com*

Bicycle Tours
Enjoy Rome also runs very cheap, four-hour bike tours of Rome, including bike and helmet rental. Or rent a mountain bike (the ancient cobbles are very rough) to ride down Via Appia Antica on a Sunday *(see p61)*.

Italian Lessons
A company aimed at holiday-makers is Italiaidea, offering courses lasting two to eight weeks, a 15-hour "survival Italian" crash course, walking tours and weekend trips, as well as cooking classes geared towards language skills. ℵ *Italiaidea: 06 6994 1314, www.italiaidea.com*

Art Lessons
Rome certainly doesn't lack for inspiration. To bring out the Michelangelo in you contact Atelier Alupi who run week-long workshops three times a year in drawing, oil and watercolour painting. The Istituto Italiano Arte Artigianato e Restauro will teach you about art restoration in a weekend course, or the techniques of fresco or stained glass in two-week courses. ℵ *Istituto Italiano Arte Artigianato e Restauro: 335 7201671, www. scuolarestauro.it*

On-Site Tours
Some churches, museums and ancient sites offer guided visits, often for free. Many museums also feature self-guided tours on portable tape players or MP3s for a nominal fee.

Private Guides
The tourist office *(see p158)* keeps lists of several licensed private guides available for hire. The rates vary widely; expect to pay at least €15–20 an hour.

Left **Fiumicino Airport** Right **Termini Railway Station**

Getting to Rome

By Air from Great Britain
British Airways (www.britishairways.com), Ryanair (www.ryanair.com), easyJet (www.easyjet.com) and Alitalia (www.alitalia.com) all fly direct from London to Rome. Jet2 (www.jet2.com) fly from Leeds and Manchester, while FlyGlobespan (www.flyglobespan.com) fly from Edinburgh. From Ireland, Aer Lingus (www.aerlingus.ie) flies direct from Dublin.

By Air from North America
There are several direct flights on US carriers, plus Italy's Alitalia.

By Air from Australasia
Alitalia flies from Melbourne to Rome twice weekly. Qantas (www.qantas.com) flies thrice weekly from Sydney, Melbourne, Brisbane and Cairns (plus Auckland, Wellington and Christchurch in New Zealand) to Rome, via Milan. All flights have a least one stopover.

By Air from Europe
Most major European carriers fly to Rome from their main hub cities.

Internet Bargains
Most airlines now use websites to promote last-minute bargains and internet-only fares. Most have banded together on www.orbitz.com and collate the best regular fares offered, but only from the US, UK or Canada. Flexible schedules can take advantage of E-savers fares (weekly emails of bargain rates for trips over the coming weekend) and sites such as www.lastminute.com, or for European flights try www.skyscanner.com.

Fiumicino (Leonardo da Vinci) Airport
Rome's international airport is 30 km (18 miles) west of the city. There's a €40 flat fee between Fiumicino and the centre, which includes four passengers with bags. Hourly express trains to Termini take 30 minutes and cost €11. The local train to Trastevere station costs €5.50, then take the No. 8 tram to central Trastevere or across the bridge to Largo Argentina (see p99). ◎ Fiumicino Airport: 06 65951

Ciampino Airport
Ciampino, Rome's smaller airport which is used mainly for domestic and European charter flights, is 15 km (9 miles) south of town. Terravision, Atral and Sitbusshuttle all run frequent buses to Termini station. Taxis are not allowed to charge more than €30 between the centre and Ciampino (four passengers with bags). Report any problems to the taxi company. ◎ Ciampino Airport: 06 794 941, www.adr.it

By Train
From London, you can take the Channel tunnel to Paris and pick up a daily or overnight train to Rome (13 hours). The Eurostar (ES) bullet train speeds in 4.5 hours from Milan to Rome via Florence. Regular Italian trains range from express EC/IC/EN (all require high-speed supplements), to the speedy freccia-rossa, to stop-everywhere regionale trains.

Termini Railway Station
Rome's main railway station has ticket windows and automated machines in the outer hall, shops, restaurants and travel agents in the inner hall and a shopping centre in the basement. The tourist office is in the inner hall (see p158). It also has a left-luggage office and 24-hour pharmacy.

By Car
Italy's trunk road, the A1 autostrada, travels from Milan in the north through Bologna and Florence to Rome, then continues on to Naples. They all intersect Rome's G.R.A. (Grande Raccordo Anulare) ring highway, which allows you to circle the city or enter it from any direction you wish.

Left **City centre bus** Centre **Pedestrian signs** Right **Roman taxis**

⑩ Getting around Rome

City Buses
Rome's ATAC bus network has central hubs at Termini, Piazza Venezia, Largo Argentina and Piazza San Silvestro. Newsagents sell maps; *fermata* (bus stop) signs list the routes of the lines which stop there. Buy tickets at newsstands, tobacconists or machines at major stops. Stamp the ticket in the machine on the bus; they are valid for 75 minutes with unlimited transfers (but only one metro ride).

Metro
Two lines intersect at Termini, mainly serving the suburbs. Good tourist stops include Spagna (Spanish Steps), Colosseo, San Paolo (basilica), Ottaviano (six blocks from St Peter's), and Cipro (six blocks from Vatican Museums). Tickets for bus and metro are the same. A third metro line is currently under construction.

Walking
The historic centre is increasingly pedestrianized, but many streets are narrow, clogged with traffic and lack pavements. The cobblestones are hard on your feet, so wear sturdy shoes.

Taxis
Taxi ranks are found at the airports, train stations, major squares and tourist sights. Base rate is €2.80, plus 92 cents per kilometre in 1-cent increments. Extra fees are charged for luggage, from 10pm to 7am, and on Sundays. Tip the driver by rounding up to the nearest Euro.

Rental Cars
Traffic is bad in Rome, and parking expensive and rare. Local outfits are rarely cheaper than international ones. Most companies require theft protection; check if your credit card covers this insurance. Petrol is expensive but diesel is available everywhere. Most petrol stations close on Sunday but many have automated machines.

Road Rules
Official speed limits are 30–50 kmph (18–30 mph) in town, 80–110 kmph (50–70 mph) on two-lane roads outside town, and 130 kmph (90 mph) on highways, where left lanes are for passing only or heavy goods vehicles.

Parking
Few hotels have garages, although many have agreements with local ones or a few free spaces on the street. Round blue signs with a red slash mean no parking; white-lined spaces are free (though often restricted to residents); yellow spaces off-limits; blue spaces available for an hourly fee (pay at meter). Parking rates are best at Parcheggio Borghese under Villa Borghese park and Gianicolo under that hill.

Bicycles and Scooters
Roman traffic makes cycling or scootering dangerous. Sundays are calmest and several roads close to traffic for bikers. Rental outfits include Roma in Scooter and, offering discounts to those with train tickets, Treno e Scooter. ✆ *Roma in Scooter: Via Cavour 80, 06 481 5669, www.scooterhire.it • Treno e Scooter: Termini's Piazza dei Cinquecento exit, 06 4890 5823, www.trenoescooter.191.it*

Daytrips
Although for far-flung sights you catch trains at Termini, some sights within Lazio are serviced by local train lines including Ostia Antica *(see pp36–7)* from Porta San Paolo station, near Piramide Metro stop. Many are also accessible by CO.TRA.L coaches, including Tivoli *(see p154)*.

Maps
TCI (Touring Club Italiano) maps are best and widely available. Road signs (green for motorways, blue for state roads) indicate destinations more often than route numbers; know the name of the first village, town and city on your route.

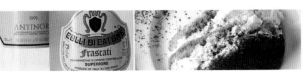

Left **Italian white wine** Right **Italian dessert**

Eating and Drinking Tips

Restaurant Types
Traditionally, a *ristorante* is the most formal and expensive eatery; a *trattoria* is a family-run, moderately priced place; an *osteria* anything from a simple *trattoria* to the equivalent of a pub with a few dishes of mixed meats and cheeses along with wine.

The Italian Meal
Italian meals, especially dinner, are drawn-out affairs of two to four hours, followed by an *espresso* (small, strong coffee) and liqueur *(digestivo)* such as *grappa* (see p77). Breakfast is traditionally just an *espresso* or *cappuccino* (coffee with steamed milk) with a sweetened croissant *(cornetto)*. Many hotels lay out a large breakfast buffet.

Antipasto
The appetizer course is traditionally *bruschetta* in pizzerias (toasted bread rubbed with garlic, olive oil, salt and often topped with tomatoes) and/or cured meats such as *prosciutto* and salami. And most places have a buffet table of vegetables where you can help yourself.

Primo
The first course. Pastas include *bucatini all'amatriciana*, *spaghetti alla carbonara*, *gnocchi di patate* and *cacio e pepe* (see p76). Soups *(minestre)* include *minestrone*

(vegetable) and *stracciatella* (egg with Parmesan in chicken broth). *Risotto* (creamy rice) is usually cooked with vegetables.

Secondo
The main course. Meats include *bistecca* or *manzo* (beef), *vitello* (veal), *agnello/abbacchio* (mutton/lamb), *pollo* (chicken), *maiale* (pork), *cinghiale* (boar), *coniglio* (rabbit) and *anatra* (duck). They are usually grilled *(alla griglia)* or roasted *(arrosto)*. Fish include *branzino* (bass), *acciughe* (anchovies), *baccalà* (cod), *sogliola* (sole), *orata* (bream) and *rombo* (turbot), usually grilled, roasted, or *all'acqua pazza* (simmered in white wine and seasonings).

Dolce
The dessert. Most popular are simple *cantucci con vin santo* (biscuits with dessert wine) or ice cream such as the *tartufo* ice cream ball. Custards of milk *(panna cotta, latte portugese)* and egg *(crème caramel)* are also favourites, as is *tiramisù* (trifle of sponge fingers soaked in *espresso* and perhaps alcohol and layered with mascarpone cheese and dusted with cocoa).

Wine and Water
No Italian meal is complete without red *(rosso)* or white *(bianco)* wine *(vino)*, either a carafe

(un litro) or a half-carafe *(mezzo litro)* of the house wine *(vino della casa)*, or a labelled bottle *(see p77)*. Italians sometimes temper their wine with water, either fizzy *(gassata)* or still *(non-gassata)*.

Cover Charges and Tipping
The *pane* (bread) charge of €1–€4 per person can be avoided, but this won't endear you to the waiters. If the menu says *"servizio incluso"* service charge is built in, although it is customary to round up by a few coins each. If not, tip a discretionary 10 per cent.

Restaurant Etiquette
Jacket and tie are almost never required, although in more up-market places reservations often are. Waiters expect you to linger over your meal, and won't rush you (some mistake this for slow service).

Bars, Pizza Rustica and Tavole Calde
Most Italian bars serve morning *cappuccino* and *cornetto*, *espresso* all day, and apéritifs *(aperitivi)* in the evening, along with sandwiches *(panini)*, pastries and ice cream *(gelato)*. A *tavola calda* is a glorified bar/cafeteria with prepared dishes behind a counter. A *pizza rustica* or *pizza a taglio* sells pizza by the slice, priced by the *etto* (100 grams).

For more traditional Roman dishes See pp76–7

Left **Hotel doorman** Right **Hotel garden**

10 Accommodation Tips

Hotels

1 Italian hotels are categorized from 1-star (basic) to 5-star (deluxe), based largely on the amenities offered rather than location. At 3 stars and above, all rooms have at least private bathroom, TV and telephone.

Rental Rooms

2 The tourist office *(see p158)* has a list of these invariably cheap options which can range from a lovely room with semi-private access or a cramped spare bedroom in someone's modern apartment. Amount of contact with the family varies, but it can be a great way to meet locals.

Apartments

3 The best sources to help you find an apartment (for a week, a month, or a year) are the English-language twice-monthly *Wanted in Rome* (www.wantedinrome.com) and the twice-weekly *Porta Portese* (www.portaportese.it) want-ad magazine. People also post apartment notices on message boards at English-language bookshops and Trastevere's Pasquino cinema.

Residences

4 Self-catering apartments, with limited maid service, are popular with long-term tourists (two weeks or more) and those who prefer more privacy. Rome's official websites (www.turismoroma.it and www.060608.it) list several residential options.

Camping and Caravaning

5 Rome has several camp sites *(campeggi)* ringed around the periphery, including Camping Flaminio, Seven Hills, Camping Tiber and Roma Camping. Italians tend to eschew tents for camper vans. You end up paying almost as much as for a cheap hotel: a fee per person and for the camp site itself. ❧ *Flaminio Village: via Flaminia Nuova 821, 06 333 2604, www.villageflaminio.com* • *Seven Hills: Via Cassia 1216, 06 3031 0826, www.sevenhills.it* • *Camping Tiber: Via Tiberina km 1400, 06 3361 0733, www.campingtiber.com* • *Roma Camping: Via Aurelia 831, 06 662 3018, www.camping.it*

Hostels

6 Cheap beds in single-sex, shared dorms cost about €18 per night. They are full of students, and usually impose a curfew of midnight. The official IYH hostel is in the bleak Foro Italico *(see p152)*. There are better, private hostels listed at www.hostels.com and www.europeanhostels.com. ❧ *IYH hostel: Viale delle Olimpiadi 61, 06 323 6267*

Bed-and-Breakfast

7 The newest category of Italian lodging falls somewhere between rental rooms and hotels, a sort of reincarnation of the old *pensione*, offering a handful of rooms along with breakfast and, usually, a friendly family reception.

Should You Reserve?

8 Reserving the first and last nights of a trip is always wise. The best-known hotels can fill up months in advance, so book ahead. Rome tends to be very crowded in May and June, but you should have no problem finding a room when you arrive, either calling around from the train station payphone or asking the tourist office.

Booking Services

9 The HR hotel consortium at Fiumicino airport and Termini railway station *(see p158)* will book you rooms for free, as will the private agency Enjoy Rome *(see p159)*. As yet, Internet booking services have highly erratic stables of hotels in their databases.

Hidden Charges

10 Rooms with private bath, a view or for stays less than three days are more costly. An extra bed is usually 30–35 per cent more. Breakfast may not be included, parking almost always extra, and prices on minibar items and phone calls shockingly high.

Left **Leather designer gloves** Right **Antiques shop**

TOP 10 Shopping Tips

1 Shop Hours
Most shops follow normal business hours (see p158) and open at 8–9am, shut for lunch until 3–4pm, and close around 6–8pm. In tourist areas and at larger stores, the lunch break (riposo) is slowly disappearing in favour of orario continuato (open all day).

2 Haggling
Expected in markets (see p69), but hardly ever in shops. Many market stall-holders now hail from Middle Eastern countries where bargaining is an art form, so be ready to do the full ritual, including acting less and less interested, while the merchant acts ever more offended and claims he can go no lower. He will not sell it for less than a profit, so any price agreed upon is acceptable.

3 VAT Refunds
Italy's Value Added Tax (IVA) is a sales tax already added on to the sticker price of every item. If you are a non-EU resident and spend more than €155 in a single shop, you can get the tax refunded. Ask the store to help you fill out the forms; then take these and the receipts to the customs office at the airport of the last EU country you'll be visiting to complete the paperwork. Your refund will be posted but it may take months. Stores marked

"Tax-Free Shopping for Tourists" speed up the process, giving you a cheque for the customs office to stamp, then you redeem it at the airport's Tax-Free Shopping desk.

4 Customs Limits
UK and Irish citizens can bring home virtually anything duty-free (although theoretical amounts such as 90 litres of wine apply). US citizens are limited to $400 worth of goods duty-free, including 200 cigarettes and 50 cigars. Canadian, Australian and New Zealand limitations are similar. Only British and EU residents may export flowers, fruits, vegetables, meats (unless tinned) and soft cheeses.

5 Wine
New anti-terrorism legislation means that you can no longer take on board wine that is purchased outside the airport. Shipping wine home is a good alternative but can be expensive.

6 Fashion and Stock Houses
Designer fashion is rarely cheaper than back home, but there is the cachet of having found those great shoes in Rome. Stock houses sell last year's styles, overstock, slight irregulars or items that won't sell in boutiques, offering a variety of labels at prices from 40–80 per cent lower than normal.

7 Art and Antiques
As the heart of the Roman Empire and an epicentre of the Renaissance and Baroque, Rome is full of antiquities, paintings and sculpture from the Middle Ages to today. There's also a good market in furnishings from Renaissance-era to Art Nouveau to simple, country-style pieces. Note that exporting goods requires correct paperwork.

8 Design Objects
Italians are masters of industrial design, from Ferraris to Alessi kettles. If the Ferrari doesn't fit your budget, consider shopping for kitchen implements, homewares or lighting systems, many sketched out by top international designers.

9 Religious Objects
Religious mementos, from kitsch, to solemn, to the classy, are hawked from stands and shops around the Vatican and, to some extent, across Rome. You can bring your purchase to the Wednesday Papal audience, during which he issues a mass blessing.

10 Crafts
Italy is renowned for hand-painted ceramics – a souvenir with a practical use. Rome is also home to many fine jewellers, from big names such as Bulgari to artisans labouring in small boutiques.

Left **Termini railway station** Right **No. 64 bus**

Things to Avoid

1 Rome in August
Rome is a ghost town in August and unbearably hot. Most Italians go on holiday for the month and while most sights are open and hotels are emptier, many shops and restaurants are closed, and you're only seeing the tourist side of the city, not its true nature *(see p158)*.

2 Pickpocket Bottlenecks
Pickpockets infest many of Rome's streets, squares and metro stations but are worst and at their most aggressive at a few prime tourist bottlenecks: the narrow pavement around the Vatican walls from the museums to St Peter's; around the Forum, especially the road from the back of the Capitoline; and the pedestrianized via dei Pastini and via di Pietra from the Pantheon to the Trevi Fountain.

3 Vatican Museums when they're Free
Yes, you get in for free the last Sunday of each month, but the trade-off is that the museums – often claustrophobic even on a good day – become a crush of bodies.

4 Restaurants around the Vatican and Forum
With rare exceptions, the restaurants that cluster around Rome's two prime tourist spots, advertising menus in six languages and often planted with a waiter waving you over, put the Roman dining experience to shame. No self-respecting Italian patronizes them, and you would be wise to avoid them.

5 Termini Area after Dark
The homeless and dispossessed congregating in the dull train station neighbourhood, home to a glut of budget hotels, make it unsavoury after dark. Generally, the streets south of the station are darker and more dangerous than those to the north.

6 The No. 64 Bus
The "Pickpocket Express" or "Wallet Eater" trundling from Termini to St Peter's has long held the title for the worst pickpocketing bus in Rome. It now faces competition from the No. 40, an express bus on the same route. Keep your wits about you, and one hand on your wallet or purse.

7 Wearing Belt Packs
The worst travel accessory ever invented. Nothing has pleased the world's pickpockets more than the popularity of these pouches, which place all of your most important belongings discreetly below eye-level and at the perfect height for a light-fingered thief to rifle through at his leisure.

8 Driving in Rome
A car is utterly unnecessary in Rome: many of its sights are on pedestrian roads so you can't drive to them anyway, and parking spaces at those accessible by car are almost impossible to find. All parking in the city is limited and preposterously expensive, and to the uninitiated, Italians seem to drive like maniacs *(see p161)*. Save renting a car until the last day of your stay in Rome and use it only to drive out of town.

9 Piazza Navona and Pantheon Areas on Thursdays
Save these areas for a different day as two of the more important sights on the Tiber Bend are closed on Thursday: Sant' Agostino with its unmissable Caravaggio works *(see p83)* and the painting collection of the Galleria Doria Pamphilj *(see p91)*.

10 The Catacombs at Weekends
Two words: tour buses. These are actually worse on Saturday, now that all vehicular traffic save a public minibus is diverted off the Via Appia Antica (the catacombs' main access road) on Sundays *(see p151)*.

Left **Street chestnut seller** Right **Roman market**

TOP 10 Rome on a Budget

1 The Vatican for Free
The Vatican Museums *(see pp8–9)* are free the last Sunday of each month but get crowded *(see p165)*. However, the free day is useful if you want to return to tour the less popular museums and collections.

2 Sightseeing for Free
Churches are free and hold some of Rome's greatest art and architecture. However, you often pay for entry into crypts, archaeological excavations and treasuries. Rome's squares are free theatres of life for the price of a *cappuccino*.

3 Sightseeing Discounts
Sights and museums are run by a variety of agencies (national, municipal or private) so prices vary. National and city museums are free for EU citizens under 18 and over 65. This also applies to citizens of Norway, Liechtenstein, Iceland and Switzerland. The Roma Pass (€25) is valid for three days and includes free public transport. The *Roma Archeologia* Card, a €23 7-day ticket, is valid for the Colosseum, the Palatine, monuments along the Via Appia and the museums of the Museo Nazionale.

4 Travel Discounts
Those under 26 can buy a *Carta Verde* for about €40 that offers a 10 per cent discount on any train ticket. The discount covers basic fares only and not the "fast" supplement added to most journeys. The same deal for over 60s is called *Carta Argento*. Available from railway stations.

5 Accommodation
Generally, prices get higher as you move towards the centre of the city and the hotel has more stars to its rating. A 1- or 2-star hotel (fewer amenities) or taking a room without a private bathroom will save you money, and is preferable to looking outside the centre or in the Termini neighbourhood where cheap hotels congregate *(see p174)*. If you can get out of paying for the hotel's breakfast, the same thing at a café costs a quarter of the price. Avoid making phone calls or using the minibar; both are overpriced.

6 Cheap Eats
In food-loving Italy, price or category of restaurant has little to do with how good the food is, so a cheaper *osteria* or *trattoria* is just as tasty as a fancy *ristorante*. Appetizers cost almost as much as first courses for less food. House wine is cheaper than bottled; tap water *(acqua dal rubinetto)* is free. *Tavole calde* and bars offer cheap meals quickly *(see p162)*.

7 Picnics
You can visit a string of small grocery stores *(alimentari)*, greengrocers *(fruttivendolo)*, bread and pastry shops *(panetteria* or *pasticceria)*, wine stores *(vini olii, enoteca* or *fiaschetteria)* or simple street stalls and create your own picnic to eat on a square, take on a daytrip, or enjoy back in your hotel room.

8 Pay in Cash
Cash is sometimes preferable to credit, and will often secure you a discount in shops and smaller hotels. Just make sure you leave with some kind of receipt.

9 Travel Off-Season
Roughly, late October to before Easter is low season in Rome, when rates on airfares and hotels can drop considerably, plus you visit without the crowds and long queues *(see p158)*.

10 Shop Wisely
Some fashion items are no cheaper in Italy than abroad. When possible, save your purchasing for one store so you can gather up the VAT limit and get a refund *(see p164)*. Go for artisan products rather than souvenirs, and purchase from the craftspeople themselves to avoid resale mark-ups. Or take advantage of the city's many markets for more bargains *(see p69)*.

Left **Disabled access** Right **Students**

🔟 Special Concerns

1 Disabled Travellers
Rome isn't fully accessible to disabled travellers, largely because many of its buildings are hundreds of years old and preservation laws prevent alteration to accommodate wheelchairs. However, most major museums have added facilities and many hotels have converted a few rooms. Some metro stops (but not the important Colosseo one) are wheelchair accessible. You'll have the best luck at restaurants during warm months, when many have tables outdoors (though bathrooms may not be accessible).

2 Resources for the Disabled
RADAR (Royal Association for Disability and Rehabilitation), based in London, publishes a series of useful pamphlets. Holiday Care Service in England offers advice on disabled-friendly accommodation. In Rome, contact Roma per Tutti or browse their useful website. ◎ *RADAR: 020 7250 3222, www.radar.org. uk • Holiday Care Service: 01293 774 535 • Roma per Tutti: 06 5717 7094, www. romapertutti.it*

3 Senior Citizens
Older travellers are treated as respected elders in a traditional society such as Italy's. EU citizens over 65 get free entry to all city and state museums and discounts at other sights and on trains.

4 Women Travellers
The Latin lover is alive and well and women can expect to receive much more attention than at home. Open staring, verbal flirtation, bottom-pinching and even inappropriate rubbing on buses are all common. Be firm. Most of this is harmless, but can be annoying and unwelcome.

5 Resources for Women
There is little in the way of official resources for women, but there is a women's bookshop, Libreria delle Donne, which acts as a reference point and resource centre for women. ◎ *Libreria delle Donne: via dei Fienaroli 31 • Map K6 • 06 581 7724*

6 Student Travellers
Rome has dozens of study abroad programmes, a huge university and tens of thousands of international students. Ask for a *"studente"* ticket to get reduced admissions on sights. Students tend to hang out in the bars of Trastevere *(see p147)* and Campo de' Fiori *(see p106)* and the clubs of Testaccio *(see p124)*, as well as around the Trevi Fountain and Spanish Steps *(see pp108–11)* after dark.

7 Resources for Students
While student ID cards are useful, the only one widely accepted is the ISIC (International Student Identity Card).

8 Families
Italians love families and will welcome your clan warmly. Most hotels will add a cot to your room for 30–35 per cent extra and restaurants often offer children's half-portions *(mezza porzione)* for 50–75 per cent less than the adult price.

9 Gay and Lesbian Travellers
Homosexuality is legal in Italy and quite broadly accepted in as cosmopolitan a city as Rome, which hosted the World Pride festival in 2000.

10 Resources for Gays and Lesbians
The national ARCI-Gay organization has offices in Rome, as does the lesbian branch, ARCI-Lesbica. The locally based Mario Mieli and Di' Gay Project groups are the most important. Useful websites include www.gay.it and www. mariomieli.org. ◎ *ARCI-Gay: Via Zabaglia 14, 06 6450 1102, www. arcigayroma.it • ARCI-Lesbica: Via Stefanini 15, 06 418 0211, www. arcilesbica. it • Di' Gay Project: Via Costantino 82, 06 513 4741, www.digayproject.org • Mario Mieli: Via Efeso 2a, 06 541 3985*

Left **Automated teller machine** Centre **Postboxes** Right **Italian bank**

TOP 10 Banking and Communications

Changing Money
Always change money at a bank (or, for American Express card-holders, at an Amex office) for the best rates and lowest commission charges. Bring your passport as ID. Exchange booths *(cambio)* are good at a pinch, but have worse rates and/or higher commission. Never exchange a travellers' cheque (or use one to pay) at a shop or hotel unless you have to; the rates are awful.

Automated Teller Machines
The fastest, easiest and cheapest way to get local currency is via an ATM *(bancomat)*, drawing money directly from your home account. No ID checks, no queues and you get a better rate than inside the bank. A fee is charged for withdrawals.

Credit Cards
MasterCard and Visa are accepted everywhere except the smallest shops, *trattorie* or hotels. American Express is also accepted in many places. Diner's Club tends to be valid only at pricier places. You can get credit card cash advances from ATMs, but interest starts accruing immediately and both credit card companies and issuing banks charge small percentage fees for the service.

Travellers' Cheques
While still the safest way to carry money (if you lose them and have kept a list of their numbers separate, you can have them speedily replaced), travellers' cheques are doomed by the evolution of ATMs. A few cheques are good for emergencies, however. Buy them in dollars, pounds sterling or euros. Personal cheques are useless, unless you're an Amex card-holder, in which case you can cash them at American Express offices.

Currency
In 2002, Italy joined most of Europe in adopting the euro (€) to replace the lira. Euro coins come in 1, 2, 5, 10, 20 and 50 euro cents and €1 and €2. Notes come in €5, €10, €20, €50, €100, €200 and €500 denominations.

Public Phones
Most payphones in Italy now accept only pre-paid phonecards *(scheda telefonica)* which you can buy in several denominations at newsstands and tobacconists *(tabacchi)*. Break off the corner before use. The newest phones also accept coins.

Calling Home
There are international phone booths in major railway stations and a range of pre-paid *carta telefonica internazionale* for making international calls, but the cheapest way is with a calling card with an international plan tied to your home phone account. To reverse the charges from any phone, dial the international operator on 170. Never call from hotels, which charge very high rates. To call Italy from abroad, dial your international prefix then Italy's country code (39), then the number, including the zero.

Internet Access
If you have your own laptop, look for a café with a Wi-Fi connection. Otherwise, the tourist office will advise you on where to find an Internet café (but bring ID).

Postal Services
Italy's post can be slow – letters might arrive home in three days or three months. You don't need to visit a post office *(ufficio postale)*; just ask any tobacconist or newsagent for stamps *(francobolli)* for the country to which you are mailing. Then drop it in the slot of the postbox (usually red) labelled *"per tutte le altre destinazioni"*.

Receiving Mail
Mail addressed to you at "FERMO POSTA/ Piazza San Silvestro 19/ 00187 Roma, Italia/ ITALY" will make it to the main post office on Piazza San Silvestro. There's a small fee to pick it up.

Left **Pharmacy sign** Centre **Roman police station** Right **Roman ambulance**

🔟 Security and Health

1 Emergency Numbers

Dial 113 for general emergencies. Dial 112 for the *carabinieri* police, 118 for an ambulance, 115 for the fire department and 803-116 for car breakdowns (a pay towing service).

2 Safety

Italy is a remarkably safe country. Aside from pickpockets, there is little to fear. Violent crime is rare, and although women (especially young foreign women) may get a lot of attention, it's mostly harmless. Italians do tend to drive aggressively, so be attentive behind the wheel or when crossing the road.

3 Pickpockets

On crowded buses, especially the No. 64 *(see p165)*, the metro, and around train stations and other areas tourists congregate, pickpockets work the crowds. Keep your wits about you and keep your passport, credit cards, plane or train tickets, and all money except for a day's worth of cash in a money belt worn under your clothes, either around the waist or on a string around the neck.

4 Young Muggers

Women dressed in colourful but dirty clothes, usually with swaddled babe in arms, tend to stick to forceful begging, but packs of small children will lift your valuables in a flash, and have been known to use force. A common ruse is to swarm you holding up pieces of cardboard with words scrawled on them while the pickpocketing happens underneath.

5 Scams

Scams, while not particularly rampant, are attempted on tourists. Act attentive and in charge and the unscrupulous are unlikely to try. Look out for taxis who might try to set the meter for "out of town" rates rather than local, and restaurants that try to pad the bill with items not ordered. They are also the most likely to try and double-charge your credit card.

6 Police

There are two main police branches you might deal with, the regular *polizia* and the more military-trained, national *carabinieri* force. A police station is called *una questura*.

7 Health Insurance

Check your personal insurance to see if it covers you abroad. Usually you must pay any hospital charges up front and file for reimbursement when you get home, although Blue Cross/Blue Shield members can visit affiliated hospitals in Rome using their card as they do at home.

8 Hospitals

Roman hospitals *(ospedale)* are efficient and semi-privatized. The emergency room is called *pronto soccorso*. For uncomplicated visits not requiring hospital admission, they'll usually give you a check-up, write a prescription if necessary and send you off with a smile, with no paperwork involved.

9 Pharmacies

Italian pharmacies *(farmacie)* are usually very well equipped and knowledgeable in helping you with minor ailments. At night and on Sundays, a sign is posted at each pharmacy listing those that are open all hours. Full-time 24-hour pharmacies include the ones at Piazza Barberini 49, Via Arenula 73 and outside Termini railway station where Via Cavour meets Piazza dei Cinquecento.

10 Food and Water Safety

Italian water is safe to drink everywhere except on trains and any source signposted *"aqua non potabile".* Food is largely safe although uncooked seafood is always chancy. The BSE (Mad Cow Disease) scare which led to a temporary ban of all beef on the bone is over, which means that the popular dish *bistecca fiorentina* can once again be made from the usual T-bone cut.

Left **Majestic** Centre **Raphael** Right **Regina Baglioni**

🔟 Bastions of Luxury

1 Eden
Perhaps Rome's most illustrious defender of the grand tradition, this hotel has been the choice of celebrities for years. Every detail of the hotel speaks of refinement, and a superb restaurant/bar tops the edifice dominating the entire city *(see p136)*. ◊ *Via Ludovisi 49 • Map E2 • 06 478 121 • www. lemeridien.com, www. starwoodhotels.com • DA • €€€€€*

2 Hassler
In one of the few genteel giants that's not yet part of a luxury chain, the honey-coloured tones of the public rooms set the mood of timeless luxury. The suites and the famous roof terrace restaurant offer some of Rome's most magnificent views. ◊ *Piazza Trinità dei Monti 6 • Map D2 • 06 699 340 • www.hotelhassler roma.com • DA • €€€€€*

3 De Russie
This historic hotel, a favourite of Picasso, has been refurbished in a sumptuous yet under-stated style. Delights include terraced garden cafés, an excellent restaurant, a spa and gym and a secret garden on the Pincio. Rooms are spacious and elegant – muted colours and sheer comfort. ◊ *Via del Babuino 9 • Map D2 • 06 328 881 • www.roccofortehotels. com • DA • €€€€€*

4 St Regis Grand
The extravagant and opulent St Regis Grand was originated by César Ritz in 1894, and it continues to live up to the illustrious hotelier's name. A world-class restaurant, Vivendo, a business centre and a fitness club complete the offerings. ◊ *Via V E Orlando 3 • Map E3 • 06 47 091 • www.stregis.com/ grandrome • DA • €€€€€*

5 Majestic
Magnificence is the keynote in the oldest of the Via Veneto hotels, founded in 1889. Rich decor is everywhere, as well as antiques and bathrooms with Jacuzzis. ◊ *Via Veneto 50 • Map E2 • 06 421 441 • www. hotelmajestic.com • DA • €€€€€*

6 Regina Baglioni
A setting fit for a king, which it has been more than once. Wall silks, Oriental carpets, paintings, marble floors, antiques – this beautiful hotel is truly a palace inside and out. Seventh-floor suites have pano-ramic views. ◊ *Via Veneto 72 • Map E2 • 06 421 111 • www.baglionihotels.com • DA • €€€€€*

7 De la Ville Inter-Continental
Certainly one of Rome's prettiest hotels, graced with fine art, marble and antiques, all lit by Venetian glass chandeliers. Each room is different in theme. Situated at the top of the Spanish Steps, it could hardly be more central. ◊ *Via Sistina 69 • Map D2 • 06 673 31 • www.inter continental.com • DA • €€€€€*

8 Grand Hotel Flora
Part of the Marriott chain, this hotel has the air of refinement you expect on Via Veneto, combined with efficiency. The decor features marble, antiques and soft colours. Extras include a roof garden restaurant and a piano bar. ◊ *Via Veneto 191 • Map E2 • 06 489 929 • www. hotelfloraroma.com • DA • €€€€€*

9 Giulio Cesare
Formerly the villa of a countess, the atmos-phere is still decidedly aristocratic. Chandeliers, antiques, paintings, Oriental carpets and a grand piano typify the public rooms. Mirror-lined hallways lead to elegant bedrooms with marble baths. ◊ *Via degli Scipioni 287 • Map B2 • 06 321 0751 • www.hotelgiulio cesare.com • €€€€€*

10 Atlante Star
Attentive service and a host of extras, such as free airport pick-up and Jacuzzis. The rooftop restaurant is famous for its panorama of St Peter's. ◊ *Via Vitelleschi 34 • Map B2 • 06 687 3233 • www. atlantehotels.com • €€€€€*

Note: *Unless otherwise stated, all hotels accept credit cards, have en-suite bathrooms and air conditioning*

Price Categories	
For a standard, double room per night (with breakfast if included), taxes and extra charges.	€ under €100
	€€ €100–150
	€€€ €150–250
	€€€€ €250–350
	€€€€€ over €350

Above **Locarno**

📏10 Romantic Charmers

1 Westin Excelsior
The grande dame of Rome's hotels, noted for its *belle époque* architecture and commanding location. Notes of grandeur abound everywhere you look, with a choice of several fine restaurants, too. ◈ *Via Veneto 125 • Map E2 • 06 470 81 • www.westin.com/excelsior rome • DA • €€€€€*

2 Lord Byron
This refined boutique hotel was originally a monastery, but there's nothing ascetic about it nowadays. The decor is an eclectic mix of styles and periods, but all of it evokes opulence. Its location provides serene solitude that makes a perfect antidote to the hectic life of the centre. ◈ *Via G de Notaris 5 • Map B2 • 06 322 0404 • www.lordbyronhotel.com • €€€€€*

3 Raphael
Certainly one of Rome's most appealing hotels. Situated just behind Piazza Navona, the location is perfect, and the ivy-covered façade suggests timeless charm and cosiness. The foyer is full of unusual art treasures and most of the rooms are originally decorated, some with parquet floors and marble accents. Great views from the terraces. ◈ *Largo Febo 2 • Map L3 • 06 682 831 • www. raphaelhotel.com • €€€€€*

4 D'Inghilterra
Hemingway and Liszt are among the distinguished past guests of this 17th-century edifice, right in the heart of the designer boutique district *(see p114)*. The lavish rooms have antiques and the marble bathrooms are provided with fresh orchids. ◈ *Via Bocca di Leone 14 • Map D2 • 06 699 811 • www.royaldemeure.com • DA • €€€€€*

5 Farnese
This renovated *belle époque* mansion is furnished with period authenticity. Captivating *trompe-l'oeil* fresco decorations, wonderful modern bathrooms and a roof garden are just a few of its attractions. Rich fabrics and high ceilings are typical of the rooms. ◈ *Via Alessandro Farnese 30 • Map C1 • 06 321 2553 • www.hotel farnese.com • €€€€*

6 Grand Hotel del Gianicolo
Located on the hill above Trastevere, this former convent offers every amenity, including beautiful gardens with a swimming pool, and roof gardens. The location is serene, despite nearby traffic. Public rooms feature Venetian glass fixtures. ◈ *Viale delle Mura Gianicolensi 107 • Map B4 • 06 5833 3405 • www.grandhotelgianicolo. it • DA • €€€€€*

7 Hotel Piranesi
A romantic boutique hotel run by a charming family. The bedrooms have wooden floors and are beautifully decorated with brocade. Fine views from the roof terrace. ◈ *Via del Babuino 196 • Map D2 • 06 328 047 • www.hotel piranesi.com • DA • €€€€*

8 La Residenza
Occupying an elegant villa this is one of Rome's special secrets. Great atmosphere, created by a canopied entrance and the deluxe bar and terrace. Some rooms have balconies. ◈ *Via Emilia 22–4 • Map E2 • 06 488 0789 • www.hotel-la-residenza.com • €€€*

9 Locarno
An Art Nouveau hotel near Piazza del Popolo. The patio has a small fountain, and antiques punctuate the decor. Rooms have high ceilings and wooden floors, and breakfast is served on the roof terrace. ◈ *Via della Penna 22 • Map D2 • 06 361 0841 • www.hotel locarno.com • €€€€*

10 St Anselmo and Villa San Pio
Nestled on a tranquil hill, these adjacent establishments are both spacious and pleasant. Rococo decor predominates, including tapestries and chandeliers. ◈ *Piazza Sant' Anselmo 2 • Map D5 • 06 570 057 • www. aventinohotels.com • €€€€*

Left **Pantheon** Right **Bedroom, Pantheon**

Comfort, Style and Value Hotels

Pantheon
This small, tasteful establishment is less than a block from the eponymous temple *(see pp14–15)*. Public areas boast stained glass, mosaics, beamed ceilings and an imposing crystal chandelier. The door to each room sports an antique print of one of Rome's obelisks, and inside you'll find fresh flowers. ✆ *Via dei Pastini 131* • *Map M3* • *06 678 7746* • *www.hotelpantheon.com* • *DA* • *€€€€€*

Dei Borgognoni
Although just around the corner from the bustling historic centre, this thoroughly up-to-date period building feels removed from it all. Subdued lighting and colours enhance the antique accents, and the hushed garden is most inviting. Some rooms have private patios. ✆ *Via del Bufalo 126* • *Map P1* • *06-6994 1505* • *www.hotel borgognoni.it* • *DA* • *€€€€*

Condotti
Amid the designer boutiques along this street *(see p111)*, the hotel offers comfort and period furnishings. All rooms are soundproofed, and many feature views over the rooftops; one has a terrace. The staff are unfailingly attentive. ✆ *Via Mario de' Fiori 37* • *Map N1* • *06 679 4661* • *www.hotelcondotti.com* • *€€€€*

Cesàri
This little gem was famous in the 1800s, when the French writer Stendhal stayed here, and the exterior is little changed. The interior, however, has been kept up-to-date, set off with antiques and old prints. All rooms have blue marble bathrooms. ✆ *Via di Pietra 89A* • *Map N2* • *06 674 9701* • *www.albergocesari.it* • *€€€€*

Fori Imperiali Cavalieri
Just steps away from all the sights of the ancient centre. Serenity reigns supreme, with decor and service to match. The historic building has been renovated and every room is equipped with a dataport. ✆ *Via Frangipane 34* • *Map Q5* • *06 679 6246* • *www.cavalieri.it* • *€€€*

Tritone
This hotel is located very near the Trevi Fountain and many other sights. The emphasis is tranquillity, ensured by double-glazing and wall-to-wall carpeting throughout. The buffet breakfast in the roof garden is a joy. ✆ *Via del Tritone 210* • *Map P1* • *06 6992 2575* • *www.travelroma.com* • *€€€€*

Teatropace 33
In a quiet street just a few minutes from Piazza Navona, Teatropace 33 occupies a beautifully restored cardinal's palazzo. Every room in the stylish interior is different. No lift. ✆ *Via del Teatro Pace 33* • *Map L2* • *06 687 9075* • *www.hotelteatropace.com* • *€€€€*

Santa Chiara
Housed in three historic buildings and run by the same family for 200 years. Situated behind the Pantheon, all rooms are spacious and full of character. Features include marble-topped desks, oak headboards and travertine bathrooms. ✆ *Via Santa Chiara 21* • *Map M3* • *06 687 2979* • *www.albergo santachiara.com* • *€€€€*

Hotel Santa Maria
Occupying a 16th-century cloister, this peaceful hotel offers a welcome retreat from bustling Trastevere. Eighteen modern, ground-floor rooms surround a lovely garden. Both single-rate and multiple-occupancy rooms are available. ✆ *Vicolo del Piede 2* • *Map K6* • *06 589 4626* • *www.htl-santamaria.com* • *DA* • *€€€*

Des Artistes
A comfortable, no-smoking hotel. Pleasing fabrics, paintings and marble bathrooms create an air of luxury. Rooms also equipped with dataports. One of the best choices in the Termini area, there's a floor set aside for budget travellers. ✆ *Via Villafranca 20* • *Map F3* • *06 445 4365* • *www.hoteldesartistes.com* • *€€*

Note: *Unless otherwise stated, all hotels accept credit cards, have en-suite bathrooms and air conditioning*

Price Categories

For a standard,	€ under €100
double room per	€€ €100–150
night (with breakfast	€€€ €150–250
if included), taxes	€€€€ €250–350
and extra charges.	€€€€€ over €350

Above **Sole al Pantheon**

🔟 Rooms with a View

1 Sole al Pantheon

Noted as an inn since 1467, this distinguished hotel was the choice of Renaissance writer Ariosto. Facing the Pantheon, it has painted period decoration in many of the rooms and modern touches such as Jacuzzis and double-glazing. ✪ *Piazza della Rotonda 63 • Map M3 • 06 678 0441 • www.hotelsole alpantheon.com • €€€€€*

2 Victoria

Round the corner from its extravagant neighbours *(see p170)*, this hotel provides a modest alternative if you want to be near Via Veneto. However, by no means is it without its charms. A terrace bar has spectacular views of the ancient Aurelian Wall and Villa Borghese. Service is excellent. ✪ *Via Campania 41 • Map E2 • 06 423 701 • www.hotelvictoriaroma. com • DA • €€€*

3 Scalinata di Spagna

With its coveted location in an 18th-century villa at the top of the Spanish Steps, this intimate jewel boasts marvellous views from many of its rooms and from the trellis-covered terrace. The rooms are not large but are beautifully appointed. Book well in advance. ✪ *Piazza Trinità dei Monti 17 • Map D2 • 06 679 3006 • www.hotelscalinata.com • DA • €€€€*

4 Domus Aventina

A former 14th-century convent with a 17th-century façade, this serene hotel has large, softly coloured rooms. From the balconies and terrace there are great views, and prints, murals and Classical artifacts lend elegance. ✪ *Via di Santa Prisca 11B • Map D5 • 06 574 6135 • www.hotel domusaventina.com • €€€*

5 Teatro di Pompeo

Have breakfast under the arches of the first theatre in Rome, built by Pompey the Great in 55 BC. Rooms have beamed ceilings, marble-topped furniture and some have great views. The style and many of the amenities of bigger hotels. ✪ *Largo del Pallaro 8 • Map N6 • 06 68300170 • www.hotel teatrodipompeo.it • €€€*

6 Sofitel Villa Borghese

Housed in a renovated Palazzo, this luxurious hotel has an elegant, modern interior and offers superb views of the park from its top floor terrace. ✪ *Via Lombardia 47 • Map E2 • 06 478 021 • www.sofitel.com • €€€€*

7 Homs

On a quiet shopping street, this mid-size hotel is a bit plain, but antiques here and there give it a gracious feel. There are two roof terraces, one enclosed for year-round breakfasts, from which you can enjoy the panorama of Rome's skyline. ✪ *Via della Vite 71–2 • Map D2 • 06 679 2976 • www. hotelhoms.it • €€€€*

8 Inn at the Spanish Steps

This up-market hotel is in a 17th-century building – once lived in by Hans Christian Andersen. It has great views of the Spanish Steps from its attractive rooftop garden. Well-equipped rooms include satellite TV and Internet access. ✪ *Via dei Condotti 85 • Map D2 • 06 699 25657 • www.atspanishsteps.com • €€€€*

9 Albergo del Sole al Biscione

What some claim is Rome's very first hotel. Its best feature is the roof terrace, affording the fine views. Rooms are basic, but the atmosphere is cosy. No breakfast. ✪ *Via del Biscione 76 • Map L4 • 06 6880 6873 • www.solealbiscione.it • No credit cards • €€*

10 Abruzzi

Old-fashioned *pensione*-style relic. The rooms are large and clean and each has its own washbasin. Ask for a room that opens onto the dazzling view. ✪ *Piazza della Rotonda 69 • Map M3 • 06 679 2021 • www.hotelabruzzi.it • No credit cards • No en-suite bathrooms • €€€*

Above **Cavalieri Hilton**

🔟 Business Hotels

1 Grand Hotel de la Minerve
Occupying the 17th-century Palazzo Fonseca behind the Pantheon, services and quality here live up to the highest international standards. The *pièce de résistance* is the Venetian-glass-canopied lounge. Rooms are large and the view from the roof terrace encompasses all of Rome. ◉ *Piazza della Minerva 69 • Map M3 • 06 695 201 • www.grandhotel delaminerve.it • €€€€€*

2 Parco dei Principi
Just at the edge of Villa Borghese stands this modern high-rise, yet inside all is over-the-top Italian court decor. Panoramas from every room take in greenery and the city's domes. There's a gym, pool, patios, lounges and a well-equipped business centre, as well. ◉ *Via G Frescobaldi 5 • Map E2 • 06 854 421 • www.parcodeiprincipi. com • €€€€€*

3 Grand Hotel Plaza
Dating from 1860, this is one of Rome's oldest hotels, and is replete with Edwardian lavishness. Grand salons with stained-glass skylights, chandeliers, frescoes and antiques combined with modern amenities produce a comfortable ambience. Large rooftop terraces offer stunning views.

◉ *Via del Corso 126 • Map D2 • 06 674 952 • www. grandhotelplaza.com• €€€€€*

4 Cavalieri Hilton
High on a hill across the river, outside the centre, this hotel has two restaurants (one is Michelin-starred), four bars, indoor and outdoor pools, a beauty salon, spa, fitness centre, tennis courts and parks make this possibly the best place in Rome for doing business on a grand scale. ◉ *Via Cadlolo 101 • Map B1 • 06 350 91 • www.romecavalieri.it • DA • €€€€€*

5 Mecenate Palace
With views of Santa Maria Maggiore *(see p127)*, this comfortable hotel is named after a great patron of the arts under Augustus Caesar. The terrace café is ideal for small conferences and there's a meeting hall that holds up to 40 people. ◉ *Via Carlo Alberto 3 • Map F3 • 06 4470 2024 • www.mecenatepalace. com • DA • €€€€*

6 Nazionale a Montecitorio
Right next to the Italian Parliament, this 16th-century palace has hosted many politicos. A regal atmosphere, especially in the restaurant with its marble floor. ◉ *Piazza Montecitorio 131 • Map M1 • 06 695 001 • www. nazionaleroma.it • DA • €€€€€*

7 Bernini Bristol
This unprepossessing brick building faces Bernini's Triton fountain *(see p133)*. The decor is also uninspiring, but this marble-laden hotel is comfortable and has secretarial and other facilities. There's a roof garden, and top rooms have fine views. ◉ *Piazza Barberini 23 • Map Q1 • 06 488 931 • www.bernini bristol.com • DA • €€€€€*

8 Dei Consoli
Elegant and refined, with all conveniences, including Internet access, hydromassage and meeting rooms. ◉ *Via Varrone 2D • Map B2 • 06 6889 2972 • www.hotel deiconsoli.com • DA • €€€€*

9 Forum
This converted convent has a roof garden restaurant overlooking the Imperial Fora. Walnut-panelled interiors create warmth, while painted tiles decorate the bathrooms. The meeting room seats 15–80 people and is equipped with all facilities. ◉ *Via Tor de' Conti 25–30 • Map P4 • 06 679 2446 • www.hotelforum rome.com • €€€€*

🔟 Radisson SAS Hotel
Contemporary hotel offering high-tech conference facilities. ◉ *Via Fillippo Turati 171 • Map F3 • 06 444 841 • www.rome.radissonsas. com • DA • €€€€€*

⟹ ***Note:** Unless otherwise stated, all hotels accept credit cards, have en-suite bathrooms and air conditioning*

Price Categories

For a standard, double room per night (with breakfast if included), taxes and extra charges.

€	under €100
€€	€100–150
€€€	€150–250
€€€€	€250–350
€€€€€	over €350

Above **Roof terrace, Campo de' Fiori**

🔟 Budget Gems

Sant'Anna
This fashionable small hotel in the medieval Borgo next to St Peter's has frescoes in the breakfast room and a fountain in the courtyard. The rooms are spacious and those at the top have their own tiny terraces. The area is quiet and still has very much the feel of old Rome. ◊ *Borgo Pio 134 • Map B3 • 06 6880 1602 • www.hotelsantanna. com • €€€*

San Carlo
The overall decor echoes a Classical influence, with marble touches placed here and there. Situated on one of the quieter streets near the Spanish Steps, the rooms are light and commodious, and some have rooftop views and private terraces. Breakfast is offered in the top-floor garden. ◊ *Via delle Carrozze 93 • Map D2 • 06 678 4548 • www.hotel sancarloroma.com • €€€*

Alimandi
Close to the Vatican, with an attractive foyer and large rooms. Terraces and a roof garden with excellent views are outstanding features for this price range. The staff are committed to quality service. On a fairly quiet shopping street, handy to public transport. Free cable TV and airport shuttle. ◊ *Via Tunisi 1 • Map B2 • 06 3972 0843 • www.alimandi.com • €€€*

La Cisterna
The medieval heart of Trastevere at its best: comfortable rooms and a quiet position on an out-of-the-way street. Out back there's a small courtyard with a fountain, where guests can have their breakfast, or just relax. ◊ *Via della Cisterna 8 • Map K6 • 06 581 7212 • www.cisternahotel.it • €€*

Santa Prisca
A converted modern convent structure, there is a slight institutional feel to this place, but it is surrounded by its own park and leafy terraces, plus ample free parking. There's also a restaurant and an American bar. ◊ *Largo M Gelsomini 25 • Map D6 • 06 575 0009 • www.hotelsantaprisca.it • DA • €€*

Al Centro di Roma B&B
This small B&B (just three rooms) is centrally located near Piazza Navona. It has a great reputation for its service, cleanliness and value for money. ◊ *Piazza Sant'-Andrea della Valle 3 • Map L4 • 06 6813 5946 • www. bbalcentrodiroma.com • €€*

Campo de' Fiori
Friendly, clean and in a great location. The roof terrace has views of the rooftops, spires and domes of this ancient quarter. Inside, the decor is replete with touches to remind you that you are in a medieval building: mirrors, frescoes and an exposed ancient wall. ◊ *Via del Biscione 6 • Map L4 • 06 6880 6865 • www. hotelcampodefiori.com • No air conditioning • €€€*

Carmel
Old-fashioned *pensione*. The decor is spartan, but there's a vine-covered terrace and most rooms have double-glazing. A unique touch is the kosher kitchen for use by Jewish guests. ◊ *Via Goffredo Mameli 11 • Map K6 • 06 580 9921 • www. hotelcarmel.it • €€*

Smeraldo
An excellent choice for both location and quality. The name is evoked by the emerald-green marble entrance, and throughout there are marble accents. Rooms are clean and simple and there are two terraces. Some rooms have private balconies. ◊ *Vicolo dei Chiodaroli 9 • Map M4 • 06 687 5929 • www. smeraldoroma.com • €€*

Trastevere
This unassuming establishment captures the medieval charm of Trastevere. Open brickwork is an accent throughout and stencils decorate the walls. Rooms have views of the local market. ◊ *Via L Manara 24A–25 • Map K6 • 06 581 4713 • www.hotel trastevere.net • €€*

Left **Hostel Sandy** Right **Alessandro Downtown**

Hostels and Religious Institutions

1 Colors
Run by the highly experienced Enjoy Rome team and handily located in a quiet street near St Peter's. Rooms are clean, staff are friendly and multilingual. Internet access and free use of the kitchen and the terrace. No curfew. No breakfast served. Self-catering apartments are available. ✪ *Via Boezio 31 • Map B2 • 06 687 4030 • www.colorshotel.com • No credit cards • €*

2 Fawlty Towers
On the pleasanter, north side of Termini Station, efficient, clean, with Internet access, kitchen, satellite TV and terrace. Helpful English-speaking staff. No curfew, no lockout. Bookings accepted for private rooms only; otherwise first come, first served. Breakfast included. ✪ *Via Magenta 39 • Map E2 • 06 445 4802 • www.fawlty towers.org • No credit cards • No air conditioning • €*

3 M & J Place Hostel
Near Termini Station; kitchen use, Internet access, no curfew. Multilingual staff, 24-hour reception; lockers and left luggage service. Tourist information, plus discount coupons. Dormitories and private rooms. Breakfast included. ✪ *Via Solferino 9 • Map E2 • 06 446 2802 • www.mejplacehostel.com • No credit cards • No air conditioning • €*

4 Hostel Alessandro & Alessandro Downtown
Friendly, international staff, 24-hour reception, no curfew, kitchen, Internet access, free coffee, tea and pastries. Lockers, free maps and tourist information. Hostel Alessandro is situated to the north of Termini, Alessandro Downtown on the other side, near Via Cavour. ✪ *Via Vicenza 42 & Via Carlo Cattaneo 23 • Map E2 • 06 446 1958/434 0147 • www.hostelalessandro. com • Air conditioning (Downtown only) • DA (Downtown only) • €*

5 Hotel Ottaviano
Private hotel/hostel, just outside the Vatican walls. Friendly, English-speaking staff and no curfew. Satellite TV, Internet access, lockers, tourist information and maps, but no breakfast served. Run by the same people as Hotel Sandy. ✪ *Via Ottaviano 6 • Map B3 • 06 3973 8138 • www. pensioneottaviano.com • No credit cards • No air conditioning • €*

6 Hostel Sandy
All-dormitory hostel. Rooms sleep from three to eight; many have fridges. No curfew. Lockers, tourist info, maps, free Internet access. ✪ *Via Cavour 136 • Map E3 • 06 488 4585 • www.sandyhostel.com • No credit cards • No air conditioning • €*

7 Bed & Breakfast Cicerone 28
This simple apartment near the Vatican is clean and quiet, since it's on the top floor. The basic rooms come with en suite or shared baths, and there's a breakfast room with a TV. ✪ *Via Cicerone 28 • Map B2 • 06 320 8195 • www. cicerone28.it • No credit cards • €*

8 B&B Agencies
For bed-and-breakfast accommodation in Rome, contact the B&B Association of Rome. ✪ *B&B Association of Rome: Via A Pacinotti 73 • 06 5530 2248 • www.b-b.rm.it*

9 The Beehive
Run by an American couple, this contemporary part hotel and part hostel (it has one dormitory room) is near Roma Termini but is quiet with a secluded walled garden. Offers free Internet access and national phone calls. ✪ *Via Marghera 8 • Map K4 • 06 4470 4553 • www. the-beehive.com • €*

10 Centro Diffusione Spiritualità
This religious house, next to the botanical gardens in Trastevere, is a bit characterless but clean and well organized, and there's a lovely garden. Curfew 11pm. ✪ *Via dei Riari 43–4 • Map J5 • 06 6880 6122 (06 8530 1758 for bookings) • No credit cards • No air conditioning • €*

Note: *Unless otherwise stated, all hotels accept credit cards, have en-suite bathrooms and air conditioning*

Price Categories

For a standard, double room per night (with breakfast if included), taxes and extra charges.

€	under €100
€€	€100–150
€€€	€150–250
€€€€	€250–350
€€€€€	over €350

Above **View from Residence Palazzo al Velabro**

Residences and Apartments

1 Santa Chiara
The perfect location for experiencing the very heart of the city, just behind the Pantheon. It offers three apartments for two to five people. The topmost is graced by beamed ceilings, a fireplace and a terrace with an unforgettable view of the ancient dome. § *Via S Chiara 21 • Map M3 • 06 687 2979 • www.albergosantachiara. com • €€*

2 Residence Palazzo al Velabro
An elegant establishment just around the corner from Piazza Venezia. The setting offers understated luxury, privacy and convenience. Guests stay in apartments named after a Roman emperor, god, king or poet. The staff are helpful. Minimum three-day stay. § *Via del Velabro 16 • Map N4 • 06 679 2758 • www.velabro.it • DA • €€€*

3 Aldrovandi Residence
Outside the city centre, just beyond Villa Borghese in the Parioli district, full of greenery. The furnishings are handsome and the service deferential. Guests are welcome to use the pool of the Hotel Aldrovandi next door. Minimum one-week stay. § *Via Aldrovandi 11 • Tram No. 19 • 06 322 1430 • www.aldrovandiresidence.it • DA • €€*

4 Residenza Farnese
A great find. Just around the corner from the Piazza Farnese and offering space and comfort. The building is a restructured 15th-century palazzo in an area loaded with history. § *Via del Mascherone 59 • Map K4 • 06 6821 0980 • www. residenzafarneseroma.it • €€€*

5 Residence Ripetta
Located very near Piazza del Popolo, this 17th-century convent has been refurbished and offers a large range of apartment options for both short- and long-term visitors. The style of the furnishings is fairly basic but clean, and staff make every effort to see to your needs. Minimum one-week stay. § *Via di Ripetta 231 • Map D2 • 06 323 1144 • www.ripetta.it • DA • €€*

6 Trastevere
In the heart of this medieval district, just a block away from the main piazza. This modest hotel also offers small, clean apartments with kitchens. § *Via L Manara 24A–25 • Map K6 • 06 581 4713 • www. hoteltrastevere.com • €*

7 Retrome
Retrome manages 10 vintage-themed apartments in various locations, including the Navona area, Campo de' Fiori and the Colosseum neighbourhood. § *Via Marco Aurelio 47 • Map E5 • 06 955 57334 • www.retrome.net • No credit cards • €/€€*

8 Residence In Trastevere
This 17th-century mansion has been transformed into suites with open beams, painted decorations and other nice touches. The roof terrace has views of the Gianicolo and the river. Minimum one-week stay. § *Vicolo Moroni 35–6 • Map K6 • 06 808 3375 • www. romerenting.com/en/ trastevere.htm • No credit cards • No air conditioning • €€*

9 Residence Vittoria
In Rome's most fashionable shopping district, this residence emphasizes luxury. The building has a range of accommodation, from studios to penthouses. Minimum one-month stay. § *Via Vittoria 60–64 • Map D2 • 06 699 25834 • www. residencevittoria.com • No credit cards • €€€€€*

10 Apartment Rentals
Numerous services offer apartment rental. Prices vary depending on type of apartment, length of stay and number of people. § *AT@ HOME: Via del Corso 300 • 06 321 20102 • www. at-home-italy.com § Rome Sweet Home • 06 699 0667 • www.romesweet home.it § Cross-Pollinate • 06 993 69799 • www. cross-polinate.com • €*

General Index

Acknowledgments

Main Contributors

Reid Bramblett is an American writer who has lived in Rome, on and off, since childhood. He has contributed to more than half a dozen guidebooks on Italy, and is also the author of *Eyewitness Top 10 Travel Guide to Tuscany*.

Jeffrey Kennedy is American by birth, but has lived in Rome for almost 18 years. A graduate of Stanford University, he divides his time between producing, writing and acting. Most recently he has been scripting and producing museum guides in Italy and has featured on the Discovery Channel's *Must See Rome* programme.

Produced by Sargasso Media Ltd, London

Project Editor Zoë Ross
Designer Stephen Woosnam-Savage
Picture Research Monica Allende
Proofreader Stewart J Wild
Editorial Assistance Mark Livesey

Main Photographer Demetrio Carrasco
Additional Photography Max Alexander, Foto Carfagna & Associati, Giuseppe Carfagna, Mike Dunning, John Heseltine, Gorka Aduriz Lazaro, James McConnachie, Kim Sayer, Solveig Steinhard, Simone Strano
Illustrator Chris Orr & Associates

FOR DORLING KINDERSLEY
Senior Art Editor Marisa Renzullo
Senior Publishing Manager Louise Lang
Publishing Managers Kate Poole, Helen Townsend
Art Director Gillian Allan
DTP Jason Little

Cartography Co-ordinator Casper Morris
Production Joanna Bull, Marie Ingledew
Design & Editorial Assistance Beverley Ager, Rachel Barber, Michelle Crane, Nicola Erdpresser, Anna Freiberger, Katharina Hahn, Amy Harrison, Gerard Hutching, Integrated Publishing Solutions, Priya Kukadia, Leonie Loudon, Carly Madden, Nicola Malone, Sonal Modha, Marianne Petrou, Quadrum Solutions Pvt, Pete Quinlan, Rada Radojicic, Ellen Root, Marta Bescos Sanchez, Annie Shapero, Ellie Smith, Solveig Steinhard

Maps Dominic Beddow, Simonetta Giori (Draughtsman Ltd)

Special Assistance

The authors would like to thank the following for their assistance: Rob Allyn, Giulia Bernardini, Gianluca Borghese, Jeff Burden, Jolie Chain, Diletta Donati, Elizabeth Geoghegan, Suzanne Hartley, Hanja Kochansky, Clark Lawrence, Adrian McCourt, Roberta Mencucci, Odile Morin, Ruth Morss, Maria Giovanna Musso, Frances Nacman, Claudio Nigro, Elaine O'Reilly, Rachel Potts, Aloma Valentini, Lila Yawn

Picture Credits

t-top; tc-top centre; tr-top right; cla-centre left above; ca-centre above; cra-centre right above; cl-centre left; c-centre; cr-centre right; clb-centre left below; cb-centre below; crb-centre right below; bl-below left; bc-below centre; br-below right.

Every effort has been made to trace the copyright holders, and we apologize in advance for any unintentional omissions. We would be pleased to insert the appropriate acknowledgements in any subsequent edition of this publication.

The publishers would like to thank the following individuals, companies, and picture libraries for permission to reproduce their photographs:

AFP, London: 66b; AISA, Barcelona: 6tr, 8-9c, 9t; AKG, London: 28b, 38tl, 38tr, 39t, 41r, 48tl, 56c, 57r, 58tl, 58, 58tr, 112tl, "The Creation of Adam" by Michelangelo Buonarroti 10tl, "Ezekiel" by Michelangelo Buonarroti 10tr, "The Fall from Grace" by Michelangelo Buonarroti 11c, "The Life of Moses" by Sandro Botticelli 11b, "The School of Athens" by Raphael 48b, Hilbich 7br, 36-37c, Erich Lessing 19ca, 30b, 31c, 38b, 39r, "Appointment of St Matthew" by Caravaggio 49t, Jean-Louis Nou 31b; ALAMY IMAGES: Glyn Thomas 54tr; ALEX-ANDERPLATZ 147tr; THE ART ARCHIVE: Museo Capitolino Rome/Dagli Orti 24c.

BABINGTON'S ENGLISH TEA ROOM: 116tl, 116tr; BRIDGEMAN ART LIBRARY: 56tl, Galleria Borghese "Sacred and Profane Love" 1515 6b, 21b, "Apollo and Daphne" by Bernini 20b, Pinacoteca Capitolina Palazzo Conservatori "The Fortune Teller" by Caravaggio 27t, Library of Congress 56tr, Keats-Shelley Memorial House Rome 57bl,

Palazzo Massimo alle Terme 29cr, 30tr, Santa Maria del Popolo "The Crucifixion of St Peter" by Caravaggio 32b, Spirito Santo Prato 67r.

CORBIS: 25ca, 89-81c.; IL CONVIVIO: 89tl; CROCE BIANCA ITALIANA: 169tr.

IL DAGHERROTIPO, Rome: Giovanni Rinaldi 66tl, 67c; 165tr; Marco Ravasini 130tl.

JACKIE GORDON: 169tl.

HEMISPHERE IMAGES: Jean du Boisberranger 68tl; HOSTELS ALESSANDRO 176tr.

LIBRERIA BABELE: Gioris Guerrini 105tl; LIBRERIA RINASCITA: 105tr.

MARKA, Milan: Roberto Benzi 168tc; MAXXI: Roberto Galasso 152br.

NEWIMAGE S.R.L.: 68tr, 111tl.

PA PHOTOS: Epa/Ansa/Luciano del Castillo 66tr.

SCALA: 7ca, 19b, 20ca, 21t, 21c, 28c, 28-29c, 29t, 29ca, 29b, 30tl, 36t, 36cl, 36b, 37t.

All other images are © DK. For further information see www.dkimages.com

Phrase Book

In an Emergency

Help!	**Aiuto!**	eye-yoo-toh
Stop!	**Ferma!**	fair-mah
Call a doctor.	**Chiama un medico**	kee-ah-mah oon meh-dee-koh
Call an ambulance.	**Chiama un' ambulanza**	kee-ah-mah oon am-boo-lan-tsa
Call the police.	**Chiama la polizia**	kee-ah-mah lah pol-ee-tsee-ah
Call the fire brigade.	**Chiama i pompieri**	kee-ah-mah ee pom-pee-air-ee

Communication Essentials

Yes/No	**Si/No**	see/noh
Please	**Per favore**	pair fah-vor-eh
Thank you	**Grazie**	grah-tsee-eh
Excuse me	**Mi scusi**	mee skoo-zee
Hello	**Buongiorno**	bwon jor-noh
Goodbye	**Arrivederci**	ah-ree-veh-dair-chee
Good evening	**Buona sera**	bwon-ah sair-ah
What?	**Che?**	kwah-leh?
When?	**Quando?**	kwan-doh?
Why?	**Perché?**	pair-keh?
Where?	**Dove?**	doh-veh?

Useful Phrases

How are you?	**Come sta?**	koh-meh stah?
Very well, thank you.	**Molto bene, grazie.**	moll-toh beh-neh grah-tsee-eh
Pleased to meet you.	**Piacere di conoscerla.**	pee-ah-chair-eh dee-coh-noh-shair-lah
That's fine.	**Va bene.**	va beh-neh
Where is/are...?	**Dov'è? Dove sono...?**	dov-eh?/doveh soh-noh?
How do I get to...?	**Come faccio per arrivare a...?**	koh-meh fah-choh par arri-var-eh ah...?
Do you speak English?	**Parla inglese?**	par-lah een-gleh-zeh?
I don't understand.	**Non capisco.**	non ka-pee-skoh
I'm sorry.	**Mi dispiace.**	mee dee-spee-ah-cheh

Shopping

How much does this cost?	**Quant'è, per favore?**	kwan-teh pair fah-vor-eh?
I would like...	**Vorrei...**	vor-ray
Do you have...?	**Avete...?**	ah-veh-teh...?
Do you take credit cards?	**Accettate carte di credito?**	ah-chet-tah-teh kar-teh dee creh-dee-toh?
What time do you open/close?	**A che ora apre/ chiude?**	ah keh or-ah ah-preh/oo-deh?
this one	**questo**	kweh-stoh
that one	**quello**	kwell-oh
expensive	**caro**	kar-oh
cheap	**a buon prezzo**	ah bwon pret-soh
size, clothes	**la taglia**	lah tah-lee-ah
size, shoes	**il numero**	eel noo-mair-oh
white	**bianco**	bee-ang-koh
black	**nero**	neh-roh
red	**rosso**	ross-oh
yellow	**giallo**	jal-loh
green	**verde**	vair-deh
blue	**blu**	bloo

Types of Shop

bakery	**il forno /il panificio**	eel forn-oh /eel pan-ee-fee-choh
bank	**la banca**	lah bang-kah
bookshop	**la libreria**	lah lee-breh-ree-ah
cake shop	**la pasticceria**	lah pas-tee-chair-ee-ah
chemist	**la farmacia**	lah far-mah-chee-ah
delicatessen	**la salumeria**	lah sah-loo-meh-ree-ah
department store	**il grande magazzino**	eel gran-deh mag-gad-zee-noh
grocery	**alimentari**	ah-lee-men-tah-ree
hairdresser	**il parrucchiere**	eel par-oo-kee-air-eh
ice cream parlour	**la gelateria**	lah jel-lah-tair-ree-ah
market	**il mercato**	eel mair-kah-toh
newsstand	**l'edicola**	leh-dee-koh-lah
post office	**l'ufficio postale**	loo-fee-choh pos-tah-leh
supermarket	**il supermercato**	eel su-pair-mair-kah-toh
tobacconist	**il tabaccaio**	eel tah-bak-eye-oh
travel agency	**l'agenzia di viaggi**	lah-jen-tsee-ah dee vee-ad-jee

Sightseeing

art gallery	**la pinacoteca**	lah peena-koh-teh-kah
bus stop	**la fermata dell'autobus**	lah fair-mah-tah dell ow-toh-booss
church	**la chiesa la basilica**	lah kee-eh-zahy lah bas-seel-i-kah
closed for holidays	**chiuso per ferie**	kee-oo-zoh pair fair-ee-eh
garden	**il giardino**	eel jar-dee-no
museum	**il museo**	eel moo-zeh-oh
railway station	**la stazione**	lah stah-tsee-oh-neh
tourist information	**l'ufficio del turismo**	loo-fee-choh del too-ree-smoh

Staying in a Hotel

Do you have any vacant rooms?	**Avete camere libere?**	ah-veh-teh kah-mair-eh lee-bair-eh?
double room	**una camera doppia**	oona kah-mair-ah doh-pee-ah
with double bed	**con letto matrimoniale**	kon let-toh mah-tree-moh-nee-ah-leh
twin room	**una camera con due letti**	oona kah-mair-ah kon doo-eh let-tee
single room	**una camera singola**	oona kah-mair-ah sing-goh-lah
room with a bath, shower	**una camera con bagno, con doccia**	oona kah-mair-ah kon ban-yoh, kon dot-chah
I have a reservation.	**Ho fatto una prenotazione.**	oh fat-toh oona preh-noh-tah-tsee-oh-neh

Eating Out

Have you got a table for...?	**Avete un tavolo per...?**	ah-veh-teh oon tah-voh-loh pair...?
I'd like to reserve a table.	**Vorrei riservare un tavolo.**	vor-ray ree-sair-vah-reh oon tah-voh-loh
breakfast	**colazione**	koh-lah-tsee-oh-neh
lunch	**pranzo**	pran-tsoh
dinner	**cena**	cheh-nah
the bill	**il conto**	eel kon-toh
waitress	**cameriera**	kah-mair-ee-air-ah
waiter	**cameriere**	kah-mair-ee-air-eh
fixed price menu	**il menù a prezzo fisso**	eel meh-noo ah pret-soh fee-soh
dish of the day	**piatto del giorno**	pee-ah-toh dell jor-no
starter	**l'antipasto**	an-tee-pass-toh
first course	**il primo**	eel pree-moh
main course	**il secondo**	eel seh-kon-doh
vegetables	**contorni**	eel kon-tor-noh
dessert	**il dolce**	eel doll-cheh
cover charge	**il coperto**	eel koh-pair-toh
wine list	**la lista dei vini**	lah lee-stah day vee-nee
glass	**il bicchiere**	eel bee-kee-air-eh
bottle	**la bottiglia**	lah bot-teel-yah
knife	**il coltello**	eel kol-tell-oh
fork	**la forchetta**	lah for-ket-tah
spoon	**il cucchiaio**	eel koo-kee-eye-oh

Menu Decoder

l'acqua minerale gassata/ naturale	lah-kwah mee-nair-ah-leh gah-zah-tah/ nah-too-rah-leh	mineral water fizzy/still
agnello	ah-niell-oh	lamb
aglio	al-ee-oh	garlic
al forno	al for-noh	baked
alla griglia	ah-lah greel-yah	grilled
la birra	lah beer-rah	beer
la bistecca	lah bee-stek-kah	steak
il burro	eel boor-oh	butter
il caffè	eel kah-feh	coffee
la carne	la kar-neh	meat
carne di maiale	kar-neh dee mah-yah-leh	pork
la cipolla	la chip-oh-lah	onion
i fagioli	ee fah-joh-lee	beans
il formaggio	eel for-mad-joh	cheese
le fragole	leh frah-goh-leh	strawberries
il fritto misto	eel free-toh mees-toh	mixed fried seafood
la frutta	la froot-tah	fruit
frutti di mare	froo-tee dee mah-reh	seafood
i funghi	ee foon-ghee	mushrooms
i gamberi	ee gam-bair-ee	prawns
il gelato	eel jel-lah-toh	ice cream
l'insalata	leen-sah-lah-tah	salad
il latte	eel laht-teh	milk
il manzo	eel man-tsoh	beef
l'olio	loh-lee-oh	oil
il pane	eel pah-neh	bread
le patate	leh pah-tah-teh	potatoes
le patatine fritte	leh pah-tah-teen-eh free-teh	chips
il pepe	eel peh-peh	pepper
il pesce	eel pesh-eh	fish
il pollo	eel poll-oh	chicken
il pomodoro	eel poh-moh-dor-oh	tomato
il prosciutto cotto/crudo	eel pro-shoo-toh kot-toh/kroo-doh	ham cooked/cured
il riso	eel ree-zoh	rice
il sale	eel sah-leh	salt
la salsiccia	lah sal-see-chah	sausage
il succo d'arancia/ di limone	eel soo-koh dah-ran-chah/ dee lee-moh-neh	orange/lemon juice
il tè	eel teh	tea
la torta	lah tor-tah	cake/tart
l'uovo	loo-oh-voh	egg
vino bianco	vee-noh bee-ang-koh	white wine
vino rosso	vee-noh ross-oh	red wine
le vongole	leh von-goh-leh	clams
lo zucchero	loh zoo-kair-oh	sugar
la zuppa	lah tsoo-pah	soup

Numbers

1	**uno**	oo-noh
2	**due**	doo-eh
3	**tre**	treh
4	**quattro**	kwat-roh
5	**cinque**	ching-kweh
6	**sei**	say-ee
7	**sette**	set-teh
8	**otto**	ot-toh
9	**nove**	noh-veh
10	**dieci**	dee-eh-chee
11	**undici**	oon-dee-chee
12	**dodici**	doh-dee-chee
13	**tredici**	tray-dee-chee
14	**quattordici**	kwat-tor-dee-chee
15	**quindici**	kwin-dee-chee
16	**sedici**	say-dee-chee
17	**diciassette**	dee-chah-set-teh
18	**diciotto**	dee-chot-toh
19	**diciannove**	dee-chah-noh-veh
20	**venti**	ven-tee
30	**trenta**	tren-tah
40	**quaranta**	kwah-ran-tah
50	**cinquanta**	ching-kwan-tah
60	**sessanta**	sess-an-tah
70	**settanta**	set-tan-tah
80	**ottanta**	ot-tan-tah
90	**novanta**	noh-van-tah
100	**cento**	chen-toh
1,000	**mille**	mee-leh
2,000	**duemila**	doo-eh mee-lah
1,000,000	**un milione**	oon meel-yoh-neh

Time

one minute	**un minuto**	oon mee-noo-toh
one hour	**un'ora**	oon or-ah
a day	**un giorno**	oon jor-noh
Monday	**lunedì**	loo-neh-dee
Tuesday	**martedì**	mar-teh-dee
Wednesday	**mercoledì**	mair-koh-leh-dee
Thursday	**giovedì**	joh-veh-dee
Friday	**venerdì**	ven-air-dee
Saturday	**sabato**	sah-bah-toh
Sunday	**domenica**	doh-meh-nee-kah

Street Index